UNDERSTANDING ALTERNATIVE MEDIA

ISSUES in CULTURAL and MEDIA STUDIES

Series editor: Stuart Allan

Published titles:

UNDERSTANDING ALTERNATIVE MEDIA

Olga Guedes Bailey
Bart Cammaerts
Nico Carpentier

Open University Press

Open University Press
McGraw-Hill Education
McGraw-Hill House
Shoppenhangers Road
Maidenhead
Berkshire
England
SL6 2QL

email: enquiries@openup.co.uk
world wide web: www.openup.co.uk

and Two Penn Plaza, New York, NY 10121–2289, USA

First published 2008

A catalogue record of this book is available from the British Library

ISBN10: 0 335 22210 2 (pb)   0 335 2211 0 (hb)
ISBN13: 978 0 335 22210 0 (pb)   978 0 335 22211 7 (hb)

Library of Congress Cataloging-in-Publication Data
CIP data has been applied for

Typeset by RefineCatch Limited, Bungay, Suffolk
Printed in Poland by OZGraf S.A.
www.polskabook.pl

The **McGraw·Hill** Companies

CONTENTS

ACKNOWLEDGEMENTS

The idea of this book started in 2004 when we – Olga, Bart, and Stuart – were in Rio de Janeiro, Brazil on our way back to the UK after the IAMCR conference in Porto Alegre, in the South of Brazil. While enjoying the 'pleasures' of Brazilian food in Copacabana, we had an inspiring conversation about media issues which would contribute to the current debates in media and cultural studies, particularly regarding media and democracy in the current context of global politics. Alternative media, we all agreed, were a case in point. From there, the project slowly started to take shape, with Nico later joining the team, which from the beginning had a strong commitment to producing an exciting book.

This book is the result of productive and engaging conversations among us, our colleagues who read the manuscript, our editors, the anonymous external reviewers, and interviewees. The responsibility for the content is ours, but their input certainly made this a better text. To all of them our deepest thanks. We are especially grateful to S. Allan for his comments, guidance, and support which were fundamental in enabling us to dare to cross the established theoretical boundaries of what constitutes 'alternative media'.

Due to the transnational nature of this project, some expressions of gratitude are specifically linked to individual authors.

Olga is grateful to her colleagues at Nottingham Trent University for their support. She expresses her gratitude to Russell, Flavia, and David, for sharing *as dores e as delícias* of this experience.

Bart would like to express his gratitude to his colleagues at the LSE and, in particular, to Robin, Maggie, and Shani for their continued support and feedback. He also extends his gratitude to his close friends, sisters, mother, and daughter Manon for having to do without him for extended periods.

Nico wishes to thank J. Servaes and R. Lie for assisting in the development of the original theoretical model that structured this book, within the framework of a

UNESCO project. He wants to thank all collaborators of the RadioSwap evaluation, and the two RadioSwap coordinators, D. Demorcy and P. De Jaeger. Finally, his warm thanks also goes to R. Day, O. Deedniks, and S. Van Bauwel.

Last, but not least, the authors would like to thank DimensionFM, RadioSwap, MST, Mister Hepburn, the Labour Party, and Jekino Films for granting us permission to use their visual images.

SERIES EDITOR'S FOREWORD

Prefigured in any sense of the 'mainstream' media is some conception of the alternatives that fall outside of typical sorts of definitions. Western ideas about what counts as citizen journalism, for instance, look very different in countries where ordinary people lack basic access to electricity, let alone to a television set or computer. In civil war-torn Liberia, Alfred Sirleaf's efforts to perform a role akin to the citizen journalist are a case in point. As the managing editor of The Daily Talk, he writes up news and editorials on a chalkboard positioned on the street outside his 'newsroom' shed every day, thereby providing passers-by with important insights into what is happening in Monrovia. 'I like to write the way people talk so they can understand it well,' he told The New York Times. 'You got to reach the common [person].] Equipped with his 'nose for a good scoop,' this 'self-taught newshound' scours newspapers – and calls on an informal network of friends acting as correspondents – for the information necessary to keep everyone 'in the know.' For those unable to read words on a chalkboard, there are symbols – a blue helmet hanging beside the board means the story involves the United Nations peacekeeping force, while a chrome hubcap represents the president (the 'iron lady' of Liberian politics). In previous years his dedication to critical reporting has met resistance from those in power; he was arrested and spent a brief spell in prison, then went into exile while his newsstand was torn down. Today, with his plywood shed rebuilt, he remains steadfast in his belief that what he is doing matters for the country's emergent democracy. 'Daily Talk's objective is that everybody should absorb the news,' he maintains. 'Because when a few people out there make decisions on behalf of the masses that do not go down with them, we are all going to be victims.'

It is precisely this type of commitment to democratising the relations of power at the heart of communication that animates Olga Guedes Bailey, Bart Cammaerts and Nico Carpentier's *Understanding Alternative Media*. In a wide-ranging discussion, they argue that alternative media are part and parcel of the daily life of individuals, at once 'banal' and 'political' in their significance. The authors show how alternative media can be understood in different ways, from a variety of theoretical perspectives. They consider competing meanings of the 'alternative' in alternative media, including, for example, alternative in relation to mainstream media; as embedded in the citizenship politics of civil society; as a means for self-representation for communities, and as a hybrid form of independent media challenging established relations of authority and control. Across this continuum, the book examines the evolving uses of different forms and practices of alternative media, highlighting the relative extent to which they help to facilitate interactive, two-way processes of communication, connecting people and their concerns locally and globally. Important insights are generated through a number of case studies, encompassing community radio, diasporic media, civil society online forums, and blogging, amongst others. The examples depicted underscore the thesis that accounts of alternative media need to overcome the limitations of simple binaries – such as alternative versus mainstream – so as to address their status as contested spaces constructed, and reconstructed anew, according to the needs, experiences and aspirations of specific groups (particularly those otherwise underrepresented, ignored or trivialised elsewhere in the mediascape). All in all, the authors make a compelling case for re-imagining familiar approaches to alternative media, and demonstrate why the implications of such theorizing matter in real-world contexts far beyond the realm of academic debate.

The *Issues in Cultural and Media Studies* series aims to facilitate a diverse range of critical investigations into pressing questions considered to be central to current thinking and research. In light of the remarkable speed at which the conceptual agendas of cultural and media studies are changing, the series is committed to contributing to what is an ongoing process of re-evaluation and critique. Each of the books is intended to provide a lively, innovative and comprehensive introduction to a specific topical issue from a fresh perspective. The reader is offered a thorough grounding in the most salient debates indicative of the book's subject, as well as important insights into how new modes of enquiry may be established for future explorations. Taken as a whole, then, the series is designed to cover the core components of cultural and media studies courses in an imaginatively distinctive and engaging manner.

Stuart Allan

INTRODUCTION

It is summer 2006 in the countryside in the state of Ceara, Brazil. The Sunday open market is in full swing in the main square. It is a noisy, vibrant affair with crowds of shoppers going about their business. Local country music – *sertaneja* – is being broadcast, and the songs are interspersed by the DJ reading out romantic dedications, advertisements, and public announcements. This alternative radio broadcast is extremely rudimentary in terms of technology and format, but it is performing astonishingly well in terms of engaging with the local people, providing information and entertainment produced by and for the community. The scene could be any marketplace, almost anywhere in the world, and is but one example of alternative communication and its part in people's daily lives. All of which brings us to why we decided to write a book about alternative media.

We believe 'alternative' communication is important for daily life, for personal and collective politics, and for our sense of identity and belonging. This sense of belonging takes diverse forms: participation in more formal 'politics' as well as in the banality of daily life, for instance, the ability to have one's voice heard at a Sunday open market. At all those levels alternative media are inclusive of and go beyond the political realm and reach the everyday life of individuals and communities. More than ever, we are living in a world of mediated experiences where the centrality and power of mainstream media are pervasive, and where the variety of the alternative spaces of mediated communication are acquiring increasing importance as means of representation of public and private ideas and action, and as their stimuli. We argue in this book that the definition of 'alternative' media should be amplified to include a wider spectrum of media generally working to democratize information/communication. We make a case for a reimagining of the alternative media canon, for a new grammar that includes practices overlooked by the current discourses defining what constitutes 'alternative media'.

We use the established discourses as a prudent point of departure to explore a wider vision of alternative media which cross established borders. We believe this book is opportune in the context of the fundamental changes occurring in the realms of the global and local media landscapes, particularly at the level of ordinary people's daily lives (and politics). This reconfiguration has been brought about by the confluence of several features: new technology (the proliferation of cable television channels and the explosion of sites on the World Wide Web); the fragmentation and fracturing of media spaces; the liberalization of media markets; and the possibilities opened up by the reduction in the costs of producing media.

These shifts have implications for the exercise of democracy, power, inclusion, comprising the right to communicate and to be represented in the media, and public participation in the political, public sphere both through engagement with the ongoing politics of recognition of different social groups and/or the global social struggles of broader political causes.

Understanding Alternative Media thus begins from the premise that the existing genealogy of alternative media relies on an unsustainable set of distinctions such as that between non-commercial and commercial or radical and non-radical alternative media. We suggest that the identity of alternative media should be articulated as relational and contingent on the particularities of the contexts of production, distribution, and consumption. The discussion, therefore, involves a series of both intersecting and disjunctive critical case studies that disconcert the traditional investment in essentialist notions of alternative media.

Our aim is to work toward a politics of communication that is concerned with forms of mediated communication that are 'alternative', not only in relation to the mainstream but also in their potential to voice ideas which are important and distinctive in their own right, that are not necessarily counter-hegemonic, but are still of significance for different communities. Our concern is not with the 'big media', but with the 'small' media that are enabling conversation among those who might be outside the mainstream public sphere and/or 'in transit' between different public media spaces, and presenting us with new ways of conceiving a democratic-political project of communication. We are not celebrating 'alternative' media *per se*; we are exploring the plethora of alternative spaces that might allow for a renewal of what constitutes the practices of alternative communication/media in the new millennium. We are pointing to the need for greater empowerment of the large majority of ordinary people removed and disfranchised from the media and the political public spheres.

Structurally, the book is organized into two parts. Part I, the theoretical framework, contains two chapters. In Chapter 1, the central argument is for multiple approaches to account for the fluidity and array of alternative media identities. We examine what is meant by the term 'alternative media'. This exposes the elusiveness of the concept 'alternative' and shows that alternative media are articulated in many different ways – not only in relation to the mainstream media, but also as community media, as civil society media, and as rhizomatic media. This discussion is informed by existing democratic and political approaches that have theoretically sustained the identities and practices of alternative media. It also examines the relationship between power and politics, and the role of civil society as a space of empowerment and the exercise of citizenship, emphasizing the importance of media and communication in democratic societies for the promotion of a civic culture.

Chapter 2 contextualizes the argument of the multiple identities of alternative media, which is illustrated by an in-depth analysis of the Brazilian movie *Radio Favela*. This romanticized film about an alternative radio station shows how the community participates in and represents itself through Rádio Favela. It equally clearly shows how this radio station positions itself as an alternative to the mainstream media, as an alternative culture of poverty and pride towards the mainstream capitalist culture, and as a civil society alternative during the Brazilian military dictatorship. Finally, the film illustrates the interconnectedness of alternative radio stations, and their complex (rhizomatic) links with other civil society organizations, but also with the mainstream media, the state, and the market(s).

Part II situates the theoretical discussion in the context of the alternative media practices of a variety of actors, including social movements and ethnic minority groups, from both a local and a global perspective. We investigate the case studies through the production–text–consumption circuit of alternative media. This empirical part of the book is structured in terms of the four approaches to understanding alternative media, set out in Chapter 1: 'serving a community'; 'alternative media as an alternative to mainstream media'; 'linking alternative media to civil society'; and 'alternative media as rhizome'.

Chapters 3 and 4 address the category of serving the community. Chapter 3 examines the impact of media regulation and policy on alternative 'community' radio stations in three Western countries – the UK, the USA, and Belgium. We suggest that, even taking account of the different media histories and approaches in the media policies analysed, alternative radio stations have had trouble in establishing themselves alongside public and commercial broadcasters. While they are gradually coming to be recognized as complementary to public and commercial broadcasting, alternative 'community' radios are still struggling for their right to communicate. Chapter 4 presents the case of diasporic media practices looking at how diasporas and migrants use 'alternative media' to create a third space of communication – public sphericules – and to produce and sustain transnational communities and networks of diasporic groups. In their diversity, these diasporic media are paramount in the communicative landscape of diasporas, not only for their reimagining of the self and belonging within and across spaces, but for their struggles for pluralistic representations.

An alternative to the mainstream is addressed in Chapters 5 and 6. Chapter 5 explores the recent phenomenon of blogging, and particularly its role in the representation of the second Iraqi War, through three distinct sub-cases. First, we focus on the use of blogging by Iraqi citizens, which provides an alternative articulation of the experience of war. A number of these bloggers were appropriated by various mainstream media because of their alternative discourses and perspectives. Second, blog sites of US military personnel – 'mili-blogs – are analysed; they present, at times, alternative representations of war that challenge mainstream rational reporting, while at other times they merely reproduce the dominant hegemony of war. Finally, we contextualize the role of photo-blogs in the case of the worldwide dissemination of the pictures of Abu Ghraib prisoners being tortured.

Chapter 6 argues that the lack of visibility and misrepresentation of ethnic and religious minorities has generated an ongoing struggle over meaning, between the minorities at the periphery of society and the mainstream media. As a political response, ethnic-religious communities have created alternative, discursively connected public spheres, which potentially work to minimize mainstream media hegemonic power over meaning. Based on the case study of *Q-News*, a magazine catering for Muslim communities, we suggest that commercial minority media should be analysed as social actors that cross the defined borders of 'alternative' media and are located in the 'public sphericules' of multicultural societies, where they articulate the struggles for inclusion and identity recognition of minorities.

Chapters 7 and 8 present case studies illustrating alternative media as part of civil society. Chapter 7 analyses civil society mailing lists and forums as an expression of (online) participation in the public sphere. Two quite distinct cases are presented. On the one hand, we examine the use of mailing lists by civil society actors to enable participation in policy processes beyond the nation-state. Mailing lists can be considered potentially to be a (cost-)efficient means of connecting dispersed activists, networking, exchanging information and facilitating internal decision-making processes. On the other hand, we explore the use of the Internet by media activists, such as Indymedia, to facilitate debate and interaction between citizens. While the former relates to a more consensual approach, the latter is clearly conflictual in nature.

Chapter 8 centres on the very local, though connected to the global, experience of the Brazilian Landless Rural Workers' Movement (MST) and its political action and alternative communication strategies. We contend that the movement uses political action both to define a collective identity and to communicate with the Brazilian people. These actions become a communication medium, which extends our understanding of alternative communication beyond a media-centric perspective, and suggests a blurring of communication with media.

Chapters 9 and 10 argue for the alternative media as rhizome by exploring the case study of the RadioSwap project, and the practice of 'political jamming'. In Chapter 9, the focus is on the network of alternative media producers and the alliances they establish with other civil society organizations through the use of an electronic archive called RadioSwap. This network of radio producers is firmly rooted in the local, but at the same time transcends it. Through its architecture, RadioSwap becomes a translocal community of interest, based on the exchange of self-produced audio that crosses the frontiers of the local, without losing its connection to it. The analysis of the RadioSwap project not only illustrates the difficulties that alternative media have to face when striving for this translocal identity, but also shows that RadioSwap is the materialization of the need and the dream to follow the trajectory of networked global civil society, without losing its grip on its roots.

Chapter 10 investigates the phenomenon of cultural and political jamming, playfully overturning hegemonic discourses and representations. The discussion is set within a historical perspective and examines revolutionary art movements, dating back to the 1960s. Several examples of current forms of jamming the political demonstrate that activists use these techniques to produce and distribute counter-hegemonic discourses through parody and satire. In this regard, the street, alternative forums, the Internet, as well as mainstream media are examined. However, it becomes apparent that these subversive techniques are being appropriated or co-opted by both reactionary forces and formal political actors.

Finally, in the concluding chapter, we evaluate our claim for a more inclusive conceptualization of 'alternative media'. We argue that the four approaches to understanding alternative media are not mutually exclusive, as each has its own merits, and, in conjunction, form a panoptic and encompassing view of alternative media. This panoptic perspective facilitates an appreciation of the diversity and multiplicity of alternative media initiatives, acknowledging their connections to communities, their distinctiveness from mainstream media embedded in civil society, and the fluidity of the boundaries that we construct between alternative and mainstream, between civil society, the state, and the market.

PART I:
THEORIZING ALTERNATIVE MEDIA

1 | FOUR APPROACHES TO ALTERNATIVE MEDIA

Even within a single area of alternative media there is much heterogeneity (of styles, of contributions, of perspectives).

(Atton 2002: 8)

Introduction

In the aftermath of the student and workers' revolt in May 1968, *Libération* appeared as the new 'alternative' newspaper of the Left in France. Its first issue (18 April 1973) carried the following comment:

> Since May 1968, the need for a new daily paper has been felt everywhere. A whole movement of ideas seeks to express itself, a movement that cuts across all the currents of the existing left, organised or not. Admittedly, it is confused, crossed by divisions, but nevertheless glued together around a common refusal of an authoritarian conception of life and around a common aspiration: for a democracy rejecting the exploitation of work, everyday violence in the name of profits, the violence of men against women, the repressions of sexuality, racism, a spoilt environment.

> (cited in Mattelart 1983: 63)

This quote illustrates a number of issues that are of importance for this book. First, by referring to sexuality, racism, women's rights, and the environment, it signals a widening of what constitutes the political. Second, it explicitly places the political within an open democratic project. Third, in refusing an authoritarian conception of life and politics, it touches upon the notion of power. Fourth, it talks about a movement of ideas, which can be attributed to a perceived need and struggle for change, as well as to the need for a medium to string together the different currents within the movement. Finally, *Libération*'s troublesome history also illustrates how difficult it is for alternative media to survive in a market economy.[1]

The above example shows that media do not operate or function in a vacuum, but are embedded in economic, political and cultural settings, be they local, national, regional or international. That is why, to understand (the importance of) alternative media we need to situate them in the political and democratic theories that have provided theoretical and intellectual support for their identities and practices. The participatory models of democracy and the related broadening of the definition of the political especially have influenced and cross-fertilized alternative media.

Participatory models of democracy emphasize the importance of 'real' citizens' participation and their more active involvement in democracy (Barber 1984). As such, they criticize the radical separation of citizens from power, the elites and democratic institutions through representation, as argued for by more elitist democratic theorists such as Schumpeter (1942). As Pateman (1970: 42) explains:

> The existence of representative institutions at national level is not sufficient for democracy; for maximum participation by all the people at that level socialisation, or 'social training', for democracy must take place in other spheres in order that the necessary individual attitudes and psychological qualities can be developed. This development takes place through the process of participation itself.

While the extreme position of participatory democracy falls back on an idealized vision of Athenian direct democracy (Blackwell 2003; Gore 1994; White 1997), other conceptualizations try to reconcile the representative character of current liberal-democratic systems with various degrees of inclusive participatory instruments. These instruments range from public consultations, citizens' juries and so-called multi-stakeholderism (Hemmati 2002), to voluntary organizations. Contrary to the more deliberative models, direct democracy is a much more individualized form of participatory democracy in which decision-making is based on the aggregate of individual opinions, for example, referenda.

The New Left conceptualizations of participatory democracy – developed by Pateman (1970, 1985) and MacPherson (1966, 1973, 1977) – focus on the combination of the principles and practices of direct and representative democracy. The problems of coordination in large-scale communities bring them to accept representation as a necessary tool at the level of national decision-making. At the same time they plead for the (partial) introduction of direct democracy in more localized and organizational spheres such as the political party system, the workplace and the local community. Although media do not feature prominently in their work, it is self-evident that they could (and should) be included in this list of organizational spheres.

Finally, the political is approached here in a broad sense and not restricted to a specific sphere or system. The political is seen as a dimension that is 'inherent to every human society and that determines our very ontological condition' (Mouffe 1997: 3).

From this it follows that the political cannot be reduced to the formal political system, to institutions or to political procedures. Such a perspective on the political sees the whole of society in its different aspects – the school, the family, the workplace, the community and (alternative) media, as equally valid spheres for political-democratic activities. At the same time, this widening of what constitutes the political allows for the accomodation of sexual, gendered and cultural identities and struggles within the democratic project.

Defining the identity of alternative media

However relevant the above contextualization of alternative media is, these media are at the same time characterized by diversity and contingency. Even the concepts of 'alternative media', 'community media', 'civil society media' and 'rhizomatic media', which will be discussed in this chapter, have proven, in the long theoretical and empirical tradition of media research,[2] to be highly elusive. The multiplicity of media organizations that carry these names have caused most mono-theoretical approaches to focus on only certain characteristics, ignoring other aspects of the identity of alternative media. This theoretical problem necessitates the use of different approaches to defining alternative media that allow for complementary emphasis on different aspects of alternative media.

This chapter aims to combine four theoretical approaches in order to capture the diversity and specificity of alternative media, to demonstrate their importance and to show the problems they face.[3] The next chapter illustrates these four approaches by analysing the Brazilian film *Radio Favela*. This very convoluted film narrates the struggles surrounding a slum radio station in Belo Horizonte.

In the multi-theoretical combination of approaches, Laclau and Mouffe's (1985) political identity theory is used as an overarching theoretical framework. Their critique on essentialism that 'There is no single underlying principle fixing – and hence constituting – the whole field of differences' (Laclau and Mouffe 1985: 111) is used to structure the theoretical approaches to alternative media. Their position allows us to distinguish between more essentialist and more relationist approaches to provide an overview of the components that construct the identity of alternative media. The more essentialist approaches tend to see identities as stable, independent and possessing a 'true' essence. The more relationist approaches incorporate notions of fluidity and contingency, see identities as mutually dependent and ignore the existence of 'true' essences.

Despite the incorporation of these essentialist approaches in this chapter (because of their importance in alternative media theory), identities are still – following Laclau and Mouffe – basically seen as relational, contingent and the result of articulatory practices within a discursive framework, which de-essentializes the two essentialist approaches. Special attention is given to the concept of antagonism, which is seen by

Laclau and Mouffe (1985: 125) as 'the limits of every objectivity' or 'the impossibility of fully constituting [society]'. While social antagonisms are traditionally seen as confrontations between actors with fully constituted identities, Laclau and Mouffe argue that social antagonisms both threaten and constitute identities. In the case of antagonism 'the presence of the "Other" prevents me from being totally myself', which means that within an antagonistic situation 'I cannot be a full presence for myself' (Laclau and Mouffe 1985: 125). At the same time antagonism has a constitutive effect on identity (and society), as the 'other' becomes a purely negative point of identification or a constitutive outside. Howarth (2000: 106), for instance, writes that the role of antagonisms 'is thus constitutive of social objectivity, as social formations depend upon the construction of antagonistic relations between social agents "inside" and "outside" a social formation'. In this chapter we contend that these antagonisms play an important role in defining the identity of alternative media, even in traditional media-centred models.

Although the first approach to alternative media (focusing on serving the community) uses a more essentialist theoretical framework that stresses the importance of the community, others explicitly focus on the relationship between alternative and mainstream media. This approach thus puts more emphasis on the relation of interdependency between two antagonistic sets of identities (alternative and mainstream). These traditional models for theorizing the identity of alternative media are complemented by two society-centred approaches.[4] The first of these society-centred approaches defines alternative media as part of civil society. Despite the basic assumption that these civil organizations differ fundamentally from market and state organizations, some emphasis is still put on the interdependency of these identities. In this approach the autonomy of the identity of civil society organizations nevertheless remains an important theoretical assumption. In order to incorporate the more relationist aspects of civil society theory – articulated, for instance, by Walzer (1998) – these identities are combined with the critiques of Downing et al. (2001), Rodriguez (2001) and Caldwell (2003) on alternative media, and radicalized and unified in a fourth approach, which builds on the Deleuzian metaphor of the rhizome. This approach allows the incorporation (even more) of aspects of contingency, fluidity and elusiveness in the analysis of alternative media.

The four approaches are depicted in Figure 1.1.

Multi-theoretical approaches

A promising starting point for the analysis is given by the working definition of community radio adopted by AMARC-Europe, the European branch of the World Association of Community Radio Broadcasters,[5] an organization that encompasses a wide range of radio practices in different continents. In Latin America, the AMARC constituents are popular radio, educational radio, miners' radio, and peasants' radio. In Africa, they refer to local rural radio, while in Europe the terms associative radio,

	Media-centred	Society-centred
Autonomous identity of community media (essentialist)	Approach I: Serving the community	
		Approach III: Part of civil society
Identity of community media in relation to other identities (relationalist)	Approach II: An alternative to mainstream	Approach IV: Rhizome

Figure 1.1 Positioning the four theoretical approaches.

free radio, popular free radio,[6] neighbourhood radio, alternative radio and community radio are used. Asians speak of radio for development and of community radio; in Oceania the terms aboriginal radio, public radio and community radio are used (Servaes 1999: 259). This semiotic diversity not only forces us to select one denominator (alternative media) as a starting point, but, more importantly, it also shows the diversity of identities and practices. In its attempt to encompass all these identities and practices, and to avoid a prescriptive definition that would include some and exclude others, AMARC-Europe (1994: 4) describes a 'community radio station' as 'a "non-profit" station, currently broadcasting, which offers a service to the community in which it is located, or to which it broadcasts, while promoting the participation of this community in the radio'.

Approach one: Serving a community

From AMARC's working definition it is clear that there is a strong emphasis on the concept of community. Moreover, it explicitly highlights the geographical aspect ('in which it is located'), although other types of relationships between medium and community are mentioned ('to which it broadcasts').

Given the importance of the concept of community, we need to look at its definition. Within the disciplines of sociology and anthropology, the concept of community has a long history. In the nineteenth century, Tönnies (1963) theorized a distinction between community and society, in which community is defined by the presence of close and concrete human ties and by a collective identity. The prevalent feature of society is the absence of identifying group relations (Martin-Barbero 1993: 29). Morris and Morton (1998: 12–13) exemplify Tönnies's distinction using the concepts of communion and association; community thus refers to the 'notion of a big family', while society 'represents a colder, unattached and more fragmented way of living devoid of co-operation and social cohesion. Instead of a sense of neighbourliness, people are isolated'.

A second (and related) feature is that a community does not require a formal organizing body, although it is often linked to such a body. As Williams (1976: 76) puts it in his *Keywords*:

> The complexity of community thus relates to the difficult interaction between the tendencies originally distinguished in the historical development: on the one hand the sense of direct common concern; on the other hand the materialization of various forms of common organization, which may or may not adequately express this.

Beyond geography (and ethnicity)

Leunissen (1986) argues that conceptualizations of community predominantly refer to geography and ethnicity as structuring notions of the collective identity or group relations. In an early overview of community definitions, Hillery (1955: 111) emphasized the geographical dimension when he concluded that 'most students (of community) are in basic agreement that community consists of persons in social interaction within a geographic area and having one or more additional ties.'

These structural conceptualizations of community have been redefined in the following ways:

• by supplementing the geographical with the non-geographical, and
• by supplementing the structural/material with the cultural.

The first non-geographical definition of community is the 'community of interest'. Although one cannot explicitly assume that a group of people has common interests[7] (see Clark 1973: 411ff.), the communality of interest can form the conditions of possibility for the emergence or existence of a community. As Lewis (1993: 13) remarks, a community of interest can extend 'across conurbations, nations and continents' and thus bypasses the geographical definition. Popple (1995: 4) distinguishes between communities of 'locality or territory' and 'a communality of interest or interest group such as the black community or the Jewish community'. Popple adds that people sharing a common condition or problem – such as alcohol dependency – can also be seen as a community of interest.

Jean Lave and Etienne Wenger developed the related notion of 'communities of practice'. Here, emphasis is placed on the presence of shared practice. A community of practice is a joint enterprise, with mutual engagement of the members involved and with a shared repertoire of communal resources (Wenger 1998: 45). As Wenger et al. (2002: 4) put it: communities of practice are 'groups of people who share a concern, a set of problems, or a passion about a topic, and who deepen their knowledge and expertise in this area by interacting on an ongoing basis'.

Analysis of the impact of information and communication technologies (ICTs) on everyday life has shown that communities are formed not only in geographically defined spaces, but also in cyberspace. These communities are termed 'virtual' or 'online' communities. As is often the case when new technologies attract (academic or other) attention, their newness is emphasized and the 'definitory' links with the past are severed. Howard Rheingold's (2001) definition of 'his' virtual community thus includes only the following components:

> Organized around affinities, shared interests, bringing together people who did
>   not necessarily know each other before meeting on-line.
> Many to many media. . . .
> Text-based, evolving into text plus graphics-based communications. . . .
> Relatively uncoupled from face to face social life in geographic communities.

Castells (1996: 352) employs a similar definition in his *Rise of the Network Society* in which he describes the virtual community as:

> a self-defined electronic network of interactive communication organized around
> a shared interest or purpose, although sometimes communication becomes the
> goal in itself. Such communities may be relatively formalized, as in the case
> of hosted conferences or bulletin board systems, or be spontaneously formed by
> social networks, which keep logging into the network to send and retrieve mes-
> sages in a chosen time pattern (either delayed or in real time).

Jones (1995) shows that virtual or online communities and geographically based communities have similar characteristics, while Kitchin (1998: 86–97) argues that people within virtual or online communities can form strong, cohesive and supportive groupings, rendering these communities global. These 'new' communities have altered the rather fixed ideas about space and place (Casey 1997). They have clearly shown that geographical proximity is not in all cases a necessary condition for, or quality of, community. The increased emphasis on (global) space, threatening (local) place with discursive erasure, has prompted some authors to come to the defence of place, at the same time avoiding the trap of romanticizing it (see also Escobar 2000). Hollander (2000: 372), for instance, argues that place-based communities also use ICTs. Cyberspace is, in other words, complemented by cyberplace. What nevertheless remains a defining feature of community is the direct and frequent contact between members and the feeling of belonging and sharing.

A second type of reconceptualization is based on the emphasis of the subjective construction of community, in which Fish's (1980) and Lindlof's (1988) concept of 'interpretative community', Cohen's (1985) 'community of meaning' and Anderson's (1983) 'imagined community' are relevant. Although Fish developed his notion of interpretative community to deal with different interpretative frameworks in literary criticism, and Lindlof's reconceptualization was specifically aimed at redefining the audience as a community, their concepts focus on the cultural communalities that are found when texts are interpreted. Janice Radway (1991) illustrates magnificently how a female romance reading group develops into an interpretative community with shared interpretations and meanings attributed to the popular literature they are consuming.

Cohen (1985: 70), in line with the above, pleads for 'a shift away from the structure of community towards a symbolic construction of community' and, in order to do so, takes culture rather than structure as the point of departure. Communities then become 'worlds of meaning in the minds of their members' (Cohen 1985: 20). Finally, Anderson (1983) emphasizes the imaginary nature of the political community or nation, 'because the members of even the smallest nation will never know most of their fellow-members, meet them, or even hear of them, yet in the minds of each lives the image of their communion' (Anderson 1983: 15). From this perspective, community is not something that is imposed on people from the outside. A community is actively constructed by its members and those members derive an identity from this construction. This perspective also allows defining community as fluid and contingent, where the feeling of belonging to a community does not necessarily exclude affinities towards other communities or social structures.

These conceptualizations are depicted in Figure 1.2.

Access, participation, and the media
Alternative media are oriented towards a community, regardless of its exact nature (defined geographically/spatially or otherwise), but the relationship between the medium and the actual community transcends 'ordinary' one-way communication, where 'topics are chosen in the same way, by professional communicators, and targeted towards the apparent needs and interests of the audience' (Berrigan 1979: 7). As is illustrated in AMARC's working definition (especially in stating that community

Community as close and concrete human ties, as 'communion', as a collective identity, with identifying group relations.		
Traditional:	**Reconceptualization 1:** Supplementing the geographical with the non-geographical	**Reconceptualization 2:** Supplementing the structural/ material with the cultural
• geography • ethnicity	• community of interest • community of practice • virtual or online community	• interpretative community • community of meaning • imagined community

Figure 1.2 Defining community.

media should be 'promoting the participation of this community'), relationships between broadcaster and community are defined by the concept of two-way communication. Here, the concepts of access and participation become important.

When focusing more explicitly on alternative media's role in facilitating participation, we need to distinguish between participation *in* the media and *through* the media, similar to the way in which Wasko and Mosco (1992: 7) distinguished between democratization *in* and *through* the media. Both participation *in* the media and *through* the media see the (mass) communicative process not as a series of practices that are often restrictively controlled by media professionals, but as a human right that cuts across entire societies.

Participation *in* the media deals with the participation of non-professionals in the production of media output (content-related participation) and in media decision-making (structural participation). Firstly, these forms of media participation allow citizens to be active in one of the many (micro-)spheres relevant to daily life and to put into practice their right to communicate (see below). Secondly, these forms of micro-participation are considered to be important because they allow people to learn and adopt a democratic and/or civic attitude, thus strengthening (the possible forms) of macro-participation, as well as the civic culture. Verba and Nie (1987: 3) summarize it as 'a participatory polity [that] may rest on a participatory society'.

Participation *through* the media deals with the opportunities for extensive participation in public debate and for self-representation in public spaces. This immediately implies that we are now entering the realm of enabling and facilitating macro-participation, which is related to the more ritualistic approaches towards media in general (Couldry 2002). Starting from a broadly defined notion of the political, consensus-oriented models of democracy (and participation) emphasize the importance of dialogue and deliberation and focus on collective decision-making in a public sphere based on rational arguments *à la* Habermas. Other authors (Fraser 1990; Mouffe 1994) stress more conflict-oriented approaches and oppositional public spheres. They point to the unavoidability of political differences and struggles and see the media as crucial sites for struggles for hegemony (Kellner 1992: 57). Despite their differences, both consensus- and conflict-oriented models stress the need for citizens to participate in these processes of dialogue, debate, and deliberation.

Although mainstream media have attempted to organize forms of audience participation (Livingstone and Lunt 1994; McNair et al. 2003; Carpentier 2003),[8] alternative media in particular have proven to be more successful in organizing deeper forms of participation in the media, whether online or offline (Girard 1992; Downing et al. 2001; Rodriguez 2001). This position is exemplified by Berrigan, who claims that access by the community and the participation of the community should be considered key defining factors for alternative media, they:

> are media to which members of the community have access, for information, education, entertainment, when they want access. They are media in which the

community participates, as planners, producers, performers. They are the means of expression of the community, rather than for the community.

(Berrigan 1979: 8)

Defining participation

However important, access and participation are not straightforward notions. As Pateman (1970: 1) puts it (focusing on participation): 'the widespread use of the term . . . has tended to mean that any precise, meaningful content has almost disappeared; "participation" is used to refer to a wide variety of different situations by different people'. It is tempting to see this process of the emptying of the concept of participation as a neutral event or as an accident of history. A more critical analysis shows that this is actually an ideological process, which aims (or threatens) to remove the more radical meanings from the concept of participation (Carpentier 2007c).

Two perspectives have had a fundamental impact on these more radical meanings of access and participation: Freire's dialogical pedagogy and the debates in the United Nations Educational, Scientific and Cultural Organization (UNESCO) about access, participation and self-management in the 1970s.

Despite Freire's focus on the educational process and the struggle against illiteracy and injustice, in which minimal account is taken of the (mass) medial context, Freire's theory has had a considerable impact within the domain of participatory communication. Thomas (1994: 51) describes this influence as follows:

> Although he never really linked his analysis to the use of particular media, it is implicit in his writings that communication, in order to be effective, has to be participatory, dialogic and reciprocal. In fact, the entire enterprise of participatory communication projects, from the organization and production of community radio in Latin America, Australia, and parts of Africa and Asia, through the practices of popular theatre in countries like Brazil, Chile, Jamaica, South Africa, India, and the Philippines utilize[s] Freire's perspective.

Freire's (1970) 'pedagogy of the oppressed' is aimed against the traditional educational system, which he regards paternalistic and non-participative. His argument is that the traditional system considers knowledge as something that is passed on as a ready-made package rather than being the result of a dialogic meeting between subjects. The end result is that the education system is maintaining and supporting existing power imbalances. Freire aims to transform this system, allowing students (together with their teachers) to develop valid knowledge in a process of 'conscientization'. 'Authentic participation would then enable the subjects involved in this dialogic encounter to unveil reality for themselves' (Thomas 1994: 51). In other words, participation is situated in a context of reduction in power imbalances, at both the broad social, political and economic levels (the relations between oppressors and repressed), and at the level of the education system, where students and teachers strive for knowledge in a non-authoritative collaboration that fosters partnership.

A second perspective was initiated at the UNESCO debates in the 1970s about the New World Information and Communication Order (NWICO) with the plea for a 'free and balanced flow of information'. Very much at the centre of these debates was the right to communicate – referred to by Jacobson (1998) as a third-generation human right. When this right was originally proposed in 1969 – by the French civil servant, Jean d'Arcy – it aimed to broaden the right to be informed, which is embedded in Article 19 of the Universal Declaration of Human Rights.[9] In 1980 the International Commission for the Study of Communication Problems (ICSCP) produced the so-called MacBride Report, *Many Voices, One World* (see ICSCP 2004). This was the first attempt to introduce the notion of communication rights at an international level and represented the right to communicate as a fundamental human right.

This repositioning expanded the traditional Western and liberal 'right to be informed', and redefined communication as 'a *two way process*, in which the partners – individual and collective – carry on a democratic and balanced *dialogue*' (ICSCP 2004: 172; emphasis added). In practice this meant that 'a) the individual becomes an active partner and not a mere object of communication; b) the variety of messages exchanged increases; and c) the extent and quality of social representation or participation in communication are augmented' (ICSCP 2004: 166).

In the UNESCO debates on the NWICO clear definitions of (the distinction between) access and participation were formulated. While their definition of access stressed the availability of opportunities to choose relevant programmes and to have a means of feedback, participation implied 'a higher level of public involvement . . . in the production process and also in the management and planning of communication systems' (Servaes 1999: 85; see ICSCP 2004). Referring to the 1977 UNESCO meeting in Belgrade, Berrigan (1979: 18) (partially) links access to the reception of information, education, and entertainment considered relevant by/for the community: '[Access] may be defined in terms of the opportunities available to the public to choose varied and relevant programs, and to have a means of feedback to transmit its reactions and demands to production organizations.' Others limit access to mass media and see it as 'the processes that permit users to provide relatively open and unedited input to the mass media' (Lewis 1993: 12). Both the production and reception approaches are considered relevant and are included in Figure 1.3.

Participation, following Pateman (1970: 71), can thus be seen as a process in which the individual members (of a community) have a certain degree of power to influence or determine the outcome of that process. She defines partial participation as 'a process in which two or more parties *influence* each other in the making of decisions but the final *power* to decide rests with one party only' (Pateman 1970: 70; emphasis added), whereas full participation is seen as 'a process where each individual member of a decision-making body has equal *power* to determine the outcome of decisions' (Pateman 1970: 71; emphasis added).

Alternative media not only allow but also facilitate the participation (in its more radical meaning) of its members (or the community) in both the produced content and

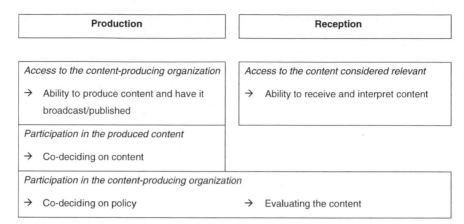

Figure 1.3 Access and participation of the community.

the content-producing organization. Prehn (1992: 259) describes the practical consequences of this definition of participation as follows: 'participation implies a wider range of activities related to involving people directly in station programming, administration and policy activities'. Although power imbalances will not totally disappear, alternative media empower community members to co-decide at both the level of media content and organization.

Access and participation of the community in alternative media
In approach one – focused on serving the community – the relationship between the broadcaster and the community is in the foreground. By choosing a specific community as a target group, the (concept of) community itself is validated and strengthened. The audience is not defined as an aggregate of individuals with common socio-demographic or economic characteristics, but instead is defined as a collective of people incorporating a series of identifying group relations. Thus, the situatedness of the audience as part of a complex set of social structures is emphasized, deepening and bridging the traditional state–citizen and medium–audience dichotomies that still tend to articulate publics and audiences as (albeit segmented) aggregates of individuals.

Moreover, the aim of alternative media in approach one – serving the community – is often translated as enabling and facilitating access and participation by members of the community. 'Ordinary people'[10] are given the opportunity for their voices to be heard, and take responsibility for distributing their own ideologies and representations. Topics that are considered relevant to the community can be discussed by members of the community. This empowers its members by signifying that their statements are considered important enough to be broadcast. Societal groups that are represented one-sidedly, disadvantaged, stigmatized, or even repressed can especially benefit from using the channels of communication opened by alternative media, to strengthen their internal identity, manifest this identity to the outside world, and thus enable social change and/or development.

On the downside, this orientation towards community also creates a situation of dependency on the community, as two-way communication requires two partners more or less equally interested in communicating. While the dominant discourse on media is based on one-way communication, raising the community's interest to go beyond this limited form of communication does not speak for itself, due to what can be called the lack of two-way communication skills and interest. This problem is exacerbated by the diffusion of specific technologies oriented towards one-way communication and the lack of technologies facilitating two-way communication. Moreover, the concept of community has often been reduced to its geographical meaning. This reduction has trapped alternative media in the position of small-scale local media, gradually de-emphasizing their role of serving the community and eventually leading to the adoption of commercial media formats in their efforts to survive.

Approach two: Alternative media as an alternative to mainstream media

A second approach to defining alternative media focuses on the notion of the alternative. This concept introduces a distinction between mainstream and alternative media, in which alternative media are seen as a supplement to mainstream media, or as a counter-hegemonic critique of the mainstream.

Alternative media are inseparable from ideology, domination and the Gramscian notion of hegemony. As Atton (2002: 15) quite rightly states:

> We might consider the entire range of alternative and radical media as representing challenges to hegemony, whether on an explicitly political platform, or employing the kinds of indirect challenges through experimentation and transformation of existing roles, routines, emblems and signs . . . at the heart of counter-hegemonic subcultural style.

Along the same lines, Downing et al. (2001: v) describe alternative – or rather, radical – media as 'generally small-scale' and expressing 'an alternative vision to hegemonic policies, priorities and perspectives'.

For this reason, we now turn first to the work of the Italian Marxist theorist Antonio Gramsci, and particularly to his ideas registered in the *Prison Notebooks* (Gramsci 1971). Gramsci's thought focused on the process of intellectual and political changes through ideologies. It is a process in which different elements of an established ideological system are (re)articulated into a new system (Mouffe 1981). Hall (1996: 32) points out that for Gramsci 'ideological struggles do not happen by displacing one whole, integral, class-mode of thought with another wholly-formed systems of ideas'. Ideological struggles work through a political strategy which involves a long and uneven struggle over the hegemony of the dominant group. They work not only when people try to contest or rupture an established ideological field in favour of an entirely new one (in the case of revolutionary struggles), but also when they disrupt the existing ideologies by transforming their meanings. According to Hall (1996: 31), 'often, ideological struggle actually consists of attempting to win some new set of meanings for an existing term or category, of disarticulating it from its place in a signifying structure'.

The concept of hegemony offers a historically contingent and negotiated view of how ideology works. Gramsci recognized the centrality of the ideological role of representation of 'common sense', the power of the 'taken-for-granted' and thus the important role of popular culture and the media in the ideological process (Turner 1992: 212). As Eagleton (1991: 115) suggests, 'if the concept of hegemony extends and enriches the notion of ideology, it also lends this otherwise somewhat abstract term a material body and political cutting edge'.

Hegemony and representation
In discussing alternative media it is important to grasp the relationship between media and representation since one reason for the very existence of alternative media is to voice the 'ideologies' of those under- or misrepresented in the mainstream channels of communication. As Fleras and Kunz (2001: 40) remind us: 'Mainstream media are framed as a contested site of competing agendas whose inner logic, institutional values, and commercial imperatives induce a reading of reality at odds with the aspirations of those outside a mainstream orbit'. Mainstream media[11] are likely to construct and grant legitimacy to 'leading' social values through constant exposure of them to the audience. In this process mainstream media become ideological as they reproduce a constructed and preferred view of 'reality'. In addition, they have the power to define which specific issues to bring to the public arena, and they become ideological by giving priority to the ideas of the main social actors such as the state, politicians, and private sector over the views of disfranchised minorities in civil society.

For example, most of the mainstream media coverage of the protests against the World Trade Organization meeting in Seattle in 2000 showed protesters as misinformed people or individuals involved in the destruction of private property and engaging in acts of violence in public spaces; their views on global capitalism and social injustice were portrayed in a condescending and dismissive manner (DeLuca and Peeples 2002; Almeida and Lichbach 2003: 264). The mainstream news media mostly used official sources for information and opinion and very often denied access to the protesters to present their views. The result of this type of media representation was a demonization of the demonstrators as ultra-violent and the construction of a general consensus in favour of economic globalization; it was a missed opportunity for the media to inform the public about the issue of free trade from various perspectives (Howley 2005).

Representation in this political context becomes a 'struggle for meaning' and is an important source of social knowledge production – a 'system, connected in more intimate ways with social practices and questions of power' (Hall 1997: 42). Reality and its meanings are constructed within language, discourse, and representation within a specific history and culture. In discursive terms this means that representation not so much distorts reality as productively provides the means by which reality is actively constructed (Hall 1997). For example, the British mainstream media have helped to reinforce a sense of national identity, of an 'us versus them' dichotomy, through their coverage of the alleged threat posed by immigrants to the British way of life. This in turn may reinforce old negative stereotypes of immigrants which might help to shape the audience's perceptions of foreigners and their inclusion or exclusion in the new country (see Bailey and Harindranath 2005). This example also highlights the relationship between media representation and the material world, that is, symbolic representations are embedded in society through language and culture and they relate to the link between meaning and processes of political decision-making.

To that end, cultural scholars have drawn attention to the political significance of constructing class, ethnic, racial, gender or sexual identities through the development of images and narratives. This remark relates to a problematization of the modes of authority embedded in practices of cultural representation (Barnett 2003). As such, it draws on Foucault's argument regarding the power of historically particular discourses,[12] often legitimized by regulatory frameworks, to define how we should define ourselves and others, and how we understand our experience and social roles or subject-positions in different sectors of life such as sexuality, psychiatry, and crime. The distinct roles attributed to the individual within a particular discourse permits different types of identity to submerge, that is, obedient and resistant (Foucault 1980).

As Foucault (1980: 114) asserted, all power implies resistance and particular languages of power imply particular languages of resistance to that power. The language of resistance can be produced because meaning is not fixed; though inscribed in the material conditions of existence it might change over time, appropriate old signifiers and carry new connotations. This dynamic allows for meaning to be contested, challenged and changed. For example, representation of Western ethnic minority groups such as black people has been characterized by a 'racialized regime of representation', which could only be contested because of the unfixed and contradictory nature of meaning (Hall 1992a).

In other words, the mainstream media play a crucial role in naturalizing dominant forms of 'common sense'. Nevertheless, subordinated groups exercise their power to contest hegemonic meanings through a discursive practice of resistance that is, to produce non-conformist and sometimes counter-hegemonic representations of the views of those marginalized, misrepresented and under-represented in the public sphere. Alternative media are one of the many available sites that provide these societal groups (and others) with the opportunity to produce these non-conformist and counter-hegemonic representations. Of course, there is no guarantee that these generated representations will necessarily be non-conformist and counter-hegemonic at all levels, simply *because* they originate from these societal groups. As Chapter 5 will show, hegemony plays at a variety of societal levels, and simultaneously resisting all hegemonies has proven to be exceptionally difficult.

The contingency of the alternative

As alternative media are defined as being in a negative relationship with mainstream media, the contingency of this concept should be emphasized: what is considered 'alternative' at a certain point in time could be defined as mainstream at another point in time. The societal context in which alternative media function is inseparable from the concept of 'alternative media' and can serve as a starting point for the definition of alternative media. Present-day mainstream media are usually considered to be:

- large-scale and geared towards large, homogeneous (segments of) audiences;
- state-owned organizations or commercial companies;
- vertically (or hierarchically) structured organizations staffed by professionals;
- carriers of dominant discourses and representations.

Alternative media can take one or more opposite positions on these matters:

- small-scale and oriented towards specific communities, possibly disadvantaged groups, respecting their diversity;
- independent of state and market;
- horizontally (or non-hierarchically) structured, allowing for the facilitation of audience access and participation within the frame of democratization and multiplicity;
- carriers of non-dominant (possibly counter-hegemonic) discourses and representations, stressing the importance of self-representation.

A more elaborate description of these different domains is given by Lewis (1993: 12); see Table 1.1.

Being a different kind of media organization

This second approach to alternative media – as an alternative to the mainstream – defines these media as alternatives to and supplementing mainstream media on an organizational and content level. At the organizational level, the existence of alternative media shows that media can exist independent of state and market. As the pressure on large-scale mainstream media to become more market-oriented tends to be considerable, alternative media show that being the 'third sector' is still an option for media organizations. This argument can be applied for the (internal) structure of the media organization, as large-scale mainstream media organizations tend to have a more vertical structure. Thus, the more horizontally structured alternative media show that alternative ways of organization, and more balanced and/or horizontal structures, remain actual possibilities.

On the content level, alternative media can offer ideologies, representations and 'discourses that vary from those originating in the mainstream media. These differences emanate from the higher level of participation of different societal groups and

Table 1.1 Defining alternative media

Domain	Examples of the domain
Motive or purpose	• Rejection of commercial motives • Assertion of human, cultural, educational, ethnic ends • Oppose the power structure and its behaviour • Building support, solidarity and networking
Sources of funding	• Rejection of state or municipal grants • Rejection of advertising revenue
Regulatory dispensation	• Supervised by distinct institutions • Independent / 'free' • Breaking somebody's rules, though rarely all of them in every respect
Organizational structure	• Horizontal organization • Allowing 'full' participation • Democratization of communication
Criticizing professional practices	• Encouraging voluntary engagement • Access and participation for non-professionals • Different criteria for news selection
Message content	• Supplementing or contradicting dominant discourses or representations • Expressing an alternative vision to hegemonic policies, priorities, and perspectives
Relationship with audience and/or consumers	• Degree of user/consumer control • Allowing the needs and goals to be articulated by the audience/ consumers themselves • Democratization of communication
Composition of the audience	• Young people, women, rural populations • Diversity and multiplicity
Range of diffusion	• Local rather than regional or national
Nature of research methodology	• Qualitative, ethnographical and long-term research

Source: adapted from Lewis (1993: 12). Some of the examples were added by us, others are based on Downing et al.'s (2001: v–xi) discussion of 'radical alternative media' characteristics.

communities and the aim to provide 'air space to local cultural manifestations, to ethnic minority groups, to the hot political issues in the neighbourhood or locality' (Jankowski 1994: 3). Mainstream media tend to be oriented towards different types of elites, as is the case, for instance, in mainstream news broadcasts favouring government sources, often resulting in what is called structural bias (see McNair 1998: 75ff.). The orientation of alternative media towards giving a voice to various (older and newer) social movements, minorities, and sub/counter-cultures and their emphasis on self-representation, can result in a more diverse content, signifying the multiplicity of societal voices.

At the same time, this rejection of the production values of the 'professional' working in mainstream media leads to a diversity of formats and genres and creates room in alternative media for experimentation with content and form. Thus, these media organizations can be rightfully seen as a breeding ground for innovation, often to be eventually adopted by mainstream media.

When alternative media are situated in an antagonistic relationship with mainstream media, alternative media may find themselves in a less advantageous position. Being small-scale, independent, and horizontally structured organizations carrying non-dominant discourses and representations hardly guarantees financial and organizational stability. This is especially the case when the antagonistic relationship between public and commercial media is placed in the context of competition, prompting these media to try to hegemonize their identities at the expense of alternative media. In such cases, alternative media are articulated as unprofessional, inefficient, limited in their capacity to reach large audiences and as marginal as some of the societal groups to whom they try to give a voice. This denies the need for an alternative, as mainstream media are deemed to cover all functions considered relevant to society. One of the main consequences of marginalizing the alternative and counter-hegemonic (or connotating it negatively, for instance, as naïve, irrelevant or superfluous) is the low political priority given to what is considered to be 'marginal', which in some countries has strengthened the downward spiral for these alternative media organizations (see Chapter 3).

Approach three: Linking alternative media to civil society

The explicit positioning of community media as independent of state and market supports the articulation of alternative media as part of civil society. Historically, civil society has produced the very ideas of citizenship, as well as the groups and pressures needed to realize these ideas and make social change happen (Janoski 1998: 17). Nevertheless, civil society is also a highly contested notion and only regained popularity as a concept after the fall of the Iron Curtain and the crucial role of civil society organizations in the demise of the old communist states (Kenney 2003). In this regard, the role of Solidarność in Poland is deemed especially relevant (see Arato 1981).

Defining civil society

From a theoretical perspective civil society can, broadly speaking, be conceived in two ways (Cohen and Arato 1992; Pérez-Díaz 1998: 211–13): as a generalist conception, drawing on the legacies of Hegel and Marx; or as a minimalist model, referring to Gramsci and Habermas (see Figure 1.4).

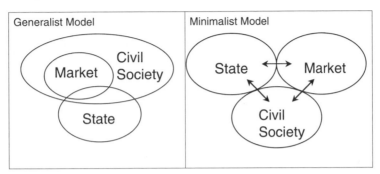

Figure 1.4 Generalist and minimalist models of civil society.

Hegel saw the sphere of civil society as constitutive of and constructive in integrating both perspectives, including the market as part of civil society and the state and a legal framework to safeguard the balance between private and public interests. While following Hegel in his conceptualization of civil society, which included the market, Marx passionately disagreed with the positive connotations attached to this notion. Marx saw the state and the legal system as prime instruments under the control of the bourgeois elite. He argued that this automatically led to private interests determining public interests. Marx therefore saw civil society very much as a site where domination was organized, as the arena where a human being 'acts as a private individual, regards other men as means, degrades himself into a means and becomes a plaything of alien powers' (Marx 1975: 153).

Gramsci accepted that civil society is a site where domination by consent, or hegemony (to use his term), is produced and reproduced. But by analytically separating civil society from the market and the state, he pointed out that it is also a sphere where hegemony can be challenged and contested. As such, civil society is the space in which alternative conceptualizations of the political and economic system can develop and thrive. Gramsci's dialectical understanding of civil society, seeing it as an arena of struggle over hegemony, 'permits an analysis of contradiction and conflict . . . rather than viewing the primary contradiction as lying between state and civil society' (Macdonald 1994: 276).

Neo-Gramscian perspectives on civil society consider this sphere to be relatively autonomous of state and market, overlapping slightly and engaging with state and market actors, but nevertheless fairly independent. It relates both to organized citizens mobilizing for social change and counter-hegemony, and to reactionary forces resisting change, reproducing hegemony. It represents 'a sphere of social interaction between economy and state, composed above all of the intimate sphere (especially the family), the sphere of associations (especially voluntary associations), social movements, and form of communication' (Cohen and Arato 1992: ix).

Civil society should, however, not be conceived as being necessarily separate from, independent of or in opposition to the state or the market at all times. In mature democracies a complex interplay and overlap between non-institutional and institutional politics can be observed, which will be thematized as rhizomatic later. As such they cannot be construed as a dichotomy, but oscillate between convergence and contention. The state is not an entity separated from society and neither is there a clear distinction between what is called civil society, and institutional and formal politics.

Civil society itself is characterized by a high degree of differentiation and fragmentation. Civil society is by no means a single actor, although certainly in policy processes it is often presented in that way. For this reason Cox (1999: 10–11), following Gramsci, distinguishes a 'top-down' conception of civil society from a 'bottom-up' one. In the former case 'the dominant forces penetrate and coopt elements of popular movements', while in the latter civil society is conceived as 'the realm in which those who are disadvantaged by globalisation of the world economy can mount their protests and seek alternatives'.

In summary, civil society is deemed important for a variety of reasons, as listed by Keane (1998: xviii):

- Civil society gives preferential treatment to individuals' daily freedom from violence;
- the importance of enabling groups and individuals freely within the law to define and express their various social identities;
- the impossibility, especially in the era of computerised networks of communication media, of nurturing 'freedom of communication' without a plurality of variously sized non-state communications media;
- the superiority of politically regulated and socially constrained markets as devices for eliminating all those factors of production that fail to perform according to current standards of efficiency.
- But of special interest . . . is the subject of democracy or, more precisely, the intellectual and political need to revive the democratic imagination.

To frame the diversity and multiplicity, but at the same time rather loose interconnectedness of current-day struggles, the 'multitude', a notion originally developed by Spinoza and reintroduced into political theory by Hardt and Negri (2004), might also be useful. According to Hardt and Negri (2004: 105) the multitude can be conceived as the 'multiplicity of all these singular differences'. As such it allows for 'the social multiplicity to manage to communicate and act in common while remaining internally different' (Hardt and Negri 2004: xiv). Active, constituent power is attributed to the multitude, while the state's power is described by Negri (1999) as constituting and reactive to the pressures of the multitude.

Also the notion of the multitude is connected to the broad approach to democracy and the political, which transcends the mere formal, institutional and procedural aspects of democracy. Democracy, from this perspective, also deals with activism, with political and cultural struggles in the process of social change that are actively performed in the sphere of civil society, and with changing political identities. Democracy is thus conceived as an open horizon without fixed content – a content that is the object of ongoing oscillations between conflict and always temporary consensus, and between inherently opposed interests within society. The democratic horizon recedes ever further, with new demands and new challenges, new political logics and new articulations of what constitutes the public interest (Laclau 1996).

Alternative media as part of civil society

By defining alternative media as part of civil society, these media can be considered the 'third voice' (Servaes 1999: 260) between state media and private commercial media. One of the clearest examples of this articulation is in the introduction to Girard's *A Passion for Radio*, where he formulates an answer to the why of this passion:

> The answer to that question can be found in a *third type of radio* – an alternative to commercial and State radio. Often referred to as community radio, its most distinguishing characteristic is its commitment to community participation at all levels. While listeners of commercial radio are able to participate in the programming in limited ways – via open line telephone shows or by requesting a favourite song, for example – community radio listeners are the producers, managers, directors and even owners of the stations.
>
> (Girard 1992: 2, emphasis added)

A starting point for defining alternative media as (part of) civil society can be found in Thompson's (1995: 122) model describing the public and private domains in contemporary Western societies, and inspired by the Gramscian model described above. A series of changes can be introduced into Thompson's model on the specificity of media organizations. Media deregulation, or, more generally, the impact of the neo-liberal discourse on media policies, has prompted public broadcasting organizations to adopt more market- and efficiency-driven approaches. This includes an increased emphasis on audience maximization (see, for example, Ang 1991), thus orienting the efforts of these companies (even) more towards the societal level, and (even) less to the community level. Alternative media still cover this terrain. Figure 1.5 depicts this reworked model and shows how this reorientation has allowed the market-driven approach to penetrate the public domain.

In his book *The Media and Democracy*, Keane (1991: 190) writes that '[f]reedom of communication is not something which can be realised in a definitive or perfect sense. It is an ongoing project without an ultimate solution. It is a project which constantly generates new constellations of dilemmas and contradictions'. Keane develops a

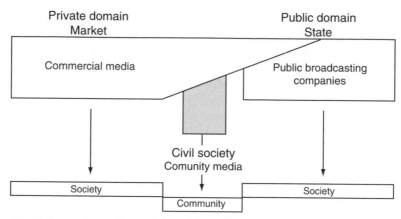

Figure 1.5 Media, market, and state (adapted from Thompson 1995: 122).

sound critique of the (neo-)liberal market-oriented conception of the media's role and position in a democracy and their ideology of limited state regulation in that regard. Concerned by the emergence of private monopolies or oligopolies, and the increasing commodification of knowledge, Keane defends a two-way strategy to overcome this 'market failure', a strong and autonomous public service broadcaster and a robust regulatory regime for commercial media. We would argue, however, that a pillar is missing in Keane's model, namely that of alternative media. It is the pillar of those watching the watchdog, and providing a complementary alternative to both public service and commercial media. Furthermore, the technological advances in terms of network-based communication tools, digital cameras and compression techniques, have provided these alternatives with new means to distribute alternative content worldwide.

Keeping alternative media embedded in civil society
The third approach defines alternative media as part of civil society, a societal segment considered crucial for the viability of democracy. Although the nature of civil society can vary extensively across nations and continents, it is argued here, following Cohen and Arato (1992: vii–viii), that this concept is relevant to most types of contemporary societies and can be seen as an important locus for the expansion or deepening of democracy by means of increasing the level of participation (see Held 1987).

Alternative media can firstly be seen as an 'ordinary' part of civil society, as one of the many types of organizations active in the field of civil society. The democratization *of* media (Wasko and Mosco 1992: 7) allows citizens to be active in one of many (micro-)spheres relevant to daily life, to organize different forms of deliberation, and to exert their rights to communicate. Secondly, as different political philosophers (from Jean-Jacques Rousseau, John Stuart Mill and Mary Wollstonecraft onwards) have pointed out, these forms of micro-participation are to be considered important, because they allow people to learn and adopt democratic and/or civic attitudes, thus strengthening (the possible forms of) macro-participation. Verba and Nie (1987: 3) summarize this as follows: 'a participatory polity may rest on a participatory society'. Held (1987: 280) exemplifies this in another catchy phrase: 'we learn to participate by participating'.

When the specificity of broadcasters and their potential role as one of the major public sphere(s) are brought into focus and alternative media are not defined as just 'ordinary' parts of civil society, these media become important because they contribute to the democratization *through* media (Wasko and Mosco 1992: 13). Alternative media can overcome the absolutist interpretation of media neutrality and impartiality, and offer different societal groups and communities the opportunity for extensive partici- pation in public debate and for self-representation in the (or a) public sphere, thus entering the realm of enabling and facilitating macro-participation.

This approach also allows a foregrounding of the struggle between alternative media (as part of civil society), the state and the market. Commercial (and public) media tend to see alternative media as 'contenders in a Darwinistic struggle among commercially oriented media' (Prehn 1992: 266). The rejection of advertising as a prime source of income by alternative media sometimes renders them financially insecure, causing them to limp from one financial crisis to another. Their situation is made worse when they (as part of civil society) are considered to be a threat to a repressive state. The objectives of alternative media can trigger interference from the state apparatus, pla- cing their staff in sometimes life-threatening situations. When focusing on the internal functioning of alternative media, it should be emphasized that *Making Democracy Work*, to use the title of one of Putnam's (1993) main publications, is a very difficult task that requires constant attention. Organizations that are horizontally structured and oriented towards participation have to deal with a certain degree of inefficiency, sometimes undermining their functioning and the realization of their objectives, or perverting these objectives.

Approach four: Alternative media as rhizome

When discussing the notion of alternative media, Downing et al. (2001: ix) critique its 'oxymoronic' nature – 'everything, at some point, is alternative to something else' – thus legitimizing their decision to focus on 'radical alternative media', and thereby excluding niche trade magazines and corporate industry bulletins. However, they still emphasize the diversity that characterizes these radical alternative media, which are to be found in a 'colossal variety of formats' (Downing et al. 2001: xi). They nevertheless serve two main purposes: to express opposition vertically and to build networking laterally. A similar argument is developed by Rodriguez (2001: 20) who suggests the notion of alternative media be abandoned in favour of citizens' media:

because 'alternative media' rests on the assumption that these media are alternative to something, this definition will easily entrap us in binary thinking: mainstream media and their alternative, that is, alternative media. Also, the label 'alternative media' predetermines the outcome the type of oppositional thinking that limits the potential of these media to their ability to resist the alienating power of mainstream media.

In discussions on civil society theory a number of authors have highlighted the interrelationship between civil society on the one hand, and state and market on the other. Though considered reductionist, the nineteenth-century Hegelian dichotomous model, conflating and fusing market and civil society, is 'still used by some Marxists and particularly by neoliberals, neoconservatives, and present-day heirs of utopian socialism' (Cohen and Arato 1992: 423). The fusion argument – proposed by Schmitt[13] and Habermas among others – deals in a variety of ways with the totalizing or colonizing effects of state interventionism. Schmitt (1980: 96 – translated by and quoted in Cohen and Arato 1992: 239), for instance, states that 'the pluralistic state becomes "total" not out of strength, but weakness; it intervenes in all areas of life because it must satisfy the claims of all those interested'. A less threatening relationist approach can be found in Walzer's (1998: 138) paradoxical civil society argument: 'the state is unlike all the other associations. It both frames civil society and occupies space within it. It fixes the boundary conditions and the basic rules of all associational activity (including political activity).' He goes on to say, using a since much quoted and contested sentence: 'Only a democratic state can create a democratic civil society; only a democratic society can sustain a democratic state' (Walzer 1998: 140).

Defining the rhizome

These relationist aspects of the civil society approach and the (critiques on the) alternative media approach are radicalized and unified in a fourth approach building on Deleuze and Guattari's (1987) metaphor of the rhizome. In the late 1970s and early 1980s both authors were heavily involved in the French alternative (free) radio scene as they saw there an opportunity to realize their 'utopie "deleuzoguattarienne" ' (Dalle 2006). Authors such as Sakolsky (1998) also used Deleuze and Guattari's metaphor to refer to alternative media as rhizomatic media.

The metaphor of the rhizome is based on the juxtaposition of rhizomatic and arbolic thinking.[14] The arbolic is a structure, which is linear, hierarchic and sedentary, and could be represented as 'the tree-like structure of genealogy, branches that continue to subdivide into smaller and lesser categories' (Wray 1998: 3). It is, according to Deleuze and Guattari, the philosophy of the state. The rhizomatic, on the other hand, is non-linear, anarchic and nomadic. 'Unlike trees or their roots, the rhizome connects any point to any other point' (Deleuze and Guattari 1987: 19).

In *A Thousand Plateaus* Deleuze and Guattari (1987) enumerate a series of characteristics of the rhizome – the principles of connection and heterogeneity, multiplicity, asignifying rupture, cartography and decalcomania. Connection and heterogeneity imply that any point of the network can be connected to any other point, despite the different characteristics of the components. The concept of multiplicity constructs the rhizome not on the basis of elements each operating within fixed sets of rules, but as an entity whose rules are constantly in motion because new elements are constantly included. The principle of the asignifying rupture means that 'a rhizome may be broken, shattered at a given spot, but it will start up again on one of its old lines, or on new lines' (Deleuze and Guattari 1987: 9). Finally, the principle of the map is juxtaposed with the idea of the copy. In contrast to the copy, the map is

> open and connectable in all of its dimensions; it is detachable, reversible, suscep-
> tible to constant modification. It can be torn, reversed, adapted to any kind of
> mounting, reworked by an individual, group, or social formation. It can be drawn
> on a wall, conceived of as a work of art, constructed as a political action or as a
> meditation. Perhaps one of the most important characteristics of the rhizome is
> that it always has multiple entryways'.
>
> (Deleuze and Guattari 1987: 12)

Rhizomatic media

The rhizomatic approach to alternative media thus focuses on three aspects: their role at the crossroads of civil society, their elusiveness, and their interconnections and link-ages with market and state. The metaphor of the rhizome firstly highlights the role of alternative media as the crossroads of organizations and movements linked with civil society. For instance, rhizomatic connections allow thinking about organizational structures where alternative media organizations can remain grounded in local com-munities and become simultaneously engaged in translocal networks (see Appadurai 1995). These translocal networks are characterized by the fluid articulation of a diver-sity of alternative media organizations. The rhizomatic approach thus becomes instru-mental in avoiding the dichotomized positioning of alternative media in relationship to the local and the global, in opening up ways to theorize how the local and global touch and strengthen each other within alternative media (see Carpentier 2007a).

The rhizomatic approach also allows the incorporation of the high level of contin-gency that characterizes alternative media. Both their embeddedness in a fluid civil society (as part of a larger network) and their antagonistic relationship towards the state and the market (as alternatives to mainstream public and commercial media) make the identity of alternative media highly elusive. In this approach it is argued that this elusiveness and contingency, which also apply to a rhizome, are their main defining elements. This elusiveness is partially related to specific organizations. For instance, activist radio stations and independent media centres (IMCs) pop up when an event requires their presence, and they often silently disappear or transform into another media activity. The Seattle Indymedia, which started its operations at the WTO Summit, is a good example. But the elusiveness of rhizomatic media also characterizes alternative media as such, as their diversity makes it very difficult to regulate and control them.

Like rhizomes, alternative media tend to cut across borders and build linkages between pre-existing gaps: 'A rhizome ceaselessly establishes connections between semiotic chains, organizations of power and circumstances relative to the arts, sciences and social struggles' (Deleuze and Guattari 1987: 7). In the case of alternative media, these connections apply not only to the pivotal role alternative media (can) play in civil society. They also apply to the linkages alternative media (and other civil organizations) can establish with (segments of) the state and the market, without losing their proper identity and becoming incorporated and/or assimilated. These more complex and contingent positions bring them sometimes to violently critique hegemony and in other cases to playfully use and abuse the dominant order. This interplay between resistance and cooperation does legitimize the utilization of the label of transhegemonic media.

Alternative media do not operate completely outside the market and/or the state, thus softening the antagonistic relationship (as being an alternative to the mainstream) towards the market and the state. They are, in other words, not merely counter-hegemonic, but engage which the market and state. In this sense they are trans-hegemonic. Alternative media do establish different types of relationships with the market and/or the state, often for reasons of survival, and in this fashion they can still be seen as potentially destabilizing – or deterritorializing as Deleuze and Guattari (1987) put it – the rigidities and certainties of public and commercial media organizations.

The elusiveness of the rhizomatic network, and its deterritorializing potential towards the more rigid media organizations in the public and private domain are depicted in Figure 1.6. It should of course be noted that even the vertically structured market and state organizations can show a fairly high degree of fluidity. But these organizations remain in most cases still considerably more rigid in comparison to civil society organizations. The deterritorializing effects of alternative media can (at least

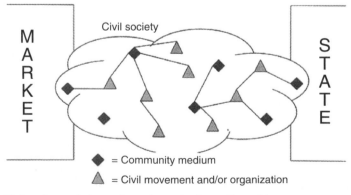

Figure 1.6 Civil society and alternative and community media as rhizome.

partially) overcome this rigidity and allow the more fluid aspects of market and state organizations to surface.

Elusive media at the crossroads, critically connected with market and state
The fourth approach builds on and extends the importance that is attributed to civil society and democracy. In contrast to the third civil society approach, the main emphasis in describing the importance of alternative media is not on their role as part of the public sphere, but on their catalytic role in functioning as the crossroads where people from different types of movements and struggles meet and collaborate. These could, for instance, be members of women's, peasants', students', and/or anti-racist movements. In this fashion alternative media not only function as an instrument giving voice to a group of people related to a specific issue, but also become a medium for rearticulating impartiality and neutrality and grouping people and organizations already active in different types of struggle for equality (or other issues).

Especially in the field of radical democratic theory, great emphasis is put on the need to link diverse democratic struggles in order to allow, as one of the proponents (Mouffe 1997: 18) puts it, the 'common articulation of, for example, antiracism, antisexism and anticapitalism'. Mouffe goes on to stress the need to establish an equivalence between these different struggles; she considers it is not sufficient to establish 'a mere alliance' (Mouffe 1997: 19) but that 'the very identity of these struggles . . . in order that the defence of workers' interests is not pursued at the cost of the rights of women, immigrants or consumers' (Mouffe 1997: 19) should be modified. This argument runs parallel with reformulations of 'the ways in which power is enacted and citizenship is expressed' (Rodriguez 2001: 19), as in radical democratic theory the political subject can experience and express the subject position of citizen in a multiplicity of forms, including political action embedded in daily life, based on economic, gender or ethnic relations (McClure 1992: 123).

The approach to alternative media as rhizomatic also makes it possible to highlight the fluidity and contingency of (community) media organizations, in contrast to the more rigid ways mainstream public and commercial media often (have to) function. The elusive identity of alternative media means that they can – by their mere existence and functioning – question and destabilize the rigidities and certainties of public and commercial media organizations. At the same time, their elusiveness makes alternative media (as a whole) hard to control and to encapsulate in legislation, thus guaranteeing their independence.

This fourth – rhizomatic – approach allows us to consider additional threats to the existence and functioning of alternative media. It is possible that its potential role at the crossroads of different social movements is simply not realized when, for instance, alternative media organizations choose an isolationist position or propagate one overpowering type of social struggle. Moreover, this role can also endanger these organizations when the objectives of (one of) these movements conflict with the objectives of the broadcaster itself, and when the independence *vis-à-vis* these movements and/or civil organizations might be threatened. Further, the complex relationships with state and market organizations create the risk of incorporation of the alternative media by these organizations and/or loss of independence, for instance financial. The approach of alternative media as rhizome uncovers a fourth potential threat to the existence of alternative media. These media signify the fluidity and contingency of media organizations, in contrast to the rigidities and certainties of public and commercial media organizations. Their very elusiveness might prevent the existence of a 'common ground' on which policy can act. This lack of a clear 'common ground' unifying and structuring alternative media complicates the functioning of the organizations representing these media (such as AMARC) and has prevented the emergence of a well-defined alternative media movement.

An overview

The four approaches and the arguments presented showing the importance and weaknesses of alternative media are summarized in Table 1.2. This overview articulates alternative media as an important but vulnerable type of media organization.

Conclusion

Alternative media research has a long theoretical and empirical tradition that has tried to capture their identity. Due to the complexity and elusiveness of this identity, this project has proven to be a very difficult task. For this reason a multi-theoretical approach is preferred, combining essentialist and relationist positions within the general framework of the (political) identity theory of Laclau and Mouffe. None of the four approaches discussed in this chapter can be considered as giving a sufficient overview when applied independently, as we postulate that the only way to capture the diversity that characterizes community media is the simultaneous application of these approaches.

Special attention in the theoretical discussion on alternative media should be directed to the fourth approach, which uses the metaphor of the rhizome in order to radicalize and unify the relationist aspects of the civil society approach, the alternative media approach and some of the critiques of this particular approach. The application of a rhizomatic approach to alternative media identities has a series of specific advantages. Firstly, this approach – together with the civil society approach – is situated within a more society-centred approach to media. Media studies and communication sciences as a whole have a very long tradition of media centrality, which in a way has to be valued, but at the same time must be considered to be reductionist as it leads to an artificial separation between media and society. Secondly, the rhizomatic approach also deepens the civil society approach. The complexity and elusiveness of alternative

Table 1.2 Summarizing the four theoretical approaches to alternative media (AM)

	1 Serving a community	2 An alternative to the mainstream	3 Linking alternative media to the civil society	4 Alternative media as rhizome
Importance of alternative media	• Validating and strengthening the community • Treating the audience as situated in a community • Enabling and facilitating access and participation by members of that community • Topics that are considered relevant to the community can be discussed by members of that community • Opening a channel of communication for misrepresented, stigmatized or repressed societal groups	• AM show that the 'third way' is still open for media organizations • Alternative ways of organization, and more balanced and/or horizontal structures remain an actual possibility • AM can offer counter-hegemonic representations and discourses that vary from those originating from mainstream media • Emphasis on self-representation, resulting in a multiplicity of societal voices • Diversity of formats and genres – room for experiment	• Importance of civil society (as such) for democracy, with AM as part of civil society • Democratization of media in relation to micro- and macro-participation • Democratization through media: extensive participation in public debate and opportunities for self-representation in the (or a) public sphere	• AM as the crossroads where people from different types of movements and struggles meet and collaborate • Deepening democracy by linking diverse democratic struggles • Highlighting the fluidity and contingency of media organizations • Questioning and destabilizing the rigidities and certainties of public and commercial media organizations, at the same time making room for transhegemonic collaborations and partnerships • Elusiveness makes AM (as a whole) hard to control and to encapsulate – guaranteeing their independence

(Continued overleaf)

Table 1.2 Continued

	1 Serving a community	2 An alternative to the mainstream	3 Linking alternative media to the civil society	4 Alternative media as rhizome
Threats to alternative media	• Dependency towards the community • Raising the community's interest in two-way communication when the dominant media discourse is based on one-way communication • Lack of two-way communication skills and interest • Lack of technology facilitating two-way communication • Reduction of community to its geographical meaning, trapping AM in the position of small-scale local media, gradually de-emphasizing their role towards serving the community	• Lack of financial and organizational stability, being small-scale, independent and horizontally structured organizations • Articulated as unprofessional, inefficient, limited in their capacity to reach large audiences and as marginal as some of the societal groups they try to give voice to • Low political priority given to the 'marginal'	• AM as contenders among commercially oriented media • Rejection of advertising as a prime source of income leads to financially hazardous situations • Dangers caused by a repressive state • Dealing with a certain degree of inefficiency • Making democracy work requires constant attention	• Not realizing its role as crossroads • Diverging or conflicting objectives with civic organizations, threatening the medium's independence towards these organizations • Incorporation by state and market organizations, loss of independence towards these organizations • Lack of a clear 'common ground' leading to lack of policy efforts, complicating the functioning of representative organizations and preventing the emergence of a well-defined AM movement

media thus become defining elements, in contrast to the more rigid state and market. The role of alternative media at the crossroads of social organizations and movements, 'connecting people' – to abuse a commercial slogan – is also brought into the picture in this fourth rhizomatic approach. Finally, this approach allows the rigid separations that are created by the antagonistic position towards mainstream media (approach two) and towards the market and the state as such (approach three) to be breached. Alternative media have attempted to resist a large number of mainstream discourses at the communicative, organizational and political level. Fighting a war of position on numerous fronts has left the alternative media movement in a rather problematic, vulnerable and isolated position. Placing the rhizomatic approach in the foreground creates more room for both the deterritorializing of mainstream identities and collaboration with state and/or market organizations. These deterritorializing effects can open (discursive) spaces for the more fluid aspects of mainstream media identities. Through different types of partnerships and strategic alliances the survival of the alternative media can be guaranteed (better), on the condition that their independence *vis-à-vis* other civil society (non-media) organizations and *vis-à-vis* state and market organizations is sufficiently protected. The rhizomatic approach can help to support a more agonistic relationship with mainstream media and with the market and the state, reducing the antagonism that has for years hounded these media organizations. A further increase in the density of the rhizome will help alternative media to combine their critical stance towards mainstream communicative, organizational and political discourses with strategic alliances with the mainstream. This will ensure the continued existence of these important media, the democratic discourses they carry, and their capacity to strengthen (communication) democracy.

Notes

1 It is rather ironic that in 2005, 39 per cent of *Libération*'s shares were purchased by the banker Édouard de Rothschild (Rimbert 2005). This did not solve *Libération*'s financial crisis – witness the public outcry in the newspaper in September 2006.
2 See for instance Janowitz's (1967) work on the community press, which was first published in 1952. Later key works on alternative media were (among others) produced by Berrigan (1977, 1979), O'Sullivan-Ryan and Kaplun (1979), Reyes Matta (1986), Jankowski et al. (1992), Girard (1992), Lewis (1993), Nostbakken and Morrow (1993), Sjöberg (1994), Husband (1994), Fraser and Estrada (2001), Downing et al. (2001), Rodriguez (2001), Gumucio (2001), Carpentier et al. (2003a, 2003b, 2003c), Jankowski (2003), Atton (2002) and Howley (2005).
3 Versions of the first (theoretical) part of this chapter were published as Carpentier et al. (2003a, 2003b, 2003c).
4 The object of this chapter – alternative media – of course complicates an unequivocal society-centred approach. This type of approach should rather be interpreted as the societal contextualization of (alternative) media.
5 The World Association of Community Radio Broadcasters is usually referred to by its French

acronym, AMARC, or the Association Mondiale des Radiodiffuseurs Communautaires. The AMARC website can be found at: http://www.amarc.org.

6 Félix Guattari (1978) uses this concept on his writings on alternative media.

7 In sociology, a group of people that is formed based on common interests is usually referred to as a 'collectivity' (Merton 1968: 353). A collectivity does not always have direct interaction, and is often only based on a common goal or interest. The people who belong to a collectivity do not need to know each other, and one cannot always identify direct interaction between them.

8 The British television and web project, 'Video Nation', illustrates that the obstacles can be effectively reduced when the media professionals involved adopt an open, honest, respectful, process-oriented and (micro-)participatory attitude, based on a thorough analysis of the power processes and imbalances (Carpentier 2003).

9 See http://www.un.org/Overview/rights.html (accessed on 17 October 2006).

10 In other words, people who are not part of a societal elite (including politicians, academics, captains of industry, and media professionals) and those not considered to be celebrities.

11 When referring to 'mainstream media' we are suggesting neither that they are monolithic nor univocal, that is, mainstream media do not always have the same concerns, the same political and ideological agendas – in fact most of the time they have contradictory and competitive interests.

12 For Foucault, discourse signified a 'group of statements which provide a language for talking about – a way of representing the knowledge about – a particular topic at a particular historical moment . . . Discourse is about the production of knowledge through language' (Hall 1992b: 291).

13 Though Schmitt (like Heidegger) turned to Nazism, his theoretical work remains of considerable importance. As Mouffe (1999a: 52) writes: 'Schmit is an adversary from whom we can learn, because we can draw on his insights. Turning them against him, we should use them to formulate a better understanding of liberal democracy.'

14 Deleuze and Guattari's work is situated within the field of epistemology. Here we focus more on organizational structures that are seen as the sedimentation of the arbolic and/or rhizomatic ways of thinking.

AN INTRODUCTORY CASE STUDY – RADIO FAVELA: REPRESENTING ALTERNATIVE MEDIA

If that radio antenna was mine, the air would carry my voice, with words like bullets, that everybody would hear. [. . .] If that antenna was mine, it would spread dreams and the voice of the favela. Once this antenna is ours, my waves will open all doors and the world will change.

(Brau, in *Radio Favela*, 0:19:35)

Introduction

The four approaches discussed in Chapter 1 can be illustrated through a discussion of *Radio Favela*, a Brazilian 'feel-good' movie directed by Helvécio Ratton. The film was first released in 2002 by Quimera Filmes as *Uma Onda no Ar*, (poorly) translated as *Something in the Air* (see Figure 2.1). Most of it is filmed in flashback and tells the story of how Rádio Favela was established by four idealist youngsters, Jorge, Brau, Roque and Zequiel (played by Alexandre Moreno, Adolfo Moura, Babu Santana and Benjamin Abras), living in the slums or favelas of Belo Horizonte, one of the largest cities in Brazil. The film offers a romanticized and celebrative narration of the authentic history of Rádio Favela, which broadcast in the slums of Belo Horizonte from 1980. The rather stereotypical filmic representation provides an exceptional insight into the core identity of alternative media, but at the same time it allows the complexities of this core identity to show through.

The opening scenes of the film are quite dramatic. They show a considerable police force making its way through the hills of the favela, accompanied by a radio technician from the Ministry of Communication, who is assisting them in tracing the radio station transmitter. Simultaneously, these opening scenes introduce two of the film's main characters, Zequiel, the station's technician and Jorge, the station's main presenter

Figure 2.1 Poster for 2002 release of *Uma Onda no Ar*.

and journalist. Jorge's first words position him and the radio station as radically involved in the community:

> Most children of the favela quit school because what they learn there has nothing to do with their reality and their interests. Their rich teachers from the city come to teach the children of their housekeepers. The children lose their interest, and the consequences are known. Today we got a letter from Nem from prison. Once we played football together and now he's in a prison cell with his head in a toilet bucket. This is what he writes: 'I wish the youngsters could only see what happened to me. I thought I was going to get rich quick, but dealing poison is not worth the effort, and you don't get rich quickly. You die young, or end up in prison, and that's something I wish for nobody. Here's only misery and humiliation.' Are you

listening, guys? Don't be stupid, the prisons are overcrowded, but there's always room for one more. [Phone rings.]

The introduction is also used to visualize the radio station's active audience. The phone call that interrupts Jorge's comments is from Rose, who asks Jorge for advice on how to trace the whereabouts of her arrested son. In a subsequent scene, a man suffering from toothache is seen entering the studio, complaining that he cannot afford a dentist. Jorge uses the airwaves to solicit help for the man, offering free publicity in return, and quickly receives a call from a dentist. Jorge warns the inhabitants of the favela to watch out for the heavily armed police force that has entered the slum, not yet realizing that they are about to raid the studio. Seconds before the police arrive at the studio, the transmitter is rushed to safety. Less lucky than the transmitter, Jorge is arrested and taken to prison, where the inmates question him about the radio station. The how-did-it-all-begin question triggers the main narrative of the film, taking the audience back to the early 1980s.

The flashback shows the four friends planning the building of the transmitter and Jorge eventually deciding to invest his life savings (meant to pay for university) in the radio equipment. They start to broadcast from Jorge's home, despite the protestations of Jorge's worried mother, Dona Neusa. Jorge is arrested for the first time, and accused of 'setting the people against the society'; he courageously denies any involvement. Meanwhile Rádio Favela has attracted the attention of a newspaper journalist, Lídia (and her lawyer friend, João), which increases the station's fame. The studio is raided by the police, and vengefully destroyed by them. The community contributes all the money it has to get the studio operational again, symbolized by the pot of money shown to Jorge when he is still weeping over the destruction. The flashback ends with Jorge being released from prison as a result of considerable societal pressure. The film ends with him in the studio, accompanied by his wife Fátima and their two children, and being visited by Brazilian representatives of the UN, which had been trying to offer Rádio Favela and Jorge a prize on behalf of the UN, and who had decided to visit the studio in person.

There are also three subplots going on in the film. The romantic one shows how Jorge met his wife. A rather dramatic second subplot narrates how the violence in the favela results in two of the four friends losing their lives. Brau, the poet, is accidentally shot by a man who set out to kill Roque. A rival gang kills Roque, who has become a criminal and a drug dealer, and three of his companions. The third subplot is related to the racism that exists in Brazilian society, exemplified by Jorge's problems at his downtown school. The second and third subplots provide the spectator with an insight into the motivations of the four youngsters to set up a radical radio station to provide a voice for the community, and to denounce violence, racism, poverty, police brutality and social injustice (in a very Freirean way).

The four approaches in *Radio Favela*

Radio Favela offers a slightly naïve narration of the history of Rádio Favela, but simultaneously provides us with the good introductory case study that allows us to illustrate the four complementary approaches that were discussed in Chapter 1. In *Radio Favela*, the radio station is clearly embedded in the community of the favela, it is portrayed as a civil society alternative to the state-controlled mainstream, and it is shown to be part of a societal (rhizomatic) network. However clear the situation of Rádio Favela seems to be, the film's narration also shows the complexities and contingencies of alternative media identities.

Serving the community

The film constructs a clear and, at first sight, unproblematic identity for alternative media. It highlights Rádio Favela's close connection with the community and the way it facilitates access and participation. The radio station is portrayed as totally immersed in the favela. The four initiators are carefully positioned as members of the favela community. They live, love, play, eat and die in the favela. When they start planning the radio station they explicitly want the 'voice of the people, the poetry of the favela' to be heard. As such, the four friends, as non-professional radio producers and owners of the radio station, are themselves the voice of the people. As radio makers from the favela, their radio work is the favela's self-representation. At the same time they open a channel of communication for the community of the favela, which is indeed a poorly represented, stigmatized and sometimes repressed group.

The symbolic ownership of the community is represented in the opening sequences of the film which show community members calling the radio station for advice, or visiting the studio to get help (or a dentist). Whilst the police are racing up the hills to raid the radio station, Zequiel is seen interviewing a mother and her three children (see figure 2.2), who are living in a house that is considered unsafe. This scene exemplifies how alternative media discuss topics that are considered relevant to the community. Zequiel speaks on her behalf, represents her interests (which no one else is willing to do) and calls for action from the city:

Zequiel: If the civil services don't intervene, we'll have a tragedy in the favela. All houses will be washed away.
Woman: I won't leave my house. Where else can we go?
Zequiel: A lot of families are in grave danger. City administration, if it rains, this will collapse. Don't say we didn't warn you.

Once the radio station is established, Jorge is seen walking through the favela, and being accosted by one neighbour after another. One wants a message passed to her son, to invite him to come to see her; another is a local shopkeeper asking for a couple of

Figure 2.2 Screenshot from *Radio Favela* (0:07:53).

commercials on the radio, as he is having a special sale (and he can 'pay in cash or use an eternal credit line'); a third, whose wife has left him, asks Jorge to tell his wife that he wants her back and that he will stop drinking. The incorporation of numerous shots of the listeners inside (and outside) the favela in these scenes signifies how firmly the audience is situated within the local community, and positioned as such by the radio station. This series of scenes also shows the often problematic centrality of radio producers, who become indispensable for the radio station's future and who risk becoming the new gate-keepers. Although the participatory attitude of all Rádio Favela's operators is beyond question, their omnipresence and their level of semi-professional expertise illustrate the always difficult relationship between alternative radio producers and their communities.

Nevertheless, the community is seen to structurally participate in the radio station. The co-ownership of the community is made evident when, after the studio has been destroyed in the police raid, the favela gets the money together to rebuild. Members of the community are granted access to the radio station to make their own programmes. One example is the local pub owner who asks Jorge permission to broadcast the work of local musicians, to 'play music that cannot be heard elsewhere, the music of the

Figure 2.3 Screenshot from *Radio Favela* (1:17:00).

favela, live and in colour.' On another occasion, five old female singers are shown on a rooftop terrace, giving the performance of a lifetime (Figure 2.3) – a scene that is cruelly disrupted by a police raid.

A *civil society alternative to the mainstream*

Rádio Favela is shown as opposing mainstream media and attempting to articulate a civic alternative to mainstream and state broadcasting, but also to state power. Here, it is important to point out that the military were in power in Brazil from 1964 to March 1985, making the establishment of a clandestine radio station more hazardous than would be the case in some other countries (in western Europe, for instance), as its counter-hegemonic presence immediately became a threat to the military and its control of the airwaves. In this sense, the film is reminiscent of Gramsci's argument that the establishment of hegemony combines the generation of consent with the possible use of force. This political specificity conflates two of the approaches mentioned in Chapter 1 – the alternative media approach and the civil society approach – in that being a civil society broadcaster immediately positioned the station as an alternative to the hegemonic state (communication) structure.

The film is built around the continuous antagonism with the repressive Brazilian state apparatus, personified by a police officer referred to as 'delegado', which could be translated as 'the one with authority' or, on a more popular note, 'a pain in the arse of poor people'. When the police enter the favela, they do so in large numbers and heavily armed (Figure 2.4). These images are juxtaposed with the ordinariness, social relevance and harmlessness of Rádio Favela's work: when one raid is about to take place, Jorge is talking on the phone to a lady whose parrot has escaped (Figure 2.5). Another raid takes place when the producers are taping the performance of five old local singers. The arbitrariness of these interventions is symbolized (and ridiculed) by one of the officers presenting a blank piece of paper, when asked to produce a search warrant. When informed by Jorge that a blank page cannot be read, he fumbles, and manages to produce the right document. Although only portrayed to a limited degree, police brutality and intimidation are evident and especially so in the scene showing Jorge being beaten during interrogation.

The police repression is represented in the film in several scenes. For instance, when Jorge and Zequiel are DJing for a group of break-dancers on a public square, only the intervention of a (white) lawyer prevents three, rather intimidating, mounted police officers from dispersing them. In another scene, Jorge and Brau are threatened with arrest for public indecency when they are discovered kissing their girlfriends in the park. These scenes focus on the resistance that these forms of (mild) repression provoke. After the incident in the park, Jorge expresses his anger in the following exchange:

Jorge: Have you seen that arsehole? What a son of a bitch.
Brau: Forget about it.
Jorge: Forget?

Figure 2.4 Screenshot from *Radio Favela* (0:07:00).

Figure 2.5 Screenshot from *Radio Favela* (0:11:00).

Brau: That piece of shit doesn't harm us, Jorge. Shit harms nobody. Shit is something you flush and forget.

Jorge: Forget. We're supposed to take this like animals. . . .

Jorge: Roque is right. I'm going to get me a gun and shoot the arsehole.

Brau: You're going to buy a microphone and make radio. Each his own way.

Apart from antagonism *vis-à-vis* the state, there are other instances of antagonism in the film that construct Rádio Favela as an alternative civil radio station. Rádio Favela is represented as an alternative to the Brazilian mainstream radio stations, which are said to 'vomit nonsense' and to produce 'trash and hollow words'. When the four friends are planning their station, they are seen sitting on the edge of a field, staring at a radio mast. The image provokes the following statement from Jorge: 'It is indeed a radio mast, but only for trash and hollow words. For us it could be a machine gun that fires words against the system.'

The Pampulha FM radio mast (Figure 2.6) had attracted Jorge's attention before, and in one of the first scenes in the film he is seen staring up at the huge mast and then sneaking into the radio building and watching a technician and a presenter at work. He is discovered by the radio station guard and thrown out. This scene constructs a clear difference between mainstream and alternative media. At the level of technical resources, the huge radio mast and the sophisticated studio are contrasted with the one-dipole antenna and one-microphone studio of Rádio Favela (Figure 2.7). But this scene highlights other differences. The mainstream studio is built in a traditional way, with glass separating the technician from the presenter (Figure 2.8). The first broadcast of Rádio Favela takes place on a terrace, in the open air, with no separation between the presenter, Jorge, and the technician, Zequiel (Figure 2.9). In the later Rádio Favela studios, this open structure is maintained, symbolizing the absence of built-in hierarchies. Finally, when he sneaks in the Pampulha radio station studio, Jorge (a member of its audience) finds himself behind glass, and denied access (Figure 2.10). When he is discovered, he is removed from the premises and even warned that he should be careful not to break something. In the case of Rádio Favela, people (listeners) are seen entering the studio, without even knocking. They are listened to, conversed with, addressed as 'neighbour' and where possible, helped, as shown in the example of the man with toothache (Figure 2.11).

The differences between state and civil society, and between mainstream and alternative media come together in the critiques on the *Voice of Brazil* (*Voz do Brasil*). This hour-long current affairs programme, which was initiated by president Vargas shortly after radio arrived in Brazil in the 1930s, focuses on information about government, parliament and the judiciary. In the film *Radio Favela* a clear antagonism is created between this programme and the Rádio Favela broadcasts. A distorted version of the *Voice of Brazil*'s musical opening theme – the 'Sinfonia' of Carlos Gomes's opera *Il Guarany* (1870), which has become, as Magaldi (2002) puts it, a symbol of Brazilianness – is used to introduce the first Rádio Favela broadcast. The *Voice of Brazil* is heavily

Figure 2.6 Screenshot from *Radio Favela*.

Figure 2.7 Screenshot from *Radio Favela*.

Figure 2.8 Screenshot from *Radio Favela*.

Figure 2.9 Screenshot from *Radio Favela*.

Figure 2.10 Screenshot from *Radio Favela*.

Figure 2.11 Screenshot from *Radio Favela*.

criticized for sending its listeners 'to sleep', and for spreading 'lies and [for] preaching'. During this first broadcast, Jorge announces that listeners will get 'instead of the voice of government, the voice of the favela'. At the end of the film, when Jorge is freed from prison and is broadcasting again, he starts his 7 p.m. broadcast with the sentence: 'It's now 7 o'clock and here comes the true voice of Brazil'.

Finally, there is antagonism towards the market. Although this film is characterized by strong antagonism towards the government and the state, it also contains references to market antagonism. This type of antagonism, which potentially positions Rádio Favela as a non-commercial station, is represented in the film in a rather specific way. As this dialogue, which takes place during the opening scenes, shows, Rádio Favela is indeed using publicity to (barely) survive:

Jorge: Do you have the figures, Zequiel?
Zequiel: I checked everything. We haven't got a penny left this month.
Jorge: Didn't the advertising company pay for the campaign of the prefect?
Zequiel: Nobody paid anything whatsoever.
Jorge: All these arrears . . .
Zequiel: We haven't gotten anything, the phone bill, the new microphone and the electricity.
Jorge: We were already in the red, but we're getting purple now.

This situation problematizes the clear-cut alternative media identity of Rádio Favela, and requires a specific narrative solution. The problem is handled by constructing a nonchalance concerning advertising. When the man with the toothache asks for help from Jorge, this help is mounted by offering free publicity, to be settled on afterwards. When a local shopkeeper asks for advertising, he is told he can pay in cash or use an 'eternal credit line'. The importance of this problematic zone is also downplayed by linking the radio station (and its people) with a general critique on poverty, criminality, and capitalism. In one scene Jorge is seen washing cars to make a living, and being harangued by Roque about 'easier' ways to make money. Jorge refuses to join Roque in his life of crime, just as he later refuses Roque's (blood) money to pay for the first transmitter, but they end up making jokes about the rich smartly dressed people passing by, calling each of them a thief. This rather unsubtle capitalist critique reunites Jorge and Roque, but also positions each of them as anti-elitist, anti-commercial and anti-capitalist.

A rhizomatic radio station

The film shows unambiguously how these various spheres overlap and interlink. The rhizomatic approach can be seen in operation on a variety of levels in the film. First, a diversity of discourses come together in the radio studio, ranging from artistic self-representations of the community (and the subcultural capital of the songs of the elders and of the moves of the break-dancers) to blatant anti-capitalist and anti-elitist discourses. Rádio Favela also is seen to be connected to a series of other – often only loosely structured – organizations in the favela, such as the break-dancers of Rock Street and BH Breakers (dancing at a street party, announced as 'our art in the streets of the city'). When Jorge is arrested, a coalition of supporters is created, exerting 'mass protest against his arrest', including 'members of parliament, journalists, lawyers, the church, etc. Even a representative of the UN' has joined the protest, as one politician is seen explaining in a phone conversation with a police officer. Also, informal (often criminal) organizations are very present in this film, and although the Rádio Favela people are very careful not to get involved, there is a clear (protective) relationship between these two spheres, as personified in the Jorge–Roque relationship.

The rhizomatic dream of a translocal network of radio stations is explicitly mentioned in the film. When Jorge is finally released from prison, he is invited to lunch by Lídia, the journalist, and João, the lawyer, who talk about their dreams and plans in the following terms:

João: The television and the other radios don't want any competition and they control the entire system. You can change the radio station in a community association. That will give you legal coverage. In the meantime we're fighting with all possible means to change the media laws. You're not the only one of your kind, Jorge. New stations like yours are seeing the daylight everywhere. We'd be a lot stronger with a national network. The elections are coming, and these radios will be very useful.

Jorge: Useful? To elect your candidate?

Lídia: You have to take sides. Preferably a side that supports you. What else purpose does your radio have?

Jorge: Why don't you write about the police raid?

Lídia: I can propose the article, but it will be refused. We're living in a dictatorship, Jorge.

Jorge: We can help each other, but our party is the party of the favela. We don't have politicians, or anyone else, just ourselves and the rest can get stuffed.

This fragment is crucial because it shows the (at least potential) connection between the radio station and the broader political struggle in Brazil. It also illustrates the risk of incorporation by other elements of the rhizomatic network, such as political (opposition) parties. In this case, the threat is recognized and deflected when Jorge remarks: 'our party is the party of the favela'. It articulates Rádio Favela as independent and elusive, as it cannot be pinned down – not by the government and not by the opposition. Other transhegemonic connections with political systems are present, for instance, Rádio Favela is financed by a campaign for the prefect – in Brazil, the prefect is the elected head of the executive branch of the municipality – and supported by members of parliament and representatives of the UN. As discussed above, there are

Figure 2.12 Screenshot from *Radio Favela* (1:12:52).

connections with the economic sphere, as illustrated by the use of commercials, and also by the (commercial) interest of Lídia's mainstream newspaper in the radio station, which results in a newspaper article about the station (Figure 2.12), much to the benefit of Rádio Favela.

Conclusion

This introductory case study on the filmic representation of *Radio Favela* shows that the application of any of the mono-theoretical approaches would have impoverished the analysis, and would have left relevant aspects under-emphasized. It is precisely the combination of approaches that enables the complex relationships among the community and the people, the state and the political system, the police, the mainstream broadcasters (and the *Voice of Brazil* programme), the market and the formal and informal economy to be dealt with.

Radio Favela shows the intimate connection of the community with the radio station, symbolized through the four initiators that are articulated as being 'ordinary' favela kids, and that are still very much in touch with the inhabitants of the favela. In allowing the community to participate in the production process, Rádio Favela becomes automatically juxtaposed to other (government, mainstream) radio stations, which do not organize a similar participatory process. This antagonism is closely related to the radio station's antagonism with the repressive Brazilian state apparatus that organizes numerous attempts to close down the radio station. Finally, *Radio Favela* shows how the technologies, discourses and practices of the radio station connect a series of societal and cultural struggles. Rádio Favela is a nodal point of a broader network of resistance, and simultaneously interacts with the mainstrain media, markets, and state and UN representatives.

Especially the tiny ruptures in the filmic story line show the complexity and contingency of the identity of alternative media. They do not stand isolated from the rest of the social and political reality, but interact with these other spheres. They are not alternative to every mainstream in society, but carefully construct transhegemonic alliances with the mainstream to ensure their survival. In some cases community media (even) manage to disrupt (or to deterritorialize) the mainstream. In the filmic narration of Rádio Favela's history we see how the mainstream political system becomes fearful of the radio station ('after all, the elections are coming', as one politician puts it), and eventually grants it legal status as educational radio (in February 2000, as a text at the end of the film reports). We also see how the mainstream journalist, Lídia (who, without any irony, states that they 'can trust her, [because she is] a journalist') becomes an avid supporter of the alternative station, going against the mainstream culture of her own newspaper. And we see how two nicely dressed UN representatives eventually make it to the studio, after being told 'to shove their prize up their arse', only to be kept waiting because the programme – 'the real voice of Brazil' as Jorge calls it – is about to start.

PART II:
CASE STUDIES

3 COMMUNITY APPROACHES IN WESTERN RADIO POLICIES

It's about community, the radio will take care of itself.
(Phil Korbel, quoted in Community Learning
and Development Partnership 2004)

Introduction

Media and (tele)communication have from the outset been the objects of government regulation and policy, from the perspective of exerting control over the media or channels of distribution, allocating the spectrum, or providing a legal framework for public broadcasting and fostering public interests. In this regard, Ó Siochrú et al. (2002: 4) state that

> regulation . . . is about the use and abuse of power. The real question is how regulation, by that name or any other, is shaped and implemented in a society, who controls it, how informed people are about it, and how they can participate in determining its priorities.

According to Van Cuilenburg and McQuail (2000: 111), three periods can be identified when a certain paradigm of media regulation was hegemonic. The first was from the invention of media and of communication technologies until the Second World War. It was characterized by the absence of policy and later by *ad hoc* policy or, as Van Cuilenburg and McQuail (2000: 111–12) put it, 'emerging' policies, clearly with national strategic and economic interests in mind. This *ad hoc* nature of emerging media policy led to distinct regulatory regimes for broadcasters, communicating one-to-many, for distributors of content, such as cable operators, and for telecommunication communicating one-to-one. The second period lasted until the 1980s and can be described as the public service era, where intervention was justified by societal and democratic concerns and the public interest. However, technological advances in telecommunication, an increased presence of satellites and the convergence of media, computer technology and telecommunication challenged the then existing (national) regulatory regimes and the existing hegemonic state monopolies in broadcasting media and telecommunication. The third period is described by Van Cuilenburg and McQuail (2000: 112) as the era of communication policy rather then media policy, signalling not only the convergence of media and telecommunication policies, but also the (relative) disengagement of the state, and the treatment of media content and communication more as a commodity than a democratic resource. This paradigmatic shift was accompanied by the privatization of state-owned telecommunication operators and the liberalization of the state monopoly on television and radio broadcasting.

State intervention in media and communication systems clearly has to be viewed in a historical context, which evidently varies from one country to another. In this regard, Hallin and Mancini's (2004) comparative model is useful. They distinguish between the Mediterranean or polarized model, the north/central European or democratic corporatist model and the North Atlantic or liberal model. In the liberal model the market clearly dominates the media system, in the corporatist model commercial and public service media are combined, while in the polarized model the state exerts a high degree of control over the media, which are usually clearly linked to the dominant political ideologies.

Despite the general trends identified by Van Cuilenburg and McQuail and by Hallin and Mancini, the differences in historical trajectories structure and shape the way in which national media systems have developed and how certain regulatory regimes were adopted and implemented. The different paradigms identified by Van Cuilenburg and McQuail confirm a general trend, but cannot be considered absolute. Historical peculiarities have resulted in a great variety of national media and communication policies.

This is why Hallin and Mancini's attempt to define different models is also necessarily a difficult exercise. The UK situation is a case in point. While it is generally seen to be part of the North Atlantic liberal model, it also has one of the strongest public service regimes in the world, which to a degree also applies to commercial media. Furthermore, these macro-accounts of media-policy paradigms, although embedded in historical analyses and accounting for different underlying political ideologies and cultures, pay little attention to a non-Western perspective, implying that the dominant Western models are applicable elsewhere in the world (Curran and Park 2000). Finally, an exclusive focus by state-controlled public broadcasting on the one hand, and commercial media on the other, on the political economy of the media and communication 'industry' leaves little space for alternative media, situated in between or relatively independent of state and market.

In this case study we focus on the element of community in alternative media (or 'community media') and how regulation and media policies relate to this. Radio is an excellent case to illustrate the participatory potentials of media. As Fraser and Estrada

(2001: 1) point out: 'To start a small radio station is not as complicated and expensive as many people think. There is enough experience in many countries to prove that it is within the reach of almost any community'. Much of the attention in the alternative radio literature (and funding for research) has been devoted to its potential for empowering communities in developing countries (see Berrigan 1979; Girard 1992; Siemering 2000; Fraser and Estrada 2001; Olorunnisola 2002).

The question addressed here relates to how different Western countries have integrated alternative radio (or not) and their focus on serving the community, in their media policies at a national level. The media policies of three Western countries – the UK, the USA and Belgium – on alternative radio will be explored briefly from a historical perspective. Whilst the USA is a prime example of a liberal media policy environment, the UK combines a strong, but highly regulated, commercial sector with an equally strong public service tradition. Belgium, in being positioned in the middle of continental Europe, presents a particular case, and is relevant for several reasons. It has a strong and dominant public service tradition, but since it is a complex federal state, regulation of the media is the responsibility of the different communities/regions. As a result there are interesting divergences between the north and south of the country; the north has modelled itself on a northern European regime and the south has adopted the pattern predominant in France and the south of Europe more generally.

Whilst these three cases have very different (media) histories and are embedded in distinct regulatory paradigms, it will become apparent that in each case alternative radio has experienced difficulties in establishing itself between the market and the state-controlled media system. We will describe the context of alternative radio in order to determine what we understand by this specific 'third' type of media, with a special focus on its relationship towards communities and their participation *in* media.

Serving the community

From the emergence of radio as a medium, its potential to be more than just a broadcasting instrument in the hands of powerful elites has been clear. Writing in 1930, Brecht (1983: 169) refers to this saying:

> Radio must be changed from a means of distribution to a means of communication. . . . Radio could be the most wonderful public communication system imaginable, a gigantic system of channels – could be, that is, if it were capable not only of transmitting but of receiving, of making the listener not only hear, but also speak, not of isolating him but of connecting him.

According to Partridge (1982: 10) the term 'community radio' was first coined in a pamphlet entitled *Possibilities for Local Radio*, written by Powell (1965). The idea of locally embedded small-scale radios produced and controlled by citizens had been around for much longer. Localism is considered to be one of the defining characteristics of alternative radio and media that serve the community. Howley (2005: 2) defines 'community media' as

> grassroots or locally oriented media access initiatives predicated on a profound sense of dissatisfaction with mainstream media form and content, dedicated to the principles of free expression and participatory democracy, and committed to enhancing community relations and promoting community solidarity.

This definition associates alternative/community media with a wider set of notions and practices, such as participation *by* communities *in* their self-controlled media, and producing content *for* the communities they serve (Kidd 1999). From this perspective the term alternative media also refers to internal democratic rules, practices of self-management, and the development of alternative 'non-mainstream' formats and content. In this regard, Prehn's (1992: 259) emphasis on participation as 'involving people directly in station programming, administration and policy activities' is highly relevant. By linking these rather strict characteristics, a clear and pure ideal-type conception of alternative media that serve a community emerges. As Chapter 1 showed, reality is, however, much messier and does not let itself be framed so easily.

Howley's definition nevertheless is useful, as it neatly describes the kind of (alternative) radio stations this chapter addresses: community-focused, non-commercial,[1] experimental, participatory, internally democratic radio initiatives driven (mainly) by volunteers. The relevance of such a narrow definition of alternative media (as community media) is most pertinent in a policy context, where this type of independent radio is often forgotten – or rather ignored – in favor of the interests of commercial local radios on the one hand, and of public service-type radios on the other. Simultaneously, the communities that are (or could be) served by these alternative media are equally quickly forgotten, in favor of markets and (national) publics.

Western policies towards alternative radios serving the community

The US case

Whereas in Europe the boom in alternative radio stations serving the community can be situated in the 1970s and 1980s, in the USA the 1960s were the period of growth for these stations. This was preceded by a long tradition in the USA of amateur radios prior to World War I. In 1927 the Radio Act was voted by Congress, aiming to end the perceived chaos on the airwaves. The act established the Federal Radio Commission, which was given the task of issuing licences. It was replaced by the Federal Communication Commission (FCC) in 1934 (see Hilliard and Keith 2005: 30–1; White, 2003). This intervention to regulate the chaos and anarchy on the airwaves provoked a fierce battle amongst commercial stations to get hold of a licence.

However, a legacy of educational radio, based in universities, assured a distinct voice over the airwaves (Sterling and Kittross 2002: 78). The educational broadcasters won a substantial victory when the FCC decided in 1941 to reserve part of the spectrum for community and other non-commercial broadcasters. Pacifica Radio (KPFA) in Berkeley, California, generally considered to be the first community radio station in the USA, took this opportunity and started transmitting in 1948. Many others would follow suit. KPFA has been described as 'an independent non-profit station supported by listeners subscribers many of whom were pacifists and anarchists' (Partridge 1982: 17). The Pacifica Foundation aimed, amongst others,

> to encourage and provide outlets for the creative skills and energies of the community [and promote] a lasting understanding between nations and between the individuals of all nations, races, creeds and colors; to gather and disseminate information on the causes of conflict between any and all of such groups.
>
> (Pacifica Foundation 1946)

The Public Broadcasting Act of 1967 provided a framework for a national public network, and also created the Corporation for Public Broadcasting, which was given the task of funding and supporting local as well as national radio. However, most of the federal money went to the National Public Radio (NPR), which served as a platform for syndicated programmes made by others and broadcasting to a national audience. Despite this, the 1970s saw a dramatic rise in the number of alternative radio initiatives, mainly run and operated by volunteers on a small scale. It is fair to say that alternative radio in the USA profited at first from the liberal ideology at the heart of US media policies, which led to a permissive and open regulatory environment for community initiatives.[2] However, this does not mean that the emergence of (local) alternative radio in the USA went uncontested. Both commercial and public broadcasting organizations persistently fought the presence of alternative radio on the airwaves. The FCC was not insensitive to the combined lobbying power of the commercial and public broadcasters, and in 1978 decided to revoke the low power (10 watt) licences. This resulted in the silencing of many smaller and poorer stations (Hilliard and Keith 2005: 186). The only way for alternative radio to survive was to obtain a 100 watt licence, which for most was too expensive.

To resist the attacks of the commercial and public broadcasters the National Federation of Community Broadcasters was set up in 1975 to represent and defend the interests of US alternative radios that serve a community. Not surprisingly, many unlicensed or pirate alternative radios emerged in the 1980s and 1990s. Pioneering examples include Black Liberation Radio in Springfield, Illinois, which went on the air in 1986, and Free Radio Berkeley, California, which started broadcasting in 1993 (Sakolsky and Dunifer 1998). These so-called micro-radio stations provoked immense resistance from both the commercial and public broadcasters who feared competition from these stations and especially frequency interference (Hilliard and Keith 2005: 191). Due to a lack of funds or because of fines and seizure of equipment by the FCC, most of these micro-radio stations had a hard time sustaining their activities. In 1996 the Grassroots Radio Coalition, a very loose association of stations, was founded to 'react against the increasing commercialization of public radio and lack of support for volunteer-based stations'.[3]

At the end of the 1990s public pressure and street protests in favour of low power FM (LPFM) stations were growing. These resulted, in 2000, in the FCC granting legal recognition to LPFM radio services and allowing them to file an application (in selected states at first, but this was extended in 2001).[4] However, Congress intervened in the FCC ruling, not only banning 'anyone who had operated an unlicensed micro-station from applying for a legal low-power station' (Hilliard and Keith 2005: 197), but also calling upon the FCC 'to study the economic impact of these new stations on corporate radio outlets as well as the . . . possibility of interference problems' (Sakolsky 2001). This provoked outrage and division within the micro-power radio movement. As a result of Congress's obstructive tactics, lobbied for by the large commercial broadcasters, only a very limited number of licences were granted. Many micro-stations continued to transmit illegally but suffered heavy police and FCC repression. For example, San Francisco Liberation Radio was raided in October 2003 after criticizing the Bush administration's war in Iraq and Free Radio Santa Cruz was closed down in October 2004.[5]

The UK case

In 1951 the UK Beveridge Report on the future of broadcasting stated: 'Use of VHF could make it possible not merely to give the existing BBC programmes to people who now fail to get them, but to establish local stations with independent programmes of their own' (Beveridge 1951: 78). Those envisaged as possibly operating such alternative stations included 'a Local Authority, a University or a specially formed voluntary agency' (Beveridge 1951: 79). However, given the hegemonic public service logic of the time (cf. Van Cuilenburg and McQuail 2000), things did not develop. The hegemony of the public broadcaster was first challenged by pirate radio stations, broadcasting from ships, for example, MV *Caroline*, MV *Olga Patricia* and MV *Mi Amigo*, anchored outside territorial waters. After a (short) period, from 1964 until 1968, of unprecedented success, they were all closed down following the voting in of the Marine and Broadcasting Offences Act in 1967.

In addition to the BBC experimenting with local stations, the Sound Broadcasting Act of 1972 had transformed the Independent Television Authority into the Independent Broadcasting Authority, giving it responsibility for radio too. However, while this theoretically allowed community stations to exist, it also provided a very strict regulatory framework that was only beneficial for commercially driven local radio. UK community initiatives that had emerged in the late 1960s and early 1970s were left operating illegally and campaigning for official recognition. Many of these pirate stations were, or soon became, advertising-funded radio, even though in many cases they were fulfilling a community role. In 1983 the Community Radio Association (CRA) was founded to represent alternative radio stations, serving a community, with government, industry and regulatory bodies. In 1997 the CRA changed its name to Community Media Association (CMA) to accommodate alternative television initiatives that serve a community.

Despite the lobby efforts of the CRA/CMA, the – by definition – illegal pirate stations were targeted repeatedly by the Department of Trade and Industry (DTI), which continually tried to shut down their broadcasting. A recent example is Dimension FM, a pirate radio in Telford in Shropshire. Dimension FM started operating in 1999 and played mainly underground electronic music that was largely ignored by mainstream radio at that time, but also had some comedy, prank and phone-in programmes. The station broadcast every weekend and as it managed to increase the power of its transmitter Dimension FM reached a growing community of loyal fans (Figure 3.1). In December 2003 the DTI organized a raid on the station, closed it down and prosecuted two of its collaborators. Their programmes are archived online.[6]

The idea of a third way, complementing the commercial and public broadcasting services, was finally accepted in 2002 when the Radio Authority issued licences for 15 of what were then called 'access radios'. These licences were renewed in 2004. The 2003 Communication Act and the 2004 Community Radio Order could be considered turning points in the history of alternative radio in the UK. After a round of consultations, the newly formed media regulator, Ofcom, began to grant full licences for alternative radios that serve a community in March 2005. Subsequently, in June 2006, 107 alternative radio stations were licensed in the UK.[7] A Community Radio Fund was introduced, managed by Ofcom and financed by the Department for Culture, Media and Sport (Ofcom 2005). It primarily funds core competencies, such as financial management, fundraising and administrative support.

An interesting example of a thriving licensed alternative radio is the East London-based Sound Radio, which claims to 'reflect, as far as is possible, the make up of the East London community to whom we broadcast'.[8] Sound Radio is partly funded by advertising, but uses this to provide access to the airwaves for 10 different (diasporic) communities in the London area. It has English, Afro-Caribbean, Latin American, Kurdish, Bangladeshi, Jewish, Turkish and African programmes. Unlike most alternative radios, Sound Radio broadcasts on AM rather than FM. This allows it to reach a much wider audience, as current FM regulations restrict alternative radios to a radius of 5-km from their antennae. In addition to their AM broadcasts, Sound Radio, similar to many other alternative stations, streams its programmes on the Internet, which is proving to be an efficient way to bypass regulatory restrictions, and to attract an international (diasporic) audience beyond the UK.

As in the USA, this limited and fairly restrictive legalization does not mean that there are no longer any pirate stations. In June 2006, some 30–40 pirate stations were active in the London area alone, mostly playing underground music. Several websites are

Figure 3.1 Support for Dimension FM (source http://www.dfmpromotions.com/radio/ courtcase.htm).

dedicated to mapping the ongoing and fluid landscape of pirate radio in the UK's capital.[9]

The Belgian case

From the outset Belgium's spectrum was guarded by the state and no non-public stations, commercial or otherwise, were allowed to broadcast. Just as in the UK, this state monopoly on broadcasting was first challenged by purely commercial initiatives, broadcasting from ships in the North Sea from the late 1960s to the early 1970s. Examples of this were the *Mi Amigo*, the *Magdalena* and the *Jeanine*, ships from which programmes produced in Belgium, the Netherlands, the UK and even Spain were broadcast; they played mostly hit parade music introduced by popular DJs. In the late 1970s and early 1980s a new challenge emerged from terrestrial local FM pirate stations. Some of these were alternative media born out of the anarchist punk movement, the environmental movement and the student movement, challenging the formats and content of the public broadcaster, but most were commercial or eventually evolved into commercial stations (Drijvers 1992: 107–8).

From a policy perspective, a distinction should be made between developments in the North and the South of Belgium, as media regulation and policy became defederalized in 1971. However, one notable exception was frequency allocation, which continued to be regulated at federal level until 1990.

In the north of the country, an opening for local non-public radio, including alternative radio, was created in May 1982, allowing some pirate stations to become legal. It is evident, however, that consecutive regional governments ignored the specificity of alternative media serving a community. For a long time media policy in the North of Belgium was based on protecting the interests of the Dutch-speaking public broadcaster. Non-public radio was by definition considered to be commercial, thereby disregarding the specificity of several alternative stations. The legislation was primarily geared to preventing commercial stations forming networks and limiting their impact on the media landscape. In the struggle to defend the interests of the public broadcaster, the demands of alternative radio stations for a distinct statute did not carry enough weight to be supported by the major political parties (Carpentier 1994; Drijvers 1992). This was confirmed when the monopoly of the public broadcaster over the territory of North Belgium was finally lifted in 2002. The fiercely competitive commercial interests involved to obtain a regional or provincial radio licence, and the lack of transparency in the allocation process, relegated the very few alternative radio stations in the north to the margins of the FM spectrum. Furthermore, their broadcasting range was severely restricted (to 15 watts).

Radio Centraal,[10] an alternative radio in Antwerp that has over 150 volunteers and runs without advertising income, has been most vocal in condemning the lack of media policies towards participatory media in consecutive North Belgian governments and the persistent conflation of alternative radio and commercial radio at a local level (Carpentier 1994). Ironically, the North Belgian media regulator, which has the power to sanction radio stations, recently condemned Radio Centraal for boosting its signal beyond the strict limits set by the law, but reduced its penalty because of the specific nature of the station. In its decision it stated: 'As it appears that Radio Centraal does not generate commercial revenues, it is accepted that in this particular case even the minimum fine would disproportionately penalize the station' (Vlaams Commissariaat voor de Media 2005, authors' translation). This amounted to an – albeit implicit – official regulatory recognition of the distinctiveness of alternative radio in the North of Belgium.

A very different picture emerges when we examine the south of the country and Brussels. First, the south was much quicker to allow commercial stations to compete with the public broadcaster at national level (1991). Some years earlier (July 1987) the French-speaking public broadcaster had been given permission to broadcast advertising, and a specific statute for alternative radio was created within the regulatory framework (Ministère de la Communauté Française 1987). This was largely due to the efforts of existing alternative stations, some of which formed the Association pour la Libération des Ondes in 1978, struggling for the 'liberation of the airwaves' and representing French-speaking alternative radios in the south and in Brussels. These included Radio Panik, Radio Air Libre and Atelier Radio Arlon. The Audiovisual Decree of 1987 even cautioned about being 'especially careful to facilitate the existence of associative creative radio[11] stations' (Art. 30, authors' translation).

A Conseil Supérieure de l'Audiovisuel (CSA) was set up as the regulator and a Fonds d'Aide à la Création Radiophonique (FACR) was created to finance specific projects. The fund has supported between 15 and 40 radiophonic projects annually since 1994 (depending on its financial position). It was initially financed from a percentage of the revenues from public service channel advertising. The new media decree voted in in February 2003 also included commercial radio networks in the funding mechanism of the FACR, although it has to be said that commercial broadcasters fiercely resisted this attack on their advertising revenues. The role of FACR is to promote:

> radiophonic creation in the French-speaking community in Belgium. It intervenes in the production costs of original and creative radio, valorizing the patrimony of the French-speaking community in the area's of information, documentaries, cultural programs, fiction and music.
>
> (FACR 2005: 7)

In addition to alternative radio organizations, individuals and other non-profit organizations can submit proposals. Furthermore, since 2002 the public broadcaster has been required to (re)transmit a minimum of 20 hours a year of productions funded by FACR.

In France, a very similar system of intra-sectorial cross-subsidies exists, whereby part of the revenues of the ads on commercial and public radio is channelled to 'les radios associatives'. A fixed (very low) percentage of the revenues goes into a fund to support, amongst others, alternative radio (Cheval 1997). This has given rise to a thriving and vibrant alternative radio sector in France (see, for example, Radio Gazelle 1992).

Conclusion

Overall, and especially in countries with a strong public service tradition, alternative radio is a recently recognized distinct media sphere, complementary to public and commercial broadcasters. In countries with a liberal tradition, such as the USA, alternative radio has a longer history, but this does not mean that there was/is no struggle or conflict regarding the right to communicate. A common thread in the cases studied is the difficulty involved in local alternative radio legitimating its existence on the FM band alongside commercial and public broadcasters. Unlike these latter, alternative radio movements have little lobbying power and are usually positioned as rogue and unprofessional actors within the broadcasting community. All too often the argument of spectrum scarcity and FM frequency interference is used against them. This has resulted in a tumultuous history of struggle both in Europe and the USA.

In many ways this is surprising given the particular attention alternative radio, serving a community, has received within international discourse on media and communication and also within developmental discourses fostering democratization in developing countries. In this regard, UNESCO has for many years been a driving force in advocating open access to the airwaves, participatory communication and the use of radio to foster development and empower disfranchised and marginalized communities (Berrigan 1979; ICSCP 2004: 55–7; Lewis 1993; Fraser and Estrada 2001). More recently, the International Telecommunication Union (ITU) sponsored World Summit on the Information Society (WSIS) rather vaguely called for 'support to media based in local communities' (WSIS 2003: Article 23j). Thus, it is high time that Western governments implement their own discourses on open access to media and communication tools aimed at democratizing developing countries within their own media environments and thereby recognize the democratic and participatory potentials of alternative radio. This would amount to allowing alternative radios 'to empower their listeners by encouraging and enabling their participation, not only in the radio, but in the social, cultural and political processes that affect the community' (Girard 1992: 2).

This case-study also shows that the theoretical models and typologies to compare media systems and regulatory regimes urgently need to be expanded to accommodate alternative radio as valuable democratic media with the right to exist separate from the public broadcasting system and the commercial market-driven radios.

Notes

1 By non-commercial we mean 'not for profit'. This does not, however, imply that no commercial activities are undertaken. Whilst most alternative radios are partly supported by those participating, as well as the audience in some cases, and in some countries by grants from the government or sponsorship deals, these funds are rarely enough to sustain a 24-hour radio station. Thus, for most alternative stations it is paramount to organize additional activities that generate funds in order to break even and invest in new equipment.

2 For a good overview of this early period of alternative radio in the USA, see Walker (2001).

3 See http://www.grradio.org/about/index.html.

4 See http://www.fcc.gov/mb/audio/lpfm/index.html.

5 For an overview of recent evolutions in the micro-power movement, see http://www.diymedia.net/.

6 See http://www.dfmpromotions.com/radio/.

7 See http://www.commedia.org.uk/about-community-media/community-radio/.

8 See http://www.soundradio.org.uk/about.php.

9 See   http://www.martinpayne.co.uk/radio/pirates/   and   http://homepage.ntlworld.com/pir8radio/.

10 See http://www.radiocentraal.be/.

11 In French, alternative radio stations are called *radios associatives* or *radios culturelles*.

4 | DIASPORAS AND ALTERNATIVE MEDIA PRACTICES

It may often be easier to live in exile with a fantasy of paradise than to suffer the inevitable ambiguities and compromise of cultivating actual, earthly places.

(Hoffman 1997: 63)

Introduction

The literature on alternative media itself is prolific, but little has been written on how audiences and readers use it. This might be viewed as a contradiction, given that 'alternative-media activists' could be seen as the most active segment of the so-called 'active audience' (Downing 2003: 625). The alternative media discussed here relate to media that are not necessarily radical, but fulfil for their audiences a fairly significant social and political role, for instance diasporic media. Diasporic media as alternative media (see Howley 2005) range from commercial to non-commercial enterprises, or a combination of both; a number are both produced and consumed by diasporic members; some are produced outside the diaspora. They are both locally and globally produced, and consumed by diasporic and migrant groups. Diasporic media are sites permeated by local and global forces and conditions, thus creating one of the many 'heterogeneous dialogues' related to globalization (Appadurai 1993) and becoming part of 'a complex form of resistance and accommodation to transnational flows' (Howley 2005: 33; Martin-Barbero 1993). These 'public sphericules' (Cunningham 2001) challenge essentialist notions of community. That is, diasporic community, through its socialization around media events, is, to a degree, constituted through media (see Hartley and McKee 2000: 84).

Diasporic media vary in their political and social aims, management, professionalism, communicative strategies, media technologies, nature (commercial or not) size,

and lifespan. They may represent a specific community, defend particularistic identities, and mediate a group's participation in national and transnational public spheres,
thus functioning to create and sustain transnational communities and networks of
diasporic groups, particularly in locations where they are minorities. As Georgiou
(2005) points out, they may be minorities in their countries of residence, but they are at
the same time part of a wider imagined community with whom they have a common
culture, language, and history. Furthermore, 'diasporic media address those audiences
both in their particularity, and also in the universality of their (imaginary) cultural
existence (e.g. Somalis in London share commonality with Somalis in France)'
(Georgiou 2005: 483). Taken together in their diversity, diasporic media constitute an
important element in the communicative landscape of diasporas not only for their
reimagining of the self and belonging within and across spaces but also for their
struggles for pluralistic representations.

The main users of alternative-diasporic media are those who are in a continuous process of cultural negotiation, i.e. migrants who are living dual lives, who have homes in
two countries, speak more than one language, and whose work and family ties involve
frequent transnational travel. (Portes et al. 1999: 217) Their reasons for using these
media vary from sustaining a bond with their home countries or connecting with the
new country, to simply engaging with the pleasures and ordinariness attached to media
consumption. Most importantly, consumption varies within diasporas according to
their different generational, gender, linguistic, and ethnic differences, and distinct
reasons for migration.

In the following, we discuss some of the findings from a sample of empirical studies
on diasporic media consumption.[1] Although these findings cannot be generalized,
given that each diasporic experience, in each locale, has its own distinctiveness, they
throw some light on diasporic groups' usage of alternative media. We present these
studies as exemplifying the importance of diasporic media practices to overcome social
and cultural exclusion through the process of identity negotiation, which the diasporic
media partly facilitate.

Diasporic audiences[2]

We shall move to consider these studies, but first, because it provides a point of reference for our argument, we briefly consider what constitutes the audience in media
studies, and how it correlates with diasporic audiences. 'Audience' relates to listeners
and viewers who are united through their shared consumption of broadcasting media,
film, music, advertising, and the Internet, and are the target of mainstream hegemonic
media institutions (Gillespie 2005: 2). The debate over audience centres on two traditions: the 'effects' one that considers audiences as passive consumers, and television
as a powerful medium, with the ability to influence them; the other that considers
audiences as active participants, that is, people making critical and/or oppositional

readings of media texts, therefore contributing to an ongoing struggle in a process of 'conflict and dialogue' over the meaning of hegemonic media texts (Martin-Barbero 1993; Carpentier 2004).

The 'effects' tradition works under the hypodermic model of media influence. This deterministic approach suggests that the media have the power to 'inject' the audiences with specific messages which will induce them to understand the world and behave in a particular manner. The assumption is that the audience is formed of a homogeneous mass of individuals who are largely acted upon by the media, implying that those people all respond in the same way to any specific 'message'. One difficulty with this tradition is its concentration on the media themselves and overlooking the conditions of viewing which might make an audience decode a particular message in a certain way (Morley 1990: 16). Studies adopting the second perspective assume that the audience is always active, and that media content is polysemic, open to interpretation. Such studies are thus criticized as being 'marred by a facile insistence on the polysemy of media products and by an undocumented presumption that forms of interpretative resistance are more widespread than subordination or the reproduction of dominant meanings' (Morley 1992: 18).

Corner (1996) argues that the emphasis on polysemy is weakening the implied determinacy in the production of meaning from media products, and overlooks the political issue of media power. However, both perspectives make intrinsic assumptions about power: 'whether power is concentrated in the hands of many or few, or whether power works on us directly, or whether it works through us in more subtle ways' (Gillespie 2005: 3). Nevertheless, Sinclair and Cunningham (2000) welcome the emphasis in audience studies on consumption, but draw attention to the fact that such studies seldom focus on cross-cultural scenarios. However, audience studies have contributed to our understanding of the ways audiences, depending on context and factors such as gender, class and ethnicity, respond to mainstream media texts.

Scholars studying diasporic media audiences and readers have employed a number of elements in audience research. A recurring trend in empirical studies of diasporic media consumption is the focus on the power of audiences and readers – diasporic communities – to shape the meaning and use of the media, both mainstream and alternative. In addition, many studies rely on qualitative methodologies – such as ethnography – to deal with the complex questions posed to diasporas regarding their mediated cultural practices, which involve concerns about the simultaneous process of hybrid identity negotiation embedded in diasporic mediated experiences, and their inclusion or exclusion in the public sphere. Diasporas are positioned in complex socio-cultural contexts characterized by diverse interactions through which their identities are formed dynamically as much through the diaspora–homeland relationship, as in response to exclusion by the host culture. As diasporic audiences, they negotiate their position from a 'third space' (Appadurai 1990) which accommodates an ongoing process of cultural and political negotiation between different hegemonies – home and abroad. This is important for understanding the ways in which diasporic groups, through their own differences, choose their media experiences and engage with media texts – mainstream and alternative – given that there seems to be an undeniable connection between the textual interpretations and social situations of viewers/readers.

Without essentializing them, it can be said that diasporic audiences tend to form 'communities' bound by some degree of common political and social interests, and by ethnicity, language and/or culture, which, in many cases, produce alternative media relevant to their lives and, in the process, reveal commonalities and interlinks among them. Through this process, diasporas create an embedded alternative, mediated cultural space through the influences of both cultures and hegemonies, generating a unique new space for self-expression and/or resistance enabled by 'alternative' discourses.

The predominant theoretical framework of diasporic cultural and media studies, which informs the research on alternative media usages by diasporas, is based on categories of national culture and identity, and generally argues that diasporic media, particularly transnational media, offer a platform to create emotional connections, or bonding and belonging, with an 'imagined' transnational community (Robins and Aksoy 2005).

Alternative media uses by diasporic communities

We now look at the consumption of diasporic media drawing upon a selective review of relevant studies. Cunningham and Sinclair's (2000) collection entitled *Floating Lives: The Media and Asian Diasporas* presents a series of in-depth analyses of different aspects of media use to sustain diasporic Asian identities. One study, conducted by Sinclair et al. (2000) on the mediascapes of Asian diasporic communities in multicultural Australia, shows that although people of Chinese origin engage with the national media, they also use, among other diasporic media, 'narrowcast'[3] channels, such as the Chinese-language service provided by pay television. The authors examine the ways members of the Chinese diaspora use these media in their daily lives to maintain cultural connections with Chinese 'imagined communities' elsewhere, while negotiating a new identity in their host country. The research used ethnographic methodology coupled with a mapping of the sources of production and distribution of videos from Great China. In relation to the media texts used by members of the diasporic group analysed, the study suggests that diasporic texts – films, music, news, and so on – are not inherently counter-hegemonic in the sense of political resistance. However, their politics 'must be grasped in the use to which they are put in the communities' (Cunningham 2001: 136) – for example, through the debates originating in the popular culture being accessed by the communities, through which they engage with political and identity formation issues.

In relation to the narrowcast television channel, The New World TV, Chinese viewers had a special relationship with news provision, even when it was 'yesterday's news'. According to the authors, this was because it created an immediate connection with 'home', a sense of here and there in which news became a space 'where the movement of separation and connection, of ambivalent and unstable points of personal and national identification, are negotiated' (Sinclair et al. 2000: 52). For example, for one mother the news gave her information about home, and also 'a strong sense of temporal and spatial connection with home' (Sinclair et al. 2000: 53). Where access to news from home is limited, all available media are consulted, though some migrants could only access news transmitted not in their original language, and which had to be translated for them by other family members. A further argument in the study relates to the establishment of daily routines and rituals in a number of families through their news viewing, which highlighted the importance of 'the temporal and the pleasures of double time for such diasporic viewers' (Sinclair et al. 2000: 54). Discussion of alternative media consumption by diasporic communities, and the need for news, can be perceived as part of a more extensive discussion on how marginalized diasporas experience their host cultures (Christiansen 2004), since mediated communication encompasses issues of representation, exclusion and inclusion.

This hunger for news among diasporic groups is evident in Bailey's (2007) analysis of the significance – if any – of diasporic media in the formation of Latin American cultural identities in Britain. Bailey's methodology centred on individual conversational interviews with 30 women from a variety of social, economic, educational and generational backgrounds, and several visits to the homes of Latin families, during 2004. Her findings on news consumption suggest that news from home is eagerly awaited and used to establish a sense of belonging and inclusion, but paradoxically, when this news is negative, also generates a process of 'demythologization' (Aksoy and Robins, 2003) by disrupting idealized notions of the homeland culture. The issue of media as ritual also emerges in this study. The viewing of transnational television is a social practice that congregates families and friends, particularly to watch special programmes about their countries. On these occasions, their sense of belonging to a distant culture is highlighted but, at the same time, it is an activity in which the sameness of television is perceived, for example, in the programme formats and types of programmes such as *Big Brother* and *Who Wants to Be a Millionaire?*, where the only difference is the language used. Thus, the appeal of these programmes is that they are about 'home', and also provide gratification from being familiar.

Overall, the diversity of the Latin American diaspora's media experience – mainstream and alternative – creates the possibility for questioning and renegotiating their identity (Bailey 2007). However, these practices are embedded in a sense of ordinariness, as an element of their daily lives influenced perhaps by their own experience of multiple belonging and awareness of the ambivalence of their diasporic existence. Whether diasporic media practices impact on the Latin Americans' feelings of inclusion or exclusion is not obvious except, perhaps, when the British media use stereotypes to misrepresent them. However, there is a disillusionment among the community with the political performance of their ethnic-diasporic media, particularly national media, in articulating their political concerns and helping shape their relationships with the wider society in terms of inclusion and acceptance.

Hamid Naficy's (1993) *The Making of Exile Culture* is a seminal work on 'exilic' television produced by Iranians in Los Angeles in the 1980s. His study encompasses the production–text–consumption circuit to explore how media uses help to shape the cultural politics of the displaced between home and host societies. He defines decentralized global narrowcasting diasporic television as 'made in the host country by liminars and exiles as a response to and in tandem with their own transitional and/or provisional status' (Naficy, 2003: 52). The Iranian exiled community produced a narrowcast television channel with programmes embedded with nostalgia and longing for the idealized homeland in genres such as fiction, variety shows, and information news. These programmes functioned to create new solidarities within the community and to mediate identity negotiation, positioning themselves in the 'spaces of liminality' where the longing for the homeland stabilized individual subjectivity and cultural identity, while raising contradictions, uncertainties, and insecurities (Naficy, 1993: 165). Thus, exile television was functioning as a ritual genre – that is, a genre with its own televisual flow, textual strategies and signifying practices, a medium produced and consumed by a community living in the liminality for whom television represents, constitutes and changes the community while helping its members to negotiate between the homeland and the host country's societies, rules and rituals. According to Naficy (1993: 91),

> part of the work of exilic popular culture is to produce a repertoire of symbols and a web of signification with which exiles can think and through which they may differentiate themselves from the host society . . . as rituals, exilic television not only aids in creating an exilic communitas but also facilitates the transformation of the communitas toward the host societas.

To sum up, Naficy's study offers an example of 'exilic' television as both a space for conscious resistance and a symptom of an exilic reality.

A similar concern with the relationship between alternative diasporic media, diasporas, and identity negotiation emerges in De Leeuw's and Rydin's (2007) study. They are particularly interested in 'media practices that attempt to overcome cultural exclusion and construct senses of home and belonging, based on the presupposition that there is a strong relationship between media use and identity construction'. They worked in 2001–4 on the European CHICAM[4] project (De Block et al., 2004), which used observation and interviews to capture the 'dailiness' of diasporic groups' media practices among 60 children (aged 10–14) and their families in six European countries. The authors looked at the uses of different media formats – mainstream and alternative.

Here, we discuss some of the findings related to diasporic media practices. Diasporic transnational television viewing was standard practice in diasporic family life, and fulfilled the roles of maintaining continuity with the past and negotiating the present. Connection with the home country was maintained, among other practices, by watching news programmes, familiar series, and movies that constituted familiar media consumption. Television was also considered important for preserving the mother tongue, an important means of maintaining ethnic identity since it is a symbol that distinguishes one group from another, thus reinforcing the feeling of belonging.

Television programmes functioned as a ritual that punctuated time and daily life, providing reassurance, or a 'comfort zone', for the diasporic subject, with the media text acquiring meaning not only with regard to its content, but also according to the circumstances of its viewers. For political refugees, for example, news programmes functioned to keep them informed about the political situation in their home countries, serving as evidence of the places they left behind and reminders of the new place – a place of a 'symbolic zone of neutrality, ambivalence and liminality' (Naficy, 2003: 8). For other types of migrants, television viewing produced a nostalgia for home, in which there was a complex difference in the feelings of parents and children. For example, as migrants or refugees, children and parents sometimes both experienced the same 'nostalgia' in watching media produced at 'home', a discourse of nostalgia focusing on 'there and then', and a discourse of desire, focusing on the 'there and now' (Dayan 1999; Christopoulou and De Leeuw 2005). However, children's perceptions of 'home' as a distant and foreign place differed from those of their parents. Overall, the authors suggest that diasporic television worked as a mediated space for experiencing different identities, both global and local, both related to youth culture and adult culture (Christopoulou and De Leeuw 2005), as well as a platform to negotiate the identity of being different, that is, being both a migrant and a new citizen.

Marie Gillespie's (1994) study also offers an in-depth ethnographic audience account of the variety of re-creative media uses by diasporic young people in the context of their cultures and daily life. Her starting point is the 'microprocesses of the construction of a British Asian identity among young people in Southhall, West London, against the backdrop of the emergence of "new ethnicities" in the context of post-colonial migration and the globalisation of communications' (Gillespie 1994: 205). She analyses the culturally diverse uses of media, arguing that they encourage cross-cultural views of media texts, resulting in an awareness of cultural differences, and increase the processes of cultural identity negotiation. Videocassette recorders were routinely used by families for the domestic family ritual of watching popular Hindi films and 'sacred' soaps – although the younger generation, when watching on their own, generally preferred to watch pop programmes.

Gillespie emphasizes gender differences in the viewing patterns of girls and boys; girls generally engaged more with Indian films and soaps, in part because their socialization revolved around the domestic sphere in which Indian films played an important social role, while, by contrast, boys were more reluctant to watch the films as they had more freedom to socialize outside the home (Gillespie 1989: 229). In generational terms, she shows that for older generations, Hindi films and programmes are a way of continuing cultural traditions and educating the younger generation about the values and beliefs of Indian culture. For the young, they are an introduction to their parents' homeland and represent a contrast with their cosmopolitan lives in England (Gillespie 1994: 82).

The sacred soaps – the *Mahabharata* and the *Ramayana* – use the myths of Indian society and interweave the philosophical basis of Hinduism and religious traditions. For the diasporic families, they provide some sort of guidance for the conduct of their everyday lives, sustaining and enhancing a commitment to religious and cultural tradition (Gillespie 1994: 95). Gillespie suggests that the identity negotiation of young people in the Indian diaspora is shaped by both cosmopolitan and diasporic experiences; they are

> both formed and transformed by their location in history and politics, language and culture. But through their material and cultural consumption and production, they are also constructing new forms of identity, shaped by but at the same time reshaping the images and meanings circulating in the media and in the market.
>
> (Gillespie 1994: 2)

All these studies show remarkable similarities in the culturally diverse media practices of diasporas in their experience of cultural dislocation. They all seem to use these media to negotiate their own identities – identities between places. They are thinking across spaces, and this signals a new type of media culture (Aksoy and Robins 2000: 343), one that is transnational, a mix of alternative and mainstream, with media uses that combine ordinariness with resistance, and media texts with multiple narratives and discourses that offer cultural survival and cultural renewal. To put it another way, in the context of multicultural societies, the way diasporas use media might be viewed as a process of 'multicultural convergence', the blurring of boundaries between different cultures and peoples (Sreberny 2005: 457).

In this process of hybrid media practices among diasporas, diasporic groups might become better tuned to the host culture – new country – and less nostalgic for the home culture – the physical space and the symbolic conceptualization of where one belongs – by constructing home as the lived experience within a locality, a space of intersection of multiple cultural references and, thus, moving towards the creation of hybrid and syncretic identities, a reimagined existence (Naficy 1993).

Conclusion

Diasporic media highlight the difficulty of defining alternative media, since they can cross the borders between mainstream and alternative media, in both the original and host cultures, and can be redefined by the particularities of production, distribution, and consumption contexts. In other words, some are mainstream media – hegemonic – in their country of production, and alternative – counter-hegemonic or fulfilling a community role – when accessed by diasporic groups elsewhere. We legitimize our choice somewhat through applying Downing et al.'s (2001: ix) argument as to the 'oxymoronic' nature of alternative media (see Chapter 1).

The social and cultural uses of diasporic media which vary among different diasporas, according to class, education, gender, religion, ethnicity, and generation, seem, to a certain extent, to shape the new identities of diasporic subjects. Their media practices are based on local, translocal, and transnational networks, which are important in sustaining community ties, challenging traditional notions of community, transforming identities, and creating new possibilities for expression and representation. Their pattern of media consumption suggests, therefore, a plethora of meanings ranging from nostalgia for the homeland to social interaction in the families and women's liberation, opening up new perceptions of their reality in between cultures.

Diasporic media work to establish a dialogue between different realities – home and host cultures – engaging with their day-to-day existence whilst they also intermingle with other cultures and media texts/contexts. In that sense, and more importantly, rather than generating a ghettoization – exclusion – of diasporas, the diasporic mediascape is providing opportunities for their engagement with other cultures and creating new networks of people where they bond (or not) with other people and institutions, therefore continuously reshaping their identities.

In this process, diasporic mediated communication enables and empowers diasporic communities to participate – inclusion – in the politics of representation and minority–majority discourses in the cultural spheres of their new homes, thus becoming a socially relevant cultural and political form of expression (Balibar 1991).

Notes

1 A considerable number of studies on diaspora and media have contributed to illuminate different aspects of the relationship between the media and the diasporic subject. However, for reasons of space, it is not possible to engage with the whole spectrum.

2 We are discussing audiences (television) and readers (print, website, and Internet) uses.

3 Narrowcast television services fragment their audience according to minority publics or markets, centring on their 'differences', while broadcast television works with mass audiences, overlooking those differences and thus homogenizing them.

4 CHICAM (Children in Communication about Migration) is a European Commission, Framework Five funded project, which was coordinated by the Institute of Education, London University.

5 | BLOGS IN THE SECOND IRAQI WAR: ALTERNATIVE MEDIA CHALLENGING THE MAINSTREAM?

War sucks big time. Don't let yourself ever be talked into having one waged in the name of your freedom. Somehow when the bombs start dropping or you hear the sound of machine guns at the end of your street you don't think about your 'imminent liberation' anymore.

(Salam Pax, posted 9 May 2003)

Introduction

Weblogs, or what is often called the blogosphere, can be deconstructed in a variety of ways: as alternative 'citizen' journalism; as participatory instruments for citizens/activists to produce their own media content; as websites of opinion; as a social platform to inform friends and family within everyday contexts; and increasingly as a new marketing and propaganda tool for elites (Deuze 2005). They challenge several dichotomies: between what is being perceived to be public and private; between alternative and mainstream media; and between the citizen/activist and the media professional. In this regard Allan (2002: 127) speaks of 'personalized journalism', with characteristics such as first-hand telling, personal accounts and two-way communicative processes between those creating content and those consuming it, whereby the latter also becomes a producer. In this regard, MacKinnon (2004: 10) even suggests replacing the signifier 'audience' with 'information community'.

In this case study we examine the use of blogs by different actors in the context of the war in Iraq and their relation to the mainstream media. Armed conflicts, of course, constitute an extreme and extraordinary situation, but that is precisely why we choose to study it, as certain (media and communication) processes become very visible and apparent in these circumstances. As Carruthers (2000: 13 and quoting Williams 1992:

158), quite rightly points out, '[w]ar should not be seen as a special case of how the media works, but rather as a magnifying glass which highlights and intensifies many of the things that happen in peace-time, albeit revealing them in exaggerated form'.

Moreover, war is the site where different hegemonies meet. First, it is the site where hegemonic mainstream media practices become highly visible, in part because alternative media fiercely (try to) resist them. Mainstream media practices and representations are stretched to their limits, and are increasingly showing cracks, fissures and internal contradictions. The mainstream (news) media's much-cherished notions of objectivity, balance, and truthfulness, in particular, are losing much of their taken-for-grantedness; the fog of war is revealing what they 'really' are: always specific constructions of ideal-typical concepts. This process of demystification has two explanations: the enormous stream of practical problems that mainstream media have to face during wartime, and the confrontation with another hegemonic level, that is, the ideological model of war, that becomes inescapable for media organizations and media professionals in times of armed conflict.

War and ideology

When a nation, or a people, goes to war, powerful mechanisms come into play, which turn the adversary into 'the enemy'. While the existence of an adversary is considered legitimate, and its right to defend its – distinct – ideas is not questioned, an enemy is excluded from the political community and has to be destroyed (Mouffe 1993: 4). The transformation of an adversary into an enemy is supported by a set of discourses, articulating the identities of all parties involved.

Following Galtung et al. (2001), we would contend that these discourses on the self and the enemy are based on a series of elementary dichotomies such as good–evil, just–unjust, innocent–guilty, rational–irrational, civilized–barbaric, organized–chaotic, superior to technology–part of technology, human–animal/machine, united–fragmented, heroic–cowardly and determined–insecure (Carpentier 2007b). These oppositions play a key role in hegemonic projects, which attempt to fix their meanings. Both sides claim to be rational and civilized, and to fight a good and just war, attributing responsibility for the conflict to the enemy. The construction of the enemy is accompanied by the construction of the identity of the self, in a clearly antagonistic relationship with the enemy's identity.

The problems in the representation of war are strengthened by the application of the specific procedures and rituals (Tuchman 1972) that media professionals use to guarantee or legitimize their truth-speaking (and objectivity). Journalistic daily practices and procedures are regulated through key concepts, such as balance, relevance and truthfulness, which have an important impact on the actual representations that journalists produce. As these fluid concepts need to be transformed into social practice, their content is rendered highly particular and specific.

The mainstream media's war coverage often contains two different hegemonies. First, they contain the ideological model of war that dominates the cultural sphere in which they operate. This hegemonic model defines 'the self' and 'the enemy', and connotates them positively or negatively. Secondly, the mainstream media's war coverage is based on procedures, rituals, and values that are themselves also hegemonic, and whose visibility in times of war increases (see Galtung et al. 2001; Tumber and Palmer 2004). The main characteristics of mainstream media's coverage of war include:

- a preference for the factual narration of the events of war, detached from individual (private) suffering, and supported by journalists' eyewitness accounts;
- a preference for elite spokespersons whose statements are considered to be of public relevance;
- a preference for (often military) experts providing contextual information about the conflict.

All these practices remain firmly embedded in the ideological model of war, which frames the images that are shown and the analyses that are made. At the same time the mainstream media's practices and preferences tend to exclude a number of other approaches that transcend the sanitized narration of war, that allow 'ordinary people' to speak, and that deconstruct the traditional dichotomies of the ideological model of war.

Alternative voices

Although the processes listed above often characterize mainstream media output, care should be taken not to homogenize the diversity of media organizations and practices. In a number of cases mainstream media have managed to produce counter-hegemonic discourses and provided spaces for critical debate, indepth analysis and humour. They have also, on a number of occasions, shown the horrors of war. Some have attempted to counter some of the basic premises of the ideological model,[1] by giving a face to Iraqi victims, by paying attention to the strong European and the less strong US popular resistance to war. Tumber and Palmer (2004: 164) summarize the situation in the UK in relation to the second Gulf War as follows: 'Unlike the anti-Vietnam protests . . . the anti-war protest over Gulf War II, consisting of a politically and socially diverse coalition, was given space and prominence in the media'.

Nevertheless, as a result of the mechanisms and characteristics of mainstream media war reporting described above, and the sensitive, emotional nature of armed conflict, alternative media organizations and communication channels offer counter-hegemonic discourses and identities that threaten the mainstream media's double hegemony, situated at the level of the hegemonic ways of covering war on the one hand, and at the level of the hegemonic ideological model of war itself on the other. Wall (2005: 166) concludes after her analysis of blogs on the Iraq war that there does appear to be a form of postmodern journalism here: one that challenges elite information control and questions the legitimacy of mainstream news, that consists not so much of grand narratives as small slices of stories which are seemingly endlessly reproduced.

These counter-hegemonic discourses are more complicated than perhaps often assumed. First, they do not always confront both hegemonies head on, but often negotiate a critical position in relation to these two dominant ones. Second, they tend to change over time, as these alternative voices sometimes become incorporated by the mainstream. To illustrate this complexity, we have selected three cases that are all related to what is now commonly called the blogosphere.

The first is the blogger Salam Pax and shows how this blogger managed to deconstruct the dichotomous model of war by expressing his reluctance to be liberated. The second case of the so-called mil-bloggers illustrates the complexity of eye-witness accounts as American soldiers are seen to enter the public space. The third case, which totally disrupts the clear-cut difference between mainstream and alternative media, private and public, concerns the Abu Ghraib pictures circulated within closed and fluid networks that were built mainly on interpersonal contacts and which take the dehumanization of the enemy to an extreme.

Salam Pax: disrupting the hegemonic definition of the Other

The Internet has emerged as (one of) the privileged channels or arenas that can be used to circulate dissenting discourses regarding the war, thereby articulating alternative representations of war (and peace). The blog written by Salam Pax, known as the Baghdad Blogger,[2] is a prime example of such representations. Salam Pax is an affluent, Western-educated architect, with a good knowledge of English, seemingly likeable from a Western perspective, neither extreme nor fundamentalist, and a member of a suppressed gay community in Iraq (Melzer 2005). He is in many ways not a typical Iraqi, but he has provided an alternative and highly personalized narrative of war. As some of the excerpts below illustrate, his personalized narrative, from the inside of Iraq, contradicts the prevailing good–evil dichotomy that classifies Iraqis either as victims of a dictatorship, who welcome the American army as liberators, or as supporters of the old Iraqi regime.

> *Last night's bombardment was very different from the nights before. It wasn't only heavier but the sound of the bombs was different. The booms and bangs are much louder; you would hear one big bang and then followed by a number of these rumbles that would shake everything. And there are of course the series of deep dob-dob-dobs from the explosions farther away.*
>
> (24 March 2003)

> *If we had a mood barometer in the house it would read 'to hell with saddam and*

may he quickly be joined by bush'. No one feels like they should welcome the American army. The American government is getting as many curses as the Iraqi.

(30 March 2003)

A conversation overheard by G. while in the Meridian Hotel – the Iraqi media center:

Female journalist 1: *oh honey how are you? I haven't seen you for ages.*
Female journalist 2: *I think the last time was in Kabul.*

Bla bla bla
Bla bla bla

Female journalist 1: *have to run now, see you in Pyongyang then, eh?*
Female journalist 2: *absolutely.*

Iraq is taken out of the headlines. The search for the next conflict is on. Maybe if it turns out to be Syria the news networks won't have to pay too much in travel costs.

(23 April 2003)

The excerpts from his blogs plainly show Salam Pax to be highly critical of the mainstream media and its practices; but his mere existence (and postings) in themselves constitute a critique of the mainstream media on a number of levels. As a witness he could – as no journalist could – write from the simultaneous positions of an expert, an independent observer and a citizen journalist. In doing so, he generated an alternative media practice that created exceptional insights and bypassed the professional journalistic culture of detachment.

During and immediately after the invasion, several newspapers in Europe and the US reprinted excerpts from Salam Pax's blog. He subsequently became a biweekly editorialist for *The Guardian* newspaper in the UK (McCarthy 2003). His critical perspectives were published in many other newspapers throughout Europe and the USA. His blog writings were also published in book form (Salam Pax 2003). Salam Pax also produced a series of documentaries for Guardian Films, using his own footage, and paying tribute to Bob Dylan's famous video clip for 'Subterranean Homesick Blues' (1965), complementing voiceovers with the written word on pan cards, as a kind of sub-text (Salam Pax 2005). These contributions have been bundled on a DVD and were aired on the BBC's *Newsnight*.

Salam Pax thus evolved from being a concerned Iraqi citizen, blogging about how Iraqi citizens were experiencing the war, into a foreign (war) correspondent, film-maker and author. He was catapulted into the mainstream, but did not lose his identity as an alternative voice.

On a book promotion tour in Australia, Salam Pax expressed his unease with his sudden celebrity status:

I'm not comfortable with the idea that I am considered a 'news source'. I am just blogging. A blog is where you can make the news more real for you . . . for me. People's lives are not news. Also, I'm not comfortable when people think I'm saying something in the name of Iraqis. I'm not.

(quoted in Coggins 2004)

This statement shows that Salam Pax still positions himself as opposed to the hegemonic structures that define professionalism and journalism, while at the same time reluctantly becoming part of them.

Mil-blogs: rendering the private self visible

US military personnel and their families also began to use blogs to connect the front with the home front and vice versa, and also (at times) as a platform to disseminate alternative representations of war, and personal accounts of how this is being experienced by the soldiers themselves and their families. These published private experiences again contradict (and implicitly critique) the mainstream media's focus on the abstract narration of war that leaves little space for the concrete narrations of the lives and experiences of individual soldiers and their focus on expert knowledge and elite representation. In this sense, these blogs are again alternatives to the mainstream media's way of covering war. As mainstream journalist John Hockenberry (2005) points out in *Wired*:

> Strong opinions throughout the military ranks in and out of wartime are nothing new. But online technology in the combat zone has suddenly given those opinions a mass audience and an instantaneous forum for the first time in the history of warfare. On the 21st-century battlefield, the campfire glow comes from a laptop computer, and it's visible around the world.

Although these sites can be seen as critiques of the mainstream media's hegemony, most simultaneously re-enforce the hegemonic discourse of war, reverting to the classic dichotomies that characterize the Western ideological model of war.[3]

An example of a hegemonic mil-blog is that of Buck Sargent,[4] an infantry officer who presents himself as 'a University of Texas graduate, a Ronald Reagan conservative, and a George Patton patriot, . . . pro-victory'. Having done tours of duty in both Afghanistan and Iraq, Buck Sargent eloquently amplifies the persuasive discourses of the war on terror and claims of bringing peace and democracy in the case of both these countries.

Some mil-blogs not only offer an alternative position towards the mainstream media, but simultaneously take a clear counter-hegemonic position in relation to the ideological model of war. These more critical mil-blogs have understandably been the object of controversy and have endowed the military establishment with uncomfortable feelings of having (partially) lost control over the flow of information.

Disturbing in this regard – at least for the US military – but difficult to discipline or control, is the use of blogs and websites by the families of soldiers on tours of duty, by members of the families of military personnel who have been killed, or by war veterans, writing to support the troops and/or to protest against or question the legitimacy of the Iraqi war.[5]

Counter-hegemonic discourses can be less obvious, more implicit, consisting of descriptions of the everyday lives of soldiers, the emotional stress, but also the banality and boredom involved in war. They contradict the heroization of American soldiers on tour in Iraq by narrating the ordinariness of their activities. One example of this is a critical blog entitled *My War: Killing Time in Iraq*, written by Spc. Colby Buzzell, based in Mosul. This blog had a hit-rate of 10,000 a day in September 2004 (Cooper 2004). On its front page it featured Picasso's *Guernica* or a 'Big Brother is Watching You' poster, which set the tone for how this soldier wrote about 'his' war (Buzzell 2005).

This example is also relevant in terms of the efforts of the military to reassert control over mil-bloggers. Due to its popularity, Buzzell's blog attracted the attention of the Pentagon's censors (Cooper 2004). He was ordered to remove two postings from his archive and to have his contributions screened by his superiors before posting. In not being ordered to stop blogging, the presence of censorship, but also a degree of tolerance on the part of his superiors, is demonstrated. It also is illustrative of the Pentagon's views on blogging, summarized in the following statement from a military spokesperson:

> We treat them [the blogs] the same way we would if they were writing a letter or speaking to a reporter: It's just information . . . If a guy is giving up secrets, it doesn't make much difference whether he's posting it on a blog or shouting it from the rooftop of a building.
>
> (Lt. Col. Barry Venable, quoted in Cooper 2004)

Not surprisingly, the removed postings re-emerged on other blogs, thus negating the attempts to delete them from the public sphere. An excerpt from one of Colby Buzzell's censored postings shows the counter-hegemonic strength of these blogs. It shows the irrationality and indiscriminateness of war, which again challenges the image of the heroic (American) soldier, who is always in control and does not indiscriminately 'shoot at everything' that might be in the area.

> Bullets were pinging off our armor all over our vehicle, and you could hear multiple RPG's [rocket-propelled grenades] being fired and flying through the air and impacting all around us. All sorts of crazy insane Hollywood explosions bullshit going on all around us. I've never felt fear like this. I was like, this is it, I'm going to die. I cannot put into words how scared I was.
>
> (Men in Black, 05 August 2004)[6]

Captain Danjel Bout, a.k.a. Thunder 6,[7] talks about the importance of exposing to his readers the day-to-day reality of war rather then the snippets of headline news we are being served by the mainstream media:

I don't purposely leave out the moments when our bodies hit the adrenal dump switch . . . For people to really understand our day-to-day experience here, they need more than the highlights reel. They need to see the world through our eyes for a few minutes.

(quoted in Hockenberry 2005)

Although the anxiety of the military authorities over, and attempts to control and screen, material posted online were apparent in the case of Colby Buzzell, there are also some more subtle mechanisms of self-censorship at work. Buck Sargent's blog, for instance, explicitly states that 'Opsec will be strictly observed in all submissions'. Sgt. Lizzie, a female soldier blogger serving in Iraq, points to the notion of operational security while demonstrating a strong desire among serving soldiers to escape the everyday reality of war through their blogging activity:

Reason you don't hear about much action from me: 1. I work in a very sensitive field, 99% of my work is classified, so I really can't talk about it. 2. Operational Security. There are certain things that I just can't talk about because it isn't wise to.

(New Lives, 20 October 2004[8])

Finally, the technology allows blogs to be relegated to the private sphere of family and friends. *The Green Side* was an example of a site, primarily directed towards family and friends, but which was publicly accessible. However, after concerns about operational security were voiced by the military establishment, the site was secured by making it password protected. In the meantime the site has gone offline.

The Abu Ghraib pictures: falling on the wrong side of the hegemonic divide

During 2003 accounts of prisoner abuse and torture began to emerge, most of which were ignored by the mainstream media, certainly in the USA. In June 2003, one month after Bush, on board the USS *Abraham Lincoln*, declared 'mission accomplished', Amnesty International (2003) was condemning the US government for its treatment of prisoners in Iraq:

The conditions of detention Iraqis are held under at the Camp Cropper Center at Baghdad International Airport – now a US base – and at Abu Ghraib Prison may amount to cruel, inhuman or degrading treatment or punishment, banned by international law.

In mid-October 2003 the International Committee of the Red Cross (ICRC) was allowed to visit the prison and reported several serious forms of 'ill-treatment' (ICRC 2004: 13). Also some US military personnel were offering eyewitness accounts of incidents of torture. One such came from Sgt. Frank 'Greg' Ford, a counter-intelligence agent, who after reporting to his superiors several incidents of what he described as war crimes, was repatriated for medical reasons and given an honourable discharge from the army (DeBatto 2004). It was another soldier who initiated investigations regarding the misconduct of military investigators and prison guards at Abu Ghraib. In January 2004, Sgt. Joseph Darby handed over photographs he had obtained from members of his company who had served in Iraq, to the US Army's Criminal Investigation Command (CID).

These photographs were acts of self-representation. The soldiers present at and involved in the acts of torture used digital cameras to document their 'everyday life' in the Abu Ghraib prison, with the explicit intent of sharing them with friends, family and other members of their social networks. They were souvenirs of the 'good times' in Iraq. This naturally highlights the increasing ubiquity of digital cameras (Kellner 2004a).

The self-representations in the Abu Ghraib photographs were not neutral, but included depictions of proud torturers in the same frame as the humiliated tortured, smiling and giving thumbs-up signs. Sontag (2004) made an analogy with photographs of lynchings,

> taken between the 1880's and 1930's, which show Americans grinning beneath the naked mutilated body of a black man or woman hanging behind them from a tree. The lynching photographs were souvenirs of a collective action whose participants felt perfectly justified in what they had done. So are the pictures from Abu Ghraib.

The sexual nature of many of the abusive photos also shows the psychology of shame and bio-politics (Foucault 1975) in their rawest form. The prisoner is reduced to what Agamben (1988) calls *homo sacer*, whose life is without value, dispensable with impunity.

Here, again, we find the ideological model of war at work. The evilness of the enemy legitimizes the dehumanization of the enemy soldiers. In warfare, this logic is used to justify the killing of these enemy soldiers, eradicating them with a total disregard for their humanity. It similarly justifies torture; these enemy bodies are no longer human, but mere containers of military information, or fragmented objects of (sadistic) pleasure.

It was not until April 2004, when Seymour Hersh reported on the ongoing investigations and published some of the photographs in *The New Yorker* (Hersh 2004), and when CBS's *60 minutes* aired a documentary on the photographs, that the Abu Ghraib scandal really gained momentum. More and more pictures appeared in the global mainstream public sphere, and in February 2006 Salon.com managed to obtain from a source who had served in Abu Ghraib and was 'familiar with the CID investigation', a DVD containing 1000 unpublished photos and an internal CID report (Benjamin 2006).

The mainstream media and their hegemonic practices were a necessary condition to turn the Abu Ghraib scandal into a media spectacle of global proportions. It was the investigative journalism of the mainstream media that catalysed the tipping of the photographs from the private to the public domain. The 'alternative' Internet was first a means used to restrict the circulation of these pictures, and kept these trophies within the social networks of the perpetrators, outside the control of the state and the military. Later, but only after the mainstream media had made the pictures public, photo-blogs allowed these pictures to be copied and pasted on multiple other websites.[9]

The publicness generated by the mainstream media also changed the nature of the Abu Ghraib pictures from trophies to legal evidence. Sontag's observation that 'the possibility of being affected morally by photographs' is determined by 'the existence of a relevant political consciousness' (Sontag 1973: 19) is highly relevant here. As the torturers transcended the cultural norms of warfare, taking the dehumanization of the enemy to the extreme and, moreover, deriving pleasure from it, they became a threat to the articulation of the American self as 'good'. In order to maintain its hegemony, the model that constructed the Iraqi soldiers as evil and the American soldiers as good had to be defended. This was done by defining these soldiers as 'bad apples' and pushing them outside the American hegemony (and the military).

Conclusion

The three cases explored in this chapter show, in their own way, how the Internet manifests itself as a medium capable of bypassing mechanisms of control imposed by either the state or the military, and generating alternative discourses capable of challenging the hegemonic ideological model of war and at times also the dichotomous frames of 'the self' versus 'the enemy'.

These blogs disrupt the hegemonic practices of the mainstream media and their focus on the rational narrative, the warring elites and the semi-military experts. Through the focus on individual and ordinary experiences, they offer alternative ways of reporting war that are embedded in daily life and that potentially offer us more insight than the detached accounts of journalists ever could. These alternative ways of reporting show that ordinary people can also perform expert roles and communicate valuable knowledges, and that these subjective experiences can be factual, relevant, truthful, and authentic. In this sense they are not so different from what we expect from professional journalists, but they do complement these more traditional forms of journalism, whilst professional journalism still remains an important truth-finding system, as is illustrated by the Abu Ghraib case.

At the same time this case study shows that these alternative channels of communication and these alternative discourses are in many cases more problematic than often assumed. First, the three examples show that it is difficult to sustain a rigid separation between alternative and mainstream, and the assumed univocal interrelationship between mainstream and hegemony. They show that while some actors use alternative media channels, such as weblogs, they in fact reproduce hegemony (cf. the patriotic blogs). Similarly, some counter-hegemonic voices are given a platform by some mainstream media in their quest for balance. Bloggers then become, in their mainstream media portrayals, the new 'real' truth-tellers, as long as they fit within the professional hegemony of the mainstream media.

Second, while the Abu Ghraib pictures scandal, ironically initiated by whistleblowers from within the military, represents the loss of control over the communicative process by the US government, re-establishing control was very much an issue in terms of the mil-blogs. It is interesting to see that the somewhat liberal attitude of the Pentagon towards blogs has changed in the last year, implementing more restrictive policies, although full control of the mil-blogosphere remains impossible. More subtle disciplining techniques are at play, often internalized by mil-bloggers and seen as common sense, for instance, not to breach operational security. In other words, hegemony can sometimes strike back.

Finally, these dynamics and interactions between the alternative and the mainstream media illustrate that the mainstream media cannot be articulated as a singular actor nor necessarily as subservient to state propaganda and control. Selected counter-hegemonic voices were given a platform and/or their blogs were referred to in mainstream online, print or broadcast media. Furthermore, sound investigative reporting revealed and initiated the Abu Ghraib scandal. It is too easy to dismiss these as mere co-option strategies and to condemn 'the media' for being a mouthpiece of US and UK propaganda. At the same time it should be noted that not all Iraqis, nor all military bloggers, were granted the same level of exposure. And, here again, hegemonic journalistic routines and codes influence which bloggers are 'selected'. Quality of writing, critical perspectives, independent views and also the ability to provide a personalized account that is relevant to a wider (Western) audience are all relevant and explain why Spc. Buzzell's blog got such high exposure while Sgt. Lizzie's did not.

Notes

1 A modest but interesting example was provided by the North Belgian newspaper *De Morgen* on 4 April 2003, when referring to the US-led coalition as a 'mini-coalition'.
2 See http://dear_raed.blogspot.com/ (with archive) and his new blog, http://justzipit.blogspot .com/.
3 To get an idea of the popularity of blogs with soldiers and their families, see, for example, http://www.military.com/blogs or http://www.milblogging.com/, which provide a gateway to a diversity of military related weblogs.
4 http://americancitizensoldier.blogspot.com/.
5 Examples of such sites and blogs carrying distinct counter-hegemonic messages and voices are Families Against the War (http://www.mfaw.org.uk/), Military Families Speak Out (http://www.mfso.org/) and Iraq Veterans Against the War (http://www.ivaw.net/).
6 http://perspective-seeker.blogspot.com/2004/09/my-war-fear-and-loathing-in-iraq.html (accessed 16 July 2006).
7 http://thunder6.typepad.com/.
8 http://sgtlizzie.blogspot.com/2004_10_01_sgtlizzie_archive.html (accessed 16 July 2006).

9 A good example in this regard is The Memory Hole (http://www.thememoryhole.org/), dedicated to archiving sensitive material that is in danger of disappearing from the public sphere. Besides this, Salon.com also archived all the Abu Ghraib photos, as did Wikipedia – see http://en.wikipedia.org/wiki/Abu_Ghraib_prisoner_abuse_reports/Gallery (accessed 16 July 2006).

6 | ETHNIC-RELIGIOUS GROUPS AND ALTERNATIVE JOURNALISM

We strongly believe that the breathtaking changes in communications technology and the new global forms of media partnerships must enhance diversity in the 21st century.

(The Minority Media and Telecommunications Council (MMTC)
web site, http://www.mmtconline.org/)

Introduction

Despite an accepted view of the potential of the mainstream media to enable minority, ethnic and religious groups to reproduce their cultural diversity and participate in the public sphere, the reality is that mainstream media, particularly public service broadcasting, have not fully catered for the communication needs of most minority groups. The systematic exclusion of ethnic and religious minorities from the public sphere – with their low share of cultural and economic capital, including access to communication technologies – has resulted in the relegation of some groups into 'zones of silence' (Rigoni 2005). Moreover, the stereotypical and ideological representation of ethnic and religious minorities in (parts of) the mainstream media has produced a negative web of signification of threat, hostility, and antagonism towards them. Currently, there is a growing tendency in the popular consciousness of Europe to blame non-European immigrants for many socio-economic problems – unemployment, housing shortages, crime, and poor performance of education and health systems. Conservative and right-wing politicians use the media to create anxiety and paranoia about race and religion, conceiving a national imaginary characterized by fear, in which 'foreigners' are the main threat to the security and well-being of a nation. (Bailey and Harindranath 2005)

In this scenario, the under-representation, one-sided representation and invisibility of ethnic and religious minorities has generated an ongoing struggle over meaning, between those minorities at the periphery of society and the mainstream media. However, the public sphere of liberal-plural societies allows for the exercise of 'alternative democratic strategies' (Calhoun 1992). This includes the possibility of minority groups in civil society exerting influence upon the media and of establishing alternative, discursively connected public spheres, potentially working to minimize mainstream media hegemonic power over meaning. Habermas (1992) reworked his concept of the public sphere, recognizing not only the existence of multiple public spheres, but also their capacity for challenging hegemonic views.

In this context of plurality of public spheres, many ethnic groups have reacted to their invisibility and one-sided representation by creating communicative spheres, that is, parallel, semi-autonomous public spheres, defined by the identities of their audiences – the 'public sphericules' suggested by Gitlin (1998). Similarly, Mouffe (1999b: 757) uses a conception of public space that takes this 'multiplicity of voices' into account, namely, the proliferation of alternative spaces of communication – print media, websites, community radio, and web-based and transnational television – where they can voice their demands for social, political, cultural, and economic inclusion in multicultural societies.

The multiplicity of 'minority media'[1] might attest to the formation of new forms of mobilization and political solidarity among a number of minority groups.[2] They all search, in different ways, for fair modes of symbolic and political representation that allow them to participate and to contribute to the construction of a multicultural, democratic society. All around the world Arab, Chinese, Indian, Afro-Caribbean, African and Latin American immigrants are accessing mainstream and alternative satellite channels broadcasting programmes[3] from their country of origin or elsewhere, and producing and accessing web pages, online radio, and printed media in their own languages. These all carry a distinct meaning for minority communities. They mainly work as providers of information and entertainment to increase a sense of belonging among ethnic and religious minorities, to promote transnational bonding, and to act as spaces for cultural expression and identity assertion. Potentially, they can offer counter-hegemonic views on current affairs, acting as a proactive agenda of positive intervention in the public sphere as well as functioning as a space of resistance to marginalization. This chapter investigates a number of distinct dimensions of minority communication, particularly the practice of journalism, focusing on *Q-News*, a Muslim magazine.

Minority media

There has been a steady increase of the minority ethnic population in the UK. The 2001 Census registered a 53 per cent increase over the 1991 figures, from 3.0 million in 1991 to 4.6 million in 2001, which corresponds to 7.9 per cent of the total population of the United Kingdom.[4] This growth has been reflected in the number of new minority media, particularly those directed at the younger generations (second and third generations of immigrants living in the UK).

The expansion of ethnic-religious minority media is an indication that these communities and their younger members, rather than fully integrating or 'assimilating', have found new identities that combine the best of their own cultures and heritage. These new-found identities bring a need to create media that understand the social and cultural compromises involved in living far from one's culture of origin, using languages that they understand and incorporating a cultural empathy that mainstream media may neither want nor be able to provide.

The growth in minority media can be understood at two levels: as a political response of minority groups to their marginalization and exclusion from equal participation in society and mainstream media industries, and as a space for identity negotiation. Both relate to the 'politics of representation' of ethnic – and religious – groups (Hall 1992a: 253) which, rather than only addressing concerns over bias, positive and negative images, and access to media institutions, centres on the production of diverse forms of media – and representation – that challenge crystallized notions of ethnic and religious minorities.

Alternative minority media work in the vacuum created by the multicultural rhetoric of assimilation or isolation, which highlights the divergent approaches to multiculturalism; the 'politics of difference' and 'liberal' politics regarding ethnic minority rights, including communication, information, and representation, which are part of the wider debate on integration, inclusion, and democracy. Liberal thinking addresses ethnic diversity and pluralism through the universalism of human rights, considered to be hostile, exclusive, or homogenizing of difference (Bailey and Harindranath 2006; Kymlicka 2001; Taylor 1992; Parekh 2000). The politics of difference, which is criticized for being anti-universalistic and anti-liberal (Barry 2001), advocates equal rights and recognition of minorities, particularly cultural and ethnic diversity.

A question relevant to this debate is how to produce a media landscape that acknowledges difference without containment and domestication of ethnic differences. In our view, minority media could be a potential solution if they are perceived as an alternative to syncretic cultures whereby identities are translated and negotiated through the fusion of different cultural interferences (Hall 1992a). Allowing for generalizations, in the confluence of immigration and multiculturalism, the global flow of media, capital, and new communication technologies, ethnic and religious minorities are using the potentials of alternative media for the affirmation and articulation of their cultures and as a way of reaffirming difference (Gilroy 1987).

There is a clear reconfiguration here of the media landscape brought about by the proliferation of cable television channels and the explosion of sites on the World Wide Web, coupled with the ongoing politics of recognition for ethnic difference (Cecil 2000). This provides an argument for a conception of alternative minority media that goes beyond existing views and becomes inclusive of alternative formations which differ and cross borders in new ways.

Caldwell (2003), based on his experience of alternative media, calls for a redefinition of alternative media, which tend to be trapped in binary oppositions (see Chapter 1). These dichotomies have tended to cultivate notions of dominant versus oppressed groups; majority versus minority discourses; and mass deception versus authentic expression (Caldwell 2003). Rodriguez (1996) also suggests that communication researchers should go beyond the binary opposition between alternative media – subordinate position – and mainstream media power. In light of these arguments, we would suggest that commercial minority media should be analysed as social actors that cross those defined borders and are located in the multiple, small public spheres of multicultural societies, where they are paramount in the articulation of minorities' struggles for inclusion and identity recognition.

Minority media journalism

Print and online minority journalism is diverse in format, content, and ethos. It can be said to belong to the category of alternative media, that is, those media that 'pursue a critical or alternative agenda, from the margins, as it were, or from the underbelly of social life' (Silverstone 1999: 103; and see discussion in Chapter 1 above). The difficulty in defining the practices of minority media lies in the fact they are not part of a uniform and homogeneous culture. On the contrary, they are enterprises characterized by fragmentation and dispersal.

Although minority media have been playing an important role in the formation and development of ethnic and religious communities in multi-ethnic societies, they have a difficult existence due to their 'high mortality rate, increasing financial difficulties, and problems in incurring criticisms . . . if they attempt to be outspoken organs in their communities' (Singer 1978, quoted in Zhang and Xiaoming 1999: 22). The short-lived reality of many minority media resonates with the negative evaluation of alternative media by Comedia (1984), which argued that their failure relates to their resistance to adopting financial and organizational principles, which would allow them to compete in the market place. The contemporary minority media landscape is characterized by a mixture of non-commercial and commercial enterprises, with some of the latter being able to achieve stable positions in the alternative market. In addition, many of these are online media, which dissipates the problems of circulation and distribution inherent in the traditional media. Minority media journalistic practice has hybrid features, combining mainstream media production elements with innovative ones. They do not mirror the mainstream and have a more meaningful and distinctive journalistic ethos, that is, political mission and/or social conscience in relation to their specific communities.

This chapter calls into question the common assumption that commercial alternative media – and their journalism practices – necessarily undermine the critical, oppositional stance of the established press (Benson 2003). Although most of minority media rely on advertising and/or subscriptions, they offer news and views ignored by the mainstream media, and encourage democratic debate and, in some cases, active political involvement. The changing mediascape, characterized by new forms of alternative media and journalistic practices, allows us to suggest an approach to alternative journalism which is beyond the traditional dichotomy of mainstream versus alternative, less 'either . . . or' (Harcup 2005) and more acceptable to new hybrid forms and practices (Atton 2003) such as those developed by ethnic-religious media.

The power of alternative media in challenging the structures of mainstream media and communication is not clear. As Rodriguez (2001) suggests, alternative media are positioned in a constant process of renegotiation over democratic media practices to strengthen democracy. So far, few would doubt the potential significance of these media, particularly considering the wider scenario of media changes occurring due to new communication technologies, economic convergence, deregulation, market pressures, and international trends towards audience segmentation (Deuze 2006a).

Nevertheless, long-term changes in the balance of power between mainstream media and alternative media are largely related to three important factors. First, the dispersal of available information, in that the excess of information accessible today might lead to a closer inspection of from where and to what end people obtain news (Couldry 2003: 51). Second, the ability of 'communities' to cross the economic barriers – high levels of capital investment and technical training – which prevent many groups from meaningful participation in the current mass media system and the production of media outputs. Contemporary media provide excellent access in terms of consumption of their outputs, but are extremely limited in terms of participation in production (McChesney 1999). Third, media and communication policies, which should be formulated to provide a multi-ethnic public media sphere inclusive of ethnic minorities. In practical terms, this means government's policy on cultural diversity should be articulated with its media policy to address the communication and media-specific needs of ethnic minorities (Downing and Husband 2005).

A major concern is the potential of minority media as a space to empower ethnic and religious minorities. Without denying the value of minority media, it remains questionable whether the struggles for social and political recognition have even influenced the inclusion and/or exclusion of minorities in society.

The focus of the rest of this chapter is twofold: we try to challenge established purist views of alternative media, and at the same time understand its political relevance beyond the constraints of its own 'ethnic-religious' boundaries, that is, a communicative space contained by its 'minority' status that might not challenge the relations of power of the mainstream politics of communication.

Case study: *Q-News*

A research project carried out by Bailey in 2005 examined the process of news production of ethnic-religious newspapers, magazines, and web pages. The aim was to clarify the complexity of journalistic practices, which seem to be dictated by the demands of commercial ventures and the 'politics of resistance', but also try to be a space for opposition and negotiation for ethnic-religious groups. Twelve journalists and editors were interviewed. They represented a number of different ethnic and religious minority backgrounds in various communities – Black, Asian, Latin American and Arab. They were chosen from a sample of 58 editors of minority media in the UK. One minority media example that was selected for this study was the Muslim magazine, *Q-News*. It was chosen for its relevance to our argument that 'alternative' media can be both critical and commercial (Comedia 1984). The magazine is representative of a new breed of alternative-commercial media with independent ownership combined with continued defence of the political mission of their founder-publisher. Not all commercial alternative media catering for minorities – ethnic and religious – are like this; many are just providers of information and news, and do not necessarily have a political agenda.

The British Muslim mediascape in the United Kingdom includes a variety of local, national, and international outlets; newspapers such as *The Muslim News, Crescent International* and *Trends*, radio stations such as Radio Ummah and Radio Ramadan, and magazines such as *Q-News, Emel, Islamica* and *Salam*. In addition, there are media committees such as the Muslim Council of Britain, Islamic Media Association, and the Forum Against Islamophobia and Racism. The printed and/or online media are produced in English and/or are bilingual, and their distribution depends on their commercial or non-commercial nature.

Q-News is a small, independent, monthly magazine, which has an online and print version. It provides a mix of lifestyle and information. The magazine is part of the British Muslim landscape.[5] The Muslim community in Britain is an established, politicized group with recognized status and rights. The magazine engages in a continuous political struggle for civil liberties, rights, political participation, and inclusion of Muslims in British society, particularly since the difficulties posed by the post 11 September 2001 'Islamophobia', a fear of and/or aversion to Islam in general and Muslims in particular (Runnymed Trust report, cited in Quraishi 2005: 60).

Philosophy, readership, staff and revenue

The magazine tends to focus on issues of common concern to Muslim communities rather than those relating to specific ethnic groups. *Q-News* was started in March 1992 by its then chief editor, Fuad Nahdi, and is published by Q-News Media Limited. According to its current editor, Fareena Alam, the magazine is politically independent since it is not financed by any one particular country or regime. On the website[6] is the statement that:

> The philosophy of *Q-News* is a combination of style, appeal and relevance to the Muslim community living in the west and around the world. Over the years, *Q-News* has repeatedly set the agenda, rather than react to it. Our chief interest lies in the development of a unique and relevant Western Muslim discourse.

Q-News provides independent analysis, critique, and review of current affairs, politics, culture, and ideas. Each issue has between 50 and 78 pages and a print run of 20,000. Reader surveys indicate that each copy is read by at least three people, increasing its reach to some 60,000 professional, educated second- and third-generation British Muslims, parliamentarians, policy-makers, and educators. Readers of *Q-News* are in the younger age range – 4 per cent are under 18, 81 per cent are aged 19–40, 14.2 per cent are 41 or over. Thirty-two per cent have household incomes between £21,000 and £34,999, while 35.2 per cent have incomes of £35,000 or above.[7]

The profile of *Q-News* readers suggests the adoption of a wider trend in minority alternative media of catering for segmented 'audiences', which is part of both an economic and a political strategy. In other words, by catering to a specific reader – the middle-class and well-educated Muslim – *Q-News* competes in the difficult minority-media market and assumes the role of the political voice of Muslim groups. It could also be suggested that Muslim communities are using minority media as part of their media diet which does not preclude the use of other existing media available to them.

Q-News has a staff of 60 unpaid people, 30 of whom are journalists, 27 are freelancers, and 3 are writers. Freelancers are frequently used; most are not trained journalists, but are experts in their subject areas. Their team of unpaid contributors is a global network of intellectuals, opinion-makers, and award-winning journalists – both Muslim and non-Muslim.

The volunteer nature of the contributors' work and the free access to online back issues for the UK audience signals the commitment to become an alternative medium that attempts to avoid ghettoization in the wider mediascape. That is, it expands its reach and appeal to a non-Muslim audience. *Q-News* producers have created a publication that is attractive to a broad range of people and organizations by blending the conventions – layout and aesthetics – of mainstream Western media with their own. To become a global magazine, its editorial agenda, its range of contributors, its orientation, and its cultural frame of reference had to be redefined to communicate in a way that was sympathetic to an international community.

Q-News receives financial support primarily from advertising and subscriptions; its advertising revenue comes mostly from private Islamic companies and charity organizations. It advertises music, shows, bookstores, Islamic designed merchandise, private Islamic bank and international investments, charities such as Ealing International Islamic Thought, the Muslim Welfare House, and the Islamic Information Centre. There are rules relating to advertising. The magazine does not carry cigarette or alcohol advertisements, or any that smack of a conspicuous consumer culture. There are no data available about the amount of revenue that is received from advertising.

Editorial autonomy seems to exist, as our analysis showed that *Q-News* carried material that constructs an image of Muslims which goes beyond the stereotypes that abound in the mainstream media. '*Q-News* has truly demonstrated that there is more to Muslims than beards, scarves and halal meat'.[8] According to its editor, Fareena Alam, the magazine aims to increase the circulation of Muslim ideas and their visibility in the public sphere. It could be argued that *Q-News* is not offensive about the religions of their advertisers, nor is it a threat to any political agenda, thus suggesting that corporate interests have little or no influence on its news process.

In terms of market media competition, that is, finance, circulation, and distribution, commercial alternative minority media tend not to compete with their mainstream counterparts, because, besides not having the necessary economic strength, they cater for specific audiences/readers. In the case of *Q-News*, their main competitors are other publications aimed at the Muslim community such as *Islamica* and *Salam*. *Q-News* is also published online, which provides advertisers with a wider platform, and overcomes the problem of local competition.

Identity and discourses

In line with their mission to provide a unique Western Muslim discourse, *Q-News* tries to achieve a balance between cultural, political, religious, and human stories, focusing on their relevance to Muslims around the world, while engaging with institutional discourses in order to offer a critique. This unique Western Muslim discourse, it could be argued, is part of the ongoing ideological counter-hegemonic struggle of the Muslim community in reclaiming and representing the meaning of Muslim identity. Marshall (1991) points out that collective identities that are articulated through alternative public spheres have a double purpose. On the internal level, this collective identity functions to create a sense of belonging to those who are marginalized. Externally, it provides a basis to change and challenge dominant ideologies. *Q-News* is clearly a commercial alternative media with a political and religious mission.

Q-News is organized around themes mostly pertinent to the Muslim community, presenting its perspective. Published articles are not time-bound because the editorial remit is not concerned with immediate news issues, although a large proportion of the magazine's content relates to current debates. It could be suggested that *Q-News* represents a new hybrid publication, which not only blurs the division between mainstream and alternative media practices, but also has the potential to open up global conversations and impact on audiences who would not otherwise be exposed to Islamic ideas.

The content of the magazine shows political commitment to the Muslim quest for visibility and participation in multicultural societies, exploring the potential of alternative media to mobilize for cultural and political ends, that is, the cultural negotiation of identities and resolution of the social problems affecting Muslim communities. By presenting an alternative Muslim perspective on national and international issues and events, the magazine can potentially become a change agent and a platform for marginalized Muslims to voice their concerns.

The structure, layout, and journalistic style of the magazine have evolved over the years to become sophisticated and modern. *Q-News* incorporates lengthy essays and uses visual material. Its political agenda remains sharp and critical, enabling political self-critique and reflection. For example, in one of his editorials Fuad Nahdi offered an assessment of the situation in the UK for Muslims; this evaluation was not what might be expected of a magazine trying to project a 'positive' image of Muslim people to its audience, particularly after 9/11.

> Two years after the traumatic events of 9/11 and decades of existence in a state of limbo it is time we made a critical assessment of our situation: the condition we are in, how we got here and where we need to go. This process has to begin with an honest appraisal. We have to start with an understanding that we, as a community, are in a mess. And that unless things change fundamentally it will continue to get messier.
>
> (Nahdi 2003: 3)

What the editorial suggests is that although the magazine works to improve the image of Muslim groups, the editors nevertheless are prepared to point out the problems created by the 'community' and to challenge them to solve the 'mess'.

The structure of the magazine varies slightly between issues, but there is a standard model, which is exemplified by issue no. 364 of November 2005. The typical range of themes varies from the political (topical issues related to the Muslim 'community' in British and global politics) to comments (features on the daily experiences of Muslim people), arts, sport, and letters from readers.

There is a persistent political tone which pervades most of the articles. The British government is frequently criticized; for example, over whom they consider to be the Muslim community's representatives. Commentator Abidullah Ansari argues in his article about the BBC *Panorama* documentary, 'A Question of Leadership', broadcast in August 2005, that

> in the wreckage of the London bombings, both successful and botched, lie some tender and immensely vulnerable pieties about the harmlessness of the radical streak in our inner city Islam. Among the casualties too has been the official belief that given the chaos of mainstream Islam in the UK, the government can safely regard representatives of tightly-organized overseas 'Islamic Movements' as the community's voice.
>
> (Ansari 2005)

Criticism of government goes beyond the national, with reportage centring on politics in other countries that affect Muslim people's interests. An instance of *Q-News*'s international political criticism is the article on the new foreign policy of Pakistan and its alignment with the American government. Alam (2005: 24) states that: 'It appears that General Pervez Musharraf is on a mission to legitimize Israel and he is going about it with the zeal of a new convert'.

The sample analysed carries a subtle message to Muslims to come out of their 'ghettos' and express their faith, 'by using every reasonable opportunity to explain Islam to those whom Allah puts in our way in our everyday lives' (Chelebi 2005). The journalistic 'voice' is often personal, humorous and intellectually challenging, with heterogeneous styles and accents. *Q-News* has developed some hybrid journalistic practices. For example, while independent of commercial interests and pressures, allowing the exploration of a plethora of themes relevant to Muslims, its primary definers – source and agenda – are mostly an elite formed by their own journalists and expert contributors, thus following a trend highlighted by Atton (2005) in relation to radical community press.

The journalism in *Q-News* seems to differ from the canon of objectivity[9] praised by mainstream journalism, as the magazine offers a mainly Islamic perspective on the issues discussed. *Q-News* might not be a case of a radical medium maintained by radical social movements (Downing et al. 2001); however, its accomplishment over the years highlights a consistent commitment to Muslim causes, which is rewarded by support from many in the Muslim global community and Muslim organizations.

In spite of its success, there could be greater cooperation, in terms of non-hierarchical or democratic practices, in fostering reader participation. There is little evidence that *Q-News* promotes a democratic and horizontal culture of communication between writers and readers. The magazine shows concern with the daily life of ordinary Muslims, but 'speaks for' (Spivak 1988) them in an act of political delegation rather than including its readers in the decision-making production process. The conversations that take place in *Q-News* might be fostering a national and global exchange of ideas, but are mostly a dialogue among Muslim elites.

Nevertheless, *Q-News* must be seen as a significant journalistic development because it represents a space both to challenge established mainstream perceptions of Muslim people, and for Muslims to discuss, reflect, and articulate their concerns over social and political inclusion and identity recognition, particularly in Western societies where Muslim people recurrently complain about their one-sided representations in mainstream media and films.

In Britain, the Islamic Human Rights Commission produced a report (Ameli et al. 2005) which argues that crude and exaggerated stereotypes of Muslim people in films and media have helped demonize Muslims as violent, dangerous, and threatening, and reinforce prejudices. A survey conducted as part of the research revealed that Muslims in Britain felt negative images of their faith in the media had consequences in their daily lives. Those interviewed 'found a direct correlation between media portrayal and their social experiences of exclusion, hatred, discrimination and violence'. Moreover, the research also established a perception of 'unashamed bias' in the media against Muslims; 4 per cent considered its representation 'fair', 62 per cent believed the media to be Islamophobic, and 16 per cent described it as racist.

The example above might help us to understand the increasing importance of alternative minority media in multicultural-democratic societies. Their value lies perhaps not only in challenging one-sided representations of ethnic-religious groups, but also in the challenges they present to the communicative political ethos of mainstream public communication as the main legitimized providers of information. The existence of *Q-News* suggests that a diversity of minority media might promote democratization of information and plurality of divergent views as well as strengthening democratic societies.

As for the political capacity of alternative media to make the voices of minorities heard in the mainstream public sphere, *Q-News* is a positive example since it has actively participated in the wider public debates concerning Muslim social inclusion. Perhaps this is because its journalists often also write for the mainstream media, and *Q-News* has become a trusted source of information, analysis, and comment, regularly consulted by main mainstream media in Britain and elsewhere. However, as Downing and Husband (2005) remind us, the reality of different types of public communication, such as alternative minority media, does not offer a solution to the inclusion of minority groups in a 'multi-ethnic public sphere'.

Conclusion

The proliferation of minority media can be related to the growth of migration patterns in Western societies. However, the example of *Q-News* also suggests that this increase relates to wider social and political worldwide trends: the emergence of all sorts of communities and groups willing to engage with the 'politics of difference', and the emergence of distinct types of alternative media and journalism practices. Situating the variety of minority media practices on a specific point (alternative or mainstream) in the media and communication spectrum, without essentializing them, is a rather daunting, if not impossible, task.

An underlying concern in this discussion, then, has been to suggest a redefinition of alternative media that is inclusive of new types of media produced by ethnic and religious minorities struggling for identity recognition and for inclusion in democratic, multicultural societies.

The case of *Q-News* indicates that commercialism does not necessarily undermine critical journalism in alternative minority media, rather, it provides a committed space for critical analysis and support for the struggles of the Muslim community. The magazine may not fulfil all the prerequisites, discussed at length in the literature, for an alternative medium. However, rather than being dismissed as a commercial enterprise, *Q-News* and other similar efforts should be viewed as a new example of hybrid format and practices. They are being used to raise awareness among the marginalized communities, to challenge the mainstream politics of communication that silences or generates one-sided representations. At the same time mainstream media create a form of 'banal transnationalism', whereas alternative media such as *Q-News* enable access to the ordinary, banal reality of Muslim life to migrant Muslims living elsewhere (Aksoy and Robins 2003; Billig 1995).

On the political role of minority media, we argue that multiple small public spheres are indeed vital to plural societies, but the proliferation of 'subaltern counter-spheres' does not lead to a multiplication of political forces, nor do they in themselves provide the conditions for social inclusion. The existence of multiple ethnic public spheres may offer a sense of belonging to a group, help shape their struggle for political rights and be central to the process of democracy. However, as Downey and Fenton (2003) point out, these multiple spheres can also be problematic from the viewpoint of democratic culture. Greater pluralism may be regarded as threatening the fragmentation of democracy rather than being its solution. Overall, though, we suggest that the existence of multiple public ethnic-religious spheres – media and journalism – might strengthen ethnic and religious minorities' participation in multicultural, democratic societies.

Notes

1 In the context of this discussion, the phrase 'minority media' refers to alternative media produced and consumed by ethnic and religious minorities.
2 'Minority' refers specifically to ethnic and religious identities of different immigrant communities living outside their home country. The Muslim community in Britain comprises at least 56 nationalities and over 100 languages (Malik 2007). The traditional meanings attributed to community are problematic in this regard as these articulations of community unify and homogenize groups that have conflicting ideas, different political interests and backgrounds, and so on (see Chapter 1). The term (as it is used here) refers to an overall profile of the Muslim group in Britain, but does recognize the diversity of the Muslim community.
3 Mainstream and alternative satellite broadcasting have different roles. Mainstream channels might play a counter-hegemonic role, which varies according to specific struggles. For example, although mainstream channels are catering to a mass audience they may also help minority groups to reassert their religious, sexual, or ethnic political and cultural struggles. Alternative channels might be produced specifically to a defined minority audience without necessarily having a counter-hegemonic role.
4 The UK Census of 2001 categorizes ethnic minorities according to 'ethnic groups': White, 'Mixed', 'Asian or Asian British' (Indian, Pakistani, Bangladeshi, and Other Asian), 'Black or Black British' (Black Caribbean, Black African, and Black Other), 'Chinese', and 'Other'. These categories define artificial boundaries and risk essentializing ideas of 'race'. Our take on ethnic minorities relates to 'ethnicity', describing different social and cultural identities of those in positions of marginality in relation to a dominant group/culture (see http://www.statistics.gov.uk/cci/nugget.asp?id=273).
5 A sample of 12 issues of the magazine from 2003 to 2005 was analysed.

6 See http://www.q-news.com/about.htm.

7 Data from http://www.q-news.com/advertising.htm.

8 Ibid.

9 There is an assumption in mainstream journalism that journalists have to achieve absolute objectivity in their reporting (see Allan 1999).

ONLINE PARTICIPATION AND THE PUBLIC SPHERE: CIVIL SOCIETY MAILING LISTS AND FORUMS

The Internet is at the forefront of the evolving public sphere, and if the dispersion of public spheres generally is contributing to the already destabilized political communication system, specific counter public spheres on the Internet are also allowing engaged citizens to play a role in the development of new democratic politics.

(Dahlgren 2005: 160)

Introduction

For civil society organizations, activists and social movements, e-mail, mailing lists and forums increasingly represent a (cost-)efficient means to distribute alternative – counter-hegemonic – information, to mobilize online as well as for offline direct action, to debate issues, and even at times to become a tool for internal decision-making. Because of this, it is often claimed that the Internet is increasingly important for strengthening the public sphere or public spaces. It is also argued that the Internet has the potential to go beyond the local or national context and construct translocal or transnational (counter-)public spaces.

This chapter examines the use and role of these interactive tools by some civil society organizations, activists and movements.[1] The case studies are situated within the civil society model outlined in Chapter 1. Within this model, alternative media are defined as part of civil society or what Servaes (1999: 260) calls the 'third voice', not only between the state media and private commercial media, but also as civil society organizations between state and market.

What is often lacking in this tradition, however, are analyses of how civil society actors, without being media organizations, increasingly adopt new media and communication technologies to 'be the media' themselves. Many of these rather loose networks of activists, social movement networks as well as more structured networks, use the Internet to control their own communication flows better, and to interact amongst themselves or with a broader (translocalized or transnationalized) constituency.

In recent years the Internet has become a crucial instrument in the media and communication strategies of civil society organizations, enabling self-representation through by-passing the mediation by mainstream media. The Internet also allows for dispersed networks of activists to interact and engage, and organize themselves locally or beyond borders. However, the importance and role of more mediated mainstream media in the processes of social change should not be minimized (Gamson and Wolfsfeld 1993; Cammaerts 2007b). Besides this, the Internet does play an intriguingly schizophrenic role in these complex socio-political evolutions.

The Internet can be considered to be inclusive in that it enables social movement organizations and networks of activists to develop common 'frames of meaning' as well as actions. Scott and Street (2001: 46) enumerate four broad reasons why the Internet is so attractive for civil society, it allows for:

(a) mesomobilization (Gerhards and Rucht 1992) – co-ordination between movement networks across borders and without the need for a transcending hierarchical organisational form;
(b) a high impact without needing major resources;
(c) the organizations to retain editorial control over content and external communication;
(d) organizations to bypass state control and communicate in a secure environment.

In addition to the reasons put forward by Scott and Street, the Internet is deemed to play an increasingly important role in relation to strengthening the public sphere through the mediation of (political) debate and expanding the political. Here we can include forums and e-mail-based mailing lists as being crucial to many current political struggles (Hill and Hughes 1998; Dahlberg 2001; Meikle 2002; Dahlgren 2005; Cammaerts and Van Audenhove 2005).

However, as these authors also show, there are serious constraints from a democratic perspective on this increased cyberization of participation. These constraints point, importantly, to the exclusionary mechanisms brought about by the Internet. One of the most prominent constraints is that access to the Internet is far from universal; nor is there an equal distribution of the capabilities and means to allow everybody to use and operate these communication tools efficiently and effectively, and certainly not if looked at from a global or transnationalized perspective (Norris 2001; Cammaerts et al. 2003). The Internet also (potentially) contributes to the fragmentation of the public sphere and/or to a ghettoization of (often male) like-minded individuals. This fragmentation is deemed by many (Gitlin 1998; Putnam 2000; Barber 2003) to be detrimental to democracy. Even Mouffe, who takes a more conflictual position towards the political, acknowledges the danger of what she calls 'a form of autism' to which the Internet may lead:

> [New media] perversely allow people to just live in their little worlds, and not being exposed anymore to the conflicting ideas that characterise the agonistic public space. [...] It reminds me of a form of autism, where people are only listening to and speaking with people that agree with them.
>
> (Mouffe, quoted in Carpentier and Cammaerts, 2006: 968)

In relation to social movements and civil society, the Internet should be treated as a political opportunity structure,[2] potentially fostering participation in the realm of primarily informal 'non-institutional' political processes and social movement networking, allowing for more fluid and short-term participation. However, at the same time we should not ignore the many constraints to the fulfilment of these potentials. The Internet is not a quick-fix for democracy or participation. While it does open up spaces for the distribution of alternative discourses, to debate life, politics and culture, or to mobilize, there remains a need to bring those discourses and interaction beyond the online to the offline world of the political.

The potentials and constraints of mailing lists and online forums are explored through an analysis of two quite different cases. The first case relates to the use of a mailing list by the Internet Governance (IG) civil society caucus active within the World Summit on the Information Society (WSIS). The second case is an analysis of a spontaneous forum on Indymedia-NL relating to the murder of the Dutch populist leader, Pim Fortuyn. The two cases will be analysed at the level of the participants, and the nature, content, and degree of interaction. In some ways, the two cases represent different ends of several dimensions: rational and policy-oriented versus emotional and political; more structured and result-oriented versus unstructured, even anarchic; translocalized and transnationalized versus localized; and civil society experts versus unorganized citizens and activists.

WSIS Internet Governance civil society caucus mailing list

With about 3000 messages over a period of just over two years, it is fair to say that the civil society WSIS IG caucus mailing list has been very active. Our analysis covered the period from 30 March 2003, when the mailing list was launched, to 3 July 2005. At the time of analysis the mailing list[3] had some 100 active participants, but there are many more who subscribe and receive the postings, constituting a broader constituency of so-called passive participants. The mailing list served as a participatory tool to communicate and interact between dispersed activists interested in the Internet governance debate within the WSIS, but also acted to link those who were active within the formal structures of the WSIS (cf. UN Working Group on Internet Governance) and the wider constituency of activists interested in these issues, but not able or willing to participate in the formal negotiations.

The most active participants in the mailing list were sent a set of questions about the list itself and its participatory potential. Some of the quotes below are taken from the responses received.

Variety of participants

According to many respondents, the e-mail-based list allowed for a broader and more global constituency to be involved, engaged and informed than would have been possible through face-to-face engagement. As one respondent put it, the mailing list had

> the capacity to involve people who could not attend and the capacity to get a wider range of viewpoints.
>
> (R-1, male)[4]

This was confirmed in part by the quantitative analysis of the mailing list. As the Internet is a global medium, it follows that the mailing-list participants will be scattered around the world and that all regions of the world will be represented (Table 7.1). However, as with Internet access, there is a clear dominance of participants from the Western hemisphere, where about 65 per cent of participants reside. Behind Europe and North America are Latin America, Asia and Africa. If the number of postings is taken into consideration, the under-representation of participants from developing countries is even more acute.

Although gender balance is considered to be 'a fundamental principle' by the Working Group on Internet Governance (WGIG 2005: 11), the gender balance within the

Table 7.1 Distribution of participation according to region

	Participants (N)	Participants (%)	Postings (N)	Postings (%)
Western Europe	36	35	1192	40
Eastern Europe	1	1	163	5
North America	29	28	831	28
Latin America	10	10	143	5
Caribbean	2	2	44	1
Asia	9	9	471	16
Australia and New Zealand	5	5	66	2
Southern and sub-Saharan Africa	8	8	56	2
Arab countries	4	4	17	1
Total	104	100	2983	100

IG mailing list itself is very skewed. More than three-quarters ($N = 80$) of participants are male. This dominance is also reflected in the number of postings, where male participants accounted for more than 80 per cent ($N = 2462$) of messages.

While the affiliations of participants of the WSIS IG mailing list reflect the different stakeholders within the IG debate, when analysing the number of postings it is clear that academics have been the most active (about 50 per cent of messages) and individual activists less so. This is related to time and resources, as well as the fact that involvement in the policy process is voluntary. The nature of international policy processes also has an effect in the sense that some degree of expertise is needed.

This fact prompted one respondent to express the criticism that the mailing list seemed

> a vehicle of a few people who want to keep in contact before and after meetings and to present some document (in the name of a larger group than they are) into the WSIS process.
>
> (R-5, female)

From this perspective those actively involved in the IG process are just another elite acting in the name of a larger constituency. Another respondent also acknowledges that gaps

> between 'insiders' who are active on the ground and people who've simply joined a listserv can occur, but under the circumstances it's not that bad.
>
> (R-6, male)

Content, degree and nature of interaction

Several respondents stated that the online interaction allows for more reflection on complex issues, as well as debate over these issues. This again comes back to expertise, both in relation to the issues being debated and in terms of political skills. Furthermore, at a global level of governance, expertise is required to make a difference and to be taken seriously by other actors.

Indeed, many respondents stressed the dynamic relationship between online and offline interaction. This can be seen in the quantitative data where the cyclical character of listserv use is clear (Figure 7.1). This confirms findings from other analyses of mailing lists (Hill and Hughes 1998; Wilhelm 2000; Cammaerts and Van Audenhove 2005).

As might be expected the summer months produce a drop in mailing list activity. Also, when it started the list had to establish itself, and there was a surge in the number of postings in the run-up to the Geneva Summit (December 2003). It is fair to say that since WSIS phase 1 the mailing list has been more active, but there are still peaks and troughs even in this period.[5]

Surges in communications on the mailing list can be attributed to preparation for physical meetings. The big surge in messages in September 2004 relates to a deliberative

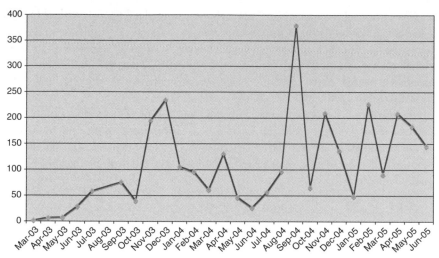

Figure 7.1 Number of postings per month.

voting procedure to nominate civil society representatives for the UN WGIG, and to the process of drafting and agreeing civil society recommendations on structure and modality of the WGIG. Subsequently, there were several WGIG meetings, and a PrepCom2[6] meeting (17–25 February 2005) for Tunis, which provoked more extreme patterns of use.

The online interaction on the mailing list thus assured 'the continuity of work in between f2f meetings' (R-4, male), but this necessary dynamic between the online and the offline also creates barriers for those who are not able to attend the meetings, or who do not have the time and resources to be heavily involved. Certainly, as one respondent pointed out, 'actual statements and agreements on particular courses of action tended to come from f2f meetings' (R-2, male). Another respondent also referred to the importance of social interaction between activists during face-to-face encounters: 'as usual, the active people had beers together f2f many times, that is why the online collaboration goes so smoothly. It's not either-or' (R-4, male). This can potentially lead to frustration, intra-movement tensions and the marginalization of minority or more radical positions.

The spontaneous Pim Fortuyn forum on the Indymedia.nl website

Indymedia can be seen as a translocal civil society organization, facilitating an exchange of (alternative) information, of different arguments, amongst citizens and activists. In this sense its relevance in terms of citizenship and civic cultures (Dahlgren

2005) is obvious. However, while the WSIS case is embedded in a consensual logic, this case exposes the conflictual nature of politics.

Indymedia provides a platform for activists and citizens to participate, by posting contributions or by reacting to contributions or events taking place in the offline world. This makes the participation in public spaces less institutionalized, very fluid and in a sense also more open than in the WSIS case.

The Indymedia websites are based on the bottom-up principle, only lightly moderated by a small volunteer staff that works mainly 'behind the screen', taking care of the technical infrastructure and layout of the website, and making editorial decisions about what features on the 'front page'. Therefore, the heart or identity of Indymedia resides in the totality of contributions made by citizens and activists. It is considered to be a platform for citizens' media. This way of integrating interactivity within an alternative news site can be considered as stimulating debate and participatory communication and has a relatively low threshold. One of the main slogans of Indymedia is *'don't hate the media, be the media'*.

Each article posted on the website has a feedback form allowing readers to react to the content of the article. Some posted articles receive a certain number of reactions, which may develop into a fierce debate among the 'readers', turning them into participants. The following short article (dated 6 May 2002) on the Dutch site of Indymedia about the murder of the Dutch right-wing populist leader, Pim Fortuyn, provoked some 270 messages in the space of a week, posted by about 110 participants.[7]

Pim Fortuyn shot dead

On May 6, Dutch popular right wing politician Pim Fortuyn was shot dead after a radio interview. This was just 9 days before general elections where Fortuyn was expected to cause an upheaval. All political parties have now ceased their campaigns.[8]

Give a short reaction to this article [link]

Variety of participants

As most postings were anonymous, signed only with nicknames, it is not easy to determine where participants hailed from. Only three posted their e-mail address and some 20 contributions had no signature at all. However, as the main language in the forum was Dutch, it is fair to assume that most participants were located in the Netherlands or the North of Belgium. From analysing the content it could also be deduced that three participants originated from the UK and Spain. Surprisingly, this did not prompt the Dutch-speaking participants to switch to another language and engage with the 'foreign' comments.

Although difficult to show empirically, the fluid character of the Indymedia format also seems to attract participants who are not politically active in the 'real' world. What is evident, however, is that, unlike some other forums, participants do not share the same or similar ideological backgrounds. This sensitizing and emotional event provoked citizens from very different political persuasions and backgrounds to interact in this spontaneously emergent forum.

Content, degree and nature of interaction

Because of the focus on the Dutch and to a lesser extent the North Belgian political context, one of the main discussion lines related to the comparison between the North Belgian neo-fascist party Vlaams Blok and Pim Fortuyn. The latter was an extreme-right populist who exuded charisma and ideas, while the former was a highly structured and hierarchical party embedded within a neo-fascist ideology and history. The discussion that was engendered between Dutch-speaking Belgians and Dutch participants in the forum was at times very lively and heated. But it can be argued that the debate went beyond the local context of the Netherlands and North Belgium, as another and perhaps more interesting line of discussion was related to the defence of democracy in the face of anti-democratic forces more generally, and, more specifically, whether the use of violence in the fight against fascism and other extreme right-wing movements in society was justified.

Most reactions were quite short, a few lines; some were longer and more argumentative. About two-thirds of participants (76) posted only one message, as a reaction to the event or to a posting by someone else. Twenty-five participants posted between two and five messages, while only nine out of 110 participants posted more than five messages, with one participant being responsible for 25 messages. Although a number of participants were considerably more active in posting than others, it could not be said that they monopolized the forum.

The way this spontaneous forum unfolded shows the fluid character of ICT-mediated participation. During the timeframe of the analysis – one week – new participants kept entering, most only posting one message, but some quickly becoming involved in the ongoing discussion.

The debate between the participants can be characterized as intense, heavy and at times very contentious. Very active participants began to address each other personally, stating why they disagreed or agreed with someone else's position(s). Most comments condemned the murder, many making abstractions of the person Fortuyn and the ideology he personified, but some participants in the spontaneous forum went so far as to justify the murder by stating, 'a good fascist is a dead fascist' or 'who's next?'. Such strong views were countered by the views of other participants, often leading to insults: 'you are a short sighted ASSHOLE' or 'Be careful, doomsday will come!!! All left-wing activists must fear for their life'.[9] Needless to say, this kind of language inflamed the ongoing debate and caused some participants to quit the forum.

In a sense, this specific case also points to the potential problematic nature of openness in posting articles and reactions. This may manifest itself in 'flaming', but also in racist or anti-Semitic opinions being voiced through the Indymedia sites. This paradox is, of course, not limited to this incident on Indymedia NL, but touches on an ongoing debate within many local Indymedia branches. In a 2002 newsletter ChuckO – a former member of the IMC Global Newswire collective – argued that (political) choices have to be made in order to address these issues:

> The IMC Network has a statement of principles and so do most local IMCs. However, the political orientation of the IMC has never been firmly established. . . . The [problem] with the IMC's vague politics is not so much what ideology it should embrace, rather what ideologies and content the IMC Network rejects and opposes. This vagueness on politics has allowed an international network of right wingers and racists to abuse and disrupt the IMC websites, which has harmed the IMC's functionality and reputation in ways that may not be fixable without stepping on lots of toes.
>
> (ChuckO 2002)

Conclusion: Relevance in relation to the public sphere and participation

The two cases presented in this chapter – the IG caucus mailing list and the spontaneous Indymedia forum – show each in their own way that the Internet potentially stimulates civic cultures, mobilizes and sustains civil society networks, or can be a platform for passionate debates. At the same time there are also several serious constraints in this regard.

The analysis of the IG caucus mailing list confirms the increasing importance of the Internet relating to intra-movement networking, to disseminating (alternative) information and to debating with a view to reaching a consensus within the network. However, it also reveals constraints, such as dominance of participants from the Northern hemisphere, and of experts and civil society professionals. This is difficult to overcome in a complex issue such as Internet Governance. In order for an actor to be taken seriously a high degree of knowledge and skills is required. This applies not only to the issue under discussion, but likewise to the ability to act strategically in the wheeling and dealing of political lobbying typical of (global) policy processes.

In addition, the analysis of the IG caucus mailing list also deepens our understanding of the dynamics between the online and the offline. While the Internet serves many functions relating to the diffusion of information beyond the direct involvement of those circulating draft proposals, choosing representatives and providing some degree of legitimation, it is during face-to-face meetings and interactions that the decisions are often made. Consensus is thus made or sought in an ongoing interaction between the online and the offline. This, in combination with expertise, creates issues of representation and exclusion that need to be addressed, not only by international organizations such as the UN, but also within civil society itself. It is also at this level that the tensions between representation, legitimization and participation emerge.

Those without easy access to the Internet and/or the skills or time to manage the vast amount of information, may feel excluded and not engage. In a policy context the use of the Internet also creates a symbolic as well as a physical distance, which can easily be (ab)used by those who hold the power, to give participants the illusion of participation. When it comes to actual decision-making, the Internet can provide access to the process, but does not facilitate the full participation that is often claimed in policy discourse. But civil society action is increasingly influencial, mainly because it builds common agendas and strives towards consensus

The rather spontaneous forum on Indymedia attracted many and diverse citizens in a limited timeframe, showing the relevance of the Internet in fostering short-term participation in public debate for citizens, allowing them to voice passionate political sentiments. Most of these participants only posted one message, but nevertheless the forum was not dominated by a small number of participants, as is often the case. This shows a relatively low threshold for people to participate. But this spontaneous forum was also mainly a Dutch-speaking affair, and comments from non-Dutch-speaking participants did not lead to other members engaging with them. This shows the importance of language in terms of inclusion or exclusion in the public space and an important constraint on the development of a so-called transnational public sphere.

Many forums tend to attract like-minded participants, leading to what we could call, paraphrasing Mouffe, digital autism. Contrary to this, a distinct feature of the Indymedia forum was the polarization and subsequent conflictual clash between ideologically opposed participants. Problematic in this regard is the anonymity of most participants, which can lead to a complete breakdown of rationality and an ignoring of the basic rules of politeness in social interaction. The flaming that occurred confirms this; such behaviour makes many people disengage. However, in many ways this relates much more to politics in the offline world, to conflicts, passions and antagonisms constitutive of political struggles. Nevertheless, there is a question as to where the limits of democracy are situated. Essentialist discourses, such as racist and other forms of discriminating language, polarize debate to such an extent that it is questionable whether we can still speak of it in terms of a debate.

Following another murder, that of the controversial Dutch film-maker, Theo Van Gogh, in November 2004 by Muslim fundamentalist activists, several forums were closed down, including the one on Indymedia NL, as a result of the strongly racist comments that were received. It is precisely here that the distinction between antagonism and agonism is exposed (Mouffe 1999b). Antagonism makes debate and thus argumentative confrontation impossible, as in this relationship 'the other' needs to be destroyed or at least humiliated. Agonism enables passionate debate to take place, ending with the parties 'agreeing to disagree', but at the same time retaining a level of respect for one another and the opposing views. As Peter van Schaik of the Dutch site condoleance.nl, hosting a condolence site for Van Gogh, eloquently put it, 'Anger is possible, but not racism' (quoted in Webwereld 2004 – authors' translation).

Notes

1 This chapter is based in part on research conducted as part of the EU 6th framework program project EMTEL II (cf. Cammaerts 2005a) and a Marie Curie Fellowship (cf. Cammaerts 2005b).

2 For more on the notion of political opportunity structure, see Meyer and Minkoff (2004).

3 The mailing list can be consulted on the World Wide Web, hosted by the Computer Professionals for Social Responsibility (CPSR), at https://ssl.cpsr.org/pipermail/governance/.

4 Respondents were anonymized.

5 The WSIS was held in two phases: phase I in 2003 (Geneva) and phase II in 2005 (Tunis).

6 Each phase of the WSIS was preceeded by three preparatory committee meetings.

7 Analysis from 6 May 2002, the day of the murder, to 15 May 2002.

8 Translation by the authors.

9 Translation by the authors.

THE BRAZILIAN LANDLESS RURAL WORKERS' MOVEMENT: IDENTITY, ACTION, AND COMMUNICATION

> Come, let us weave our freedom
> Strong arms that tear the soil
> Under the shade of our courage
> Let us spread our rebellion
> And let us plant in this land as brothers!
> (Hymn of the MST)

Introduction

The Landless Rural Workers' Movement (Movimento dos Trabalhadores Rurais Sem Terra, MST) in Brazil is one of the largest grassroots organizations in the world and one of the most important social movements in Latin America. It pursues land reform through organizing unemployed and landless farm workers to take over the uncultivated areas of land belonging to large landowners, traditionally one of the most powerful classes in Brazilian society. In Brazil, which has never undergone significant agrarian reform, the issue of landlessness is essentially political. Brazil is a country of contrasts: it has the ninth highest gross national product (GNP) and the most unequal income distribution in the world. It is a country where 3 per cent of the population own two-thirds of the cultivable land, of which 60 per cent is unused. This is the second highest ownership concentration in the world. Although Brazil is highly urbanized, agriculture continues to be important for Brazil's export agenda.

The MST reflects a strong political and social identity in its ability to mobilize its social base for contentious political actions, which has helped to increase its political and public visibility. This chapter discusses the MST's repertoire of action, communication, and alternative media, which combine the traditional instrumental forms of social movements – rational action and representation – with new experiences of embodiment and identity. The MST uses political action both to define a collective identity and to communicate with the Brazilian people. These actions become a communication medium, which extends our understanding of alternative communication beyond a media-centric perspective, and suggests a blurring between communication and media. As Downing et al. (2001: 26) suggests, 'communication and media, both within their ranks and without, play a huge role in movement trajectories'.

We chose to analyse the MST for two reasons: for its importance in the scenario of political struggles in Latin America as a voice of/for a historically excluded people, and for its innovative ways of combining different forms of symbolic communication, including the media, to express its political identity and claims for social justice. The MST's alternative media have helped in the process of reshaping politics and democratic expression in Brazil.

We next clarify what is meant by a social movement in order to situate the MST as a political social movement. Social movements have different modes of mobilization: from the rioting mob that protest without organization in a context of social crisis (Smelser 1962) to the modern politically organized movements, based on a wider understanding of action and culture (Tilly 1984; Tarrow 1999), and the new social movements, based on diffused networks organized through the Internet (Langman 2005).

Political social movements are understood as an act of representation, where rational actors are 'deliberately formed', and ordinary people, mostly the impoverished, confront elites, politicians, and the state to influence the political system and its decision-making. They operate as a public identity rather than an individual, private one. They act collectively, through organized actions with planned strategies well inserted into the cultural and political contexts, and are usually backed by social networks. The emphasis of this type of social movement, an example of which is the labour movement, is on collective action, on the association of new groups that are 'deliberately formed, specialist, manifestly political organizations as instruments of collective action' (Tilly 1982: 23) based on a common purpose, solidarity, and a collective identity. Their repertoire of action covers a combination of 'contentious politics' (Tarrow 1999: 5) (strikes, occupations, and street demonstrations) and participation in institutions (legal actions, public relations, lobbying and negotiating with authorities).

The new social movements, considered as a counter-model to the established political process type (Touraine 1981; Melucci 1996), centre on the question of identity situated in the sphere of culture and its model of creativity and knowledge, the central resource in post-industrial society (Touraine 1981).

In the process of cultural identification through new social movements, identity is 'the shared definition of a group that derives from its members' common interests, experiences and solidarity' (Taylor and Whittier 1992: 105). Thus, the identity politics of the new social movements concerns the affirmation of cultural difference where they attempt to resist and deterritorialize state and market intervention in daily life. Identity politics represents demands regarding the right of individuals to decide about their own private lives. These demands are concerned with 'new forms of emancipation such as supporting civil rights and valorising identities of minorities, advancing feminism, ecology, gay rights, etc.' (Dunn 1998: 150). These are movements where 'actors take action in the names of identities' (McAdam et al. 2001: 137) and are thus held together by identity rather than organizational structure (McDonald 2006). Downing criticizes this approach for being 'almost messianic' and reductionist in its conviction as to what constitutes a social movement, dismissing those that do not correspond to certain definitions, such as the Labour movement, as dated. He points to the Eurocentric nature of such views, exemplified by an overemphasis on Western experiences and virtually ignoring, for instance, the South African anti-apartheid and Afro-Brazilian political movements (Downing et al. 2001: 25).

Currently, many social movements work at a transnational level. They are 'global social movements', which can be characterized as supranational informal networks of social actors, based on shared beliefs and solidarity, who mobilize to protest about global issues and whose actions are organized in at least two countries (della Porta et al. 2006). In the context of globalization, social movements are the expression of civil society mobilized to achieve political outcomes at differentiated local, national, and international/transnational levels (Cammaerts 2005a; Chesters and Welsh 2006). They not only attempt to influence national political processes and organizations, but also try to reach international organizations such as the International Monetary Fund and the World Bank. In discussing the MST's media and communicative strategies, we need to briefly consider its history and the political and social conditions underlying its creation.

The Brazilian context and the history of the MST[1]

The MST is a social movement that combines a struggle for human rights from the perspective of class struggle – peasants versus landowners – with the rights of minorities – gender and ethnicities. In that sense, the MST presents characteristics that somehow challenge the rigid demarcation between 'traditional' and 'new' social movements as they, for instance, orient their politics and identities toward agendas outside, as well as within, their nation-states and countries.

The struggle for land in Brazil goes back to Portuguese colonization in the early sixteenth century, when land was distributed through processes of patronage and 'squatting' which favoured the wealthy (Johnson 1987). These ownership mechanisms are reflected in today's land distribution and have led to high levels of poverty among ordinary people, particularly in rural areas. The vast area of land held by a small landowning elite has produced a long tradition of rebellion, peasant leagues, revolutionary impulses and guerrilla movements. The MST follows the peasant movement tradition established in the 1950s.

The economic context in Brazil in the 1970s was characterized by capitalist moderni-zation of the countryside promoted by the military government, which resulted in mechanization aimed at improving agricultural exports controlled by transnational corporations. This had devastating economic and social consequences for the rural community. Masses of small farmers and agricultural day labourers found themselves without land and work, and were forced to migrate to overcrowded cities or to areas of agricultural colonization – a government programme implemented to attract peasants to the border states where there was no infrastructure, no regular work, and poor living conditions. This agricultural policy resulted in increased concentration of land-ownership and many more landless rural workers. Those who decided to stay in the countryside became the founding force of the MST (Harnecker 2003).

At the political and social levels, in the early 1980s the slow movement towards democratization was propelled by the military power's failure to deal with the econ-omy. Public demonstrations against the regime were held on the issue of human rights and other demands, which led to the mobilization of unions all over the country and to the birth of the Labour Party (Partido dos Trabalhadores). In this period of political unrest in the 1980s, most peasants were engaged in a struggle against the government's agricultural policy, through 'combative rural unionism', which incorporated the idea of a socially organized struggle, and became the basis for the MST. On an ideological level, popular demand for democratization, together with pressure from the progres-sive church motivated by the theology of liberation,[2] was fundamental in organizing the peasant movements into a single movement protesting about the right to own land (Harnecker 2003).

The MST was launched in 1984 under the motto 'Land for those who work on it';[3] its first national congress was held in 1985. The aims of the movement were to cam-paign and to struggle for land redistribution, and also to build a new society. Since its beginning the MST understood the importance of producing its own media to promote the landless cause; the newspaper *Sem Terra* was launched in 1981 to create class awareness among landless workers in ways that were impossible via the mainstream, capitalist media. The movement initially campaigned through non-violent actions and negotiation with local organizations. From 1986, when the military government lost power, to 1993, the independence and visibility of the MST increased and it adopted a new slogan, 'Occupy, resist, and produce'. This period was marked by violent clashes between peasant farmers, landowners and the police. It coincided with the coming into force of the 1985 agrarian reform, and the 1988 Constitution, which allowed uncultivated land to be expropriated for reasons of 'social interest'.

This constitutional change did not guarantee that land would be given over to the landless people since often the law was not enforced; thus, the MST continued to be very active in its demands for land. From 1994 to 1998 under the liberal government of Fernando Henrique Cardoso, the MST became an important social actor in the strug-gle for land reform, with high visibility in the mainstream media. This new status was triggered by the MST's implementing a series of actions – occupations and marches – in the rural areas of São Paulo, the most influential Brazilian state. This resulted in the settlement of thousands of landless families on expropriated land. The movement's political influence and pressure for agrarian reform were bolstered by the incidents that occurred in the Amazon region: the Corumbiara episode in August 1995, and the massacre in Eldorado dos Carajás in April 1996. Both events saw the brutal murder of farm workers by the police. Also, these events, and particularly the Carajás massacre, received worldwide television coverage, which revealed the existence in Brazil of the agrarian problem and the violence suffered by Brazil's rural poor,[4] and provided the MST with national and international support and recognition.

At this point, another new slogan was adopted: 'Agrarian reform: a struggle for all'. In 1998, in his second presidential mandate, Fernando Henrique Cardoso implemented an agricultural policy based on the North American agricultural model of internationalization of the agricultural market, a policy that was detrimental to the interests of rural workers.

The late 1990s marked the beginning of the MST's full engagement with other social movements around the world in the struggle for land, protection of the environment, and objection to neo-liberal policies. At the same time relationships between the MST and the state deteriorated, and the government began a public campaign against the movement which included its demonization in the mainstream media.

Even though state resources increased, and the Cardoso administration (1995–2003) authorized more new settlements than all the previous administrations from 1970 to 1994 put together (Seligmann 1998), the MST was the most consistent and active opposition to his government (Hammond 1999). At the movement's national congress in 2000, a new slogan was adopted: 'For a Brazil without large state' – a motto that still guides their actions in 2007, and works as a communicative sign, an 'ephemeral media' (Dale 1996).

In 2003, Luiz Inácio Lula da Silva, a Labour party activist, became president of Brazil. Lula's election, according to the MST 'represented the victory of the Brazilian people and the defeat of the elites and their project, but this was not enough to generate significant changes in the agrarian structure and agrarian model'.[5] Currently, the relationship of the MST with the state is rather ambiguous due to its paradoxical reliance on a state – which it opposes. In spite of its problems, political merits, and ambiguities, the MST continues to pressurize for a more general agrarian reform, and has become the main national reference point in the struggle against neo-liberalism.

The MST's identity

Throughout its history, the MST has continuously evolved and reaffirmed its identity as an independent[6] social-political peasant movement centred on a class struggle against landowners. The movement is essentially national in scope and works in conjunction with other rural and urban movements throughout Brazil and abroad. Its activists work to bring class awareness to the rural landless farm workers and to provide a historical understanding of their exploitation. This process of political consciousness is intrinsic to the role developed by their alternative media, which functions to inform members of the movement on wider developments of their political struggles, and to reinforce the importance of their commitment to the success of the cause. For example, an article in the *Sem Terra* newspaper (April 2006) about the perverse effects of transnational capital on the rural area of Brazil states that there is an increasing support for alternative politics against neo-liberal and transnational capital where 'our mobilization and constant action is fundamental to the struggle and must be strength'.

The MST's ideological and practical guiding principles require that each individual goes beyond the past and imagines a new social, political and economic ideal, what Wolford (2003: 503) calls the 'imagined community' of the landless. The consensus and mobilization of the landless people in Brazil depend on trust and cooperation based on mutual understanding and identities, and on the 'collective action frames that justify, dignify, and animate action' (Tarrow 1999: 21).

The ideology or 'schemata of interpretation' (Benford and Snow 2000) of the MST functions to dignify discontent, identify the 'enemy' in terms of binary oppositions – 'us' and 'the other' – and to show solidarity with other groups. Accordingly, most articles in the MST's printed media are suffused with meanings that articulate the class antagonism between the MST and the elites representing the 'imperialism of the transnational capital' (*Sem Terra* newspaper, April 2006). An instance of the 'us versus them' dichotomy can be found in a November/December 2005 feature article in the *Sem Terra* magazine, 'The agrarian reform that has not been implemented', which blames the old and new rural elites, government and politicians for stopping land reform from taking place.

The MST use its alternative media, rituals and symbols, such as hymns, music, flag, and documents embedded with historical references to the class character of the movement's struggle, to enhance internal cohesion and to project an image of unity to the outside world, a form of communication in itself. For example, the leaders emphasize the MST's connections with the national peasant struggles of the past to demonstrate its links with a line of noble fighters and global heroes, such as Marx, Che Guevara, Rosa Luxemburg, and Nelson Mandela, whose photographs are displayed on posters at meetings. This provides the movement with a sense of history and what the future holds: 'it gives an exact notion of the limitations and the temporary character of our participation . . . we want to use what has already been invented to build a better world' (Stédile and Fernandes 2005: 57–8).

As Szerzynski (2002: 55) argues, through rituals as a form of action, members of a movement can generalize beyond their specific actions to connect with universal or mystic meanings. Through the use of symbols such as its flag, the typical red caps and tee-shirts, and certain songs, the landless farm workers are declaring who they are and asserting that not only do they want to become part of a wider historic struggle of landless workers, but for a short time are part of this struggle (Wolford 2003). These rituals and symbols in turn are part of the process of public affirmation of their collective identity which gives them 'recognition as a credible political player with the capacity to make a difference in the next political struggle' (McAdam et al. 2001: 148). The MST mass demonstrations are a classical example of a combination of rituals and symbols expressing their members' identity – *sem terra* (see Figure 8.1).

Another form of communication that works to preserve the movement's identity and cohesion is through the social, symbolic practice of the 'Mystic' or 'Mysticism'. This ritual is practised at all events and communicates through symbols – flag, dance, music – rather than through complex speech, through connotation rather than denotation (Szerzynski 2002: 54). The Mystic is a 'collective manifestation of a feeling of happiness but not a metaphysic or idealistic one' (Stédile and Fernandes 2005: 130). This is an experience of personal recognition of singularity and solidarity, which confirms to the MST members that they are experiencing the struggle not as a sacrifice but as part of their lives.

This is based on liberation theology, which relied on charismatic leaders to engage people in the practices of the Catholic faith and to maintain union through its sermons. MST activists adapted this symbolic communication by imaginatively using songs, theatre, and hymns to help form new ideas and shape behaviour (see Wolford 2003). The messages of the mystic are humility, sacrifice, perseverance, gratefulness,

Figure 8.1 National March for Agrarian Reform, when more than 13 million people walked from Goiânia to Brasília, between 2 and 17 May 2005 (photo by Francisco Rojas, http://www.mstbrazil.org).

sincerity, responsibility, and discipline. According to João P. Stédile, the national coordinator of the MST, 'the Mystic motivates people to the struggle, it is not a duty but a way of materializing beliefs and ideals' (Stédile and Fernandes 2005: 132). The Mystic provides them with a moral force and faith in their eventual victory based on a conviction that socialism is the alternative to the neo-liberal and capitalist systems.

The identity of the movement works on two levels: its oppositional class nature, and the belief that within the movement all members are in theory equal, part of a class in itself (Wolford 2003: 507). Being 'landless' (*sem terra*) forms the identities of the movement's members. They see themselves as respected citizens, fighting for their rights, and no longer pariahs of society. Based on common loyalties, the *sem terra* give meaning to their own experiences. The movement also gains a 'collective identity' in which 'social actors recognize themselves – and are recognized by others – as part of broader groups' (della Porta and Diani 1999: 85).

MST: The grammar of action, communication, and media

The repertoire[7] of political and communicative actions developed by the MST works through an understanding of action as intentional and symbolic, that is, performed through signs (Bourdieu 1985), while at the same time valorizing the subjective experience of individual subjects as in the practices of the Mystic. The MST is required to address the strategic dilemmas posed by different types of action, and find a balance between the need for visibility and the danger of being stigmatized, between the power of numbers and the strengthening of identities, between bearing witness and being effective. Moreover, the movement has to think strategically about the political opportunities and political relevance of specific types of protest. The MST's heterogeneous repertoire of actions sometimes crosses the boundaries of civil society by engaging in negotiations with government, or participating in meetings with policymakers, but also includes land occupation, public demonstrations, marches, occupations of government buildings, fasts and hunger strikes. Occupations and large-scale marches tend to attract the most media attention, underlining the power of direct action as opposed to lobbying – even when in the public interest – and letter writing.

The MST decides the best way of exerting political pressure, based on the movement's needs and the local political context. For example, peaceful land occupations are one way they exert pressure despite landowners using private security measures and mobilizing the police against them, because successive governments have lacked the political will to implement agrarian reform. Occupation has proved to be the most effective form of protest in the movement's pursuit of its strategy to force agrarian reform authorities to expropriate and redistribute farmland. An occupation is well prepared for: the MST finds sites that are eligible for expropriation, and recruits and organizes the occupiers. An occupation can comprise 200 to 2500 families, who are recruited from the cities and locations proximate to the areas to be occupied. Once recruited, they meet regularly and are taught how to raise political awareness and to conduct themselves during the occupation (Hammond 2004).

During an occupation, the MST acts as the mediator between the settlers and the state. The success of the MST in winning land has resulted in a complex interplay between representatives and resources of the state. Even though national government and sectors of the media portray occupation as illegal, the local communities and local governments give some basic support to the settlers (Wolford 2003). In the 1990s, an average of 160,000 families were involved in occupations. Currently there are 180,000 encamped families awaiting government recognition. They await the government decision, which might take years, in the 'permanent camps' where they establish cooperative farms, construct houses, schools, radio stations, run arts programmes, and have functioning health clinics.[8] The power of occupation goes beyond a tactical use of media for public visibility; it relates to living the experience, enduring difficulties and disruption to daily life, living in uncomfortable and dangerous conditions.

At the subjective level, 'occupation and marches are an expression of organized rebellion and the formation of class awareness as well as building a new identity' (Harnecker 2003: 82). The success of the MST's strategy of mobilizing large numbers of people for their marches and occupations is, in part, due to the use of their own alternative media, particularly the Internet, to circulate information, to generate a forum to create consensus, and to organize and call for a protest demonstration.

In fact, the large crowds mobilized by the MST challenges Melucci's argument that in an information society the power of the action does not come from the physical mass and presence, but through the ability to challenge common sense perceptions of social issues (Melucci 1996: 76). MST marches and occupations have to be massive so that participants are protected from police brutality, to show their strength as a movement, to gather public attention, to change values and perceptions amongst the population, and ultimately to guarantee agrarian reform. The legitimacy of the movement then, depends in part on its number of supporters, since 'there is always strength in number' (DeNardo, quoted in Della Porta et al. 2006: 238).

One of the most visible actions of the MST was a 1000 km march of landless farm workers from various states, to Brasília, the capital of Brazil. They arrived there on 17 April 1997, one year after 19 workers had been massacred in Eldorado dos Carajás, Pará. 'The aim was to counter the government strategy of making us invisible to society, thus the march's objective was to have a dialogue with society, wherein the march in itself was a medium of communication to the population' (Stédile and Fernandes 2005: 152). This date has become the day of remembrance and marks the MST's continued struggle for social justice. In the MST's case, the large marches and occupations are communicative actions that contest and disrupt the dominant codes defining agrarian reform and other social issues, forcing society to think about them. In these mass events, the use of ICTs, such as radio, wireless PDAs, or text messaging and the Internet, is fundamental for self-mobilization, connections between social actors, self-representation, coordination, and the success of public demonstrations. In 1995, the

MST for the first time used mobile phones and the Internet to keep its members updated during an occupation. These technologies represent vital forms of communication for occupiers camped in remote areas waiting for news on the development of their actions (Berger 1998: 100).

The movement produces its own alternative media – newspaper, magazine, radio programmes, and website – to support and disseminate oppositional views not only related to agrarian reform, but also on wider political issues such as local elections, social struggles, transnational social movements' struggles against neo-liberalism and a free market, and the exploitation of women in Brazilian society. These alternative media function not simply as a political instrument, but as a collective good in themselves as they short-circuit corporate control of public communication and foster democratic conversation and influence public policy, helping to counterbalance distortions about the landless farm workers' movement. The alternative media also provides the *sem terra* with the opportunity to 'recodify one's own identity with one's own signs . . . the chance to become one's own story teller, regaining one's own voice; and the reconstruction of one's self-portrait of one's own community and culture' (Rodriguez 1996: 64).

In addition, they provide an important frame, outside the views of the mainstream media, for readers and writers to make sense of the world of the landless people. The reader is invited to enter the everyday life experience of landless people as they negotiate agrarian reform in the context of neo-liberalism. This is not simply a question of publicity and public relations.

By publicizing the problems of the landless people, the MST's alternative media question public perceptions of what constitutes a member of a society in which such inequalities exist. These media create a space for identity formation and suggest to their readers a way of positioning themselves in relation to the landless movement. Unfortunately, the influence of alternative media is undermined in part by the negative coverage by the Brazilian mainstream media of the MST as lawless people and violent troublemakers. For example, because they are considered lawless, sectors of the media use the word 'invasion' rather than 'occupation' to describe the movement's actions, which has connotations of violence and illegality. An opinion piece written by a former state minister of justice, in the conservative newspaper *Estado de São Paulo*, formulates this as follows:

> Of course if someone asked me whether I defend agrarian reform, I would answer yes without blinking. But [if they asked] whether I would approve an invasion, I would not give the same answer. Neither would the respondents [in a survey in which 52 percent said they approved of the MST]. Their support depended on there being no violence. Now, isn't an invasion in itself violent?
>
> (quoted in Hammond 2004: 76)

The MST website functions as a communicative space, presenting data about the movement such as its history, legal battles, occupations and so forth, and communicating information about political and economic themes, thus providing alternative knowledge on specific issues. The website can also potentially influence the traditional mass media and facilitate communication with other social movements, creating webs of interpersonal communication that 'do not operate through the media, even though they are fed by media and feed into media' (Downing et al. 2001: 203). Perhaps more importantly, the Internet has important implications for social movements in terms of the potential of democratic contestation and mobilization. It allows social movements such as the MST a 'refiguring of politics, a refocusing of politics on everyday life and using the tools and techniques of new computer and communication technology to expand the field and domain of politics' (Kellner 2004b: 8).

The radio programme *Vozes da Terra* (Voices from the Land) is streamed on the website, and the movement has low-power radio stations that they can use to broadcast to the occupied camps. These radio stations are extremely important, given that they are very popular among rural workers because they are cheap and are an instantaneous source of information, particularly for the illiterate.

The monthly newspaper *Sem Terra* has a print run of 20,000 and national distribution. The movement's magazine, also called *Sem Terra*, is published bimonthly and sold at several of the movement's state branches; it provides a deeper analysis of the political and economic situation in Brazil, and contains articles on education, arts, sports, culture, history, and the environment. MST activists and supporters produce both the newspaper and the magazine. The editorial lines of both publications demonstrate their commitment to exploring social and economic justice issues in relation to the landless. The self-image constructed in the MST's internal media is that of a 'militant movement' using innovative political strategies and actions. In its external media, MST projects a pragmatic image of itself as a 'solution to national problems' such as bringing production to unused land and providing work for large numbers of rural workers. It also includes descriptions of the violence endured by land occupiers, and a focus on the successful outcomes of their struggle (Hammond 2004). The alternative newspaper carries news of successful actions and the problems that landless farm workers encounter as a result of actions by the state, the police, and landowners. Both publications present articles and interviews with influential national left-wing figures, academics, journalists, and so on, and offer opinion and analysis that corroborate the MST ideologies and oppositional views that counterbalance the mainstream media's usual contempt for the landless cause. This is not surprising, given that the Brazilian mainstream media ownership is concentrated in the hands of elite groups closely articulated with the political system and the state.

Stédile, the MST's national coordinator, writes:

Our aim has never been to get media attention but the social struggle for land. However, the movement's demonstrations have won media attention, thus popularizing the MST symbols of communication. As much as the media owners don't like us, they can't ignore our voice forever and have to report our struggle.

(Stédile and Fernandes 2005: 134)

The MST may not always aim to get media attention with their public demonstrations; nonetheless, they are probably aware that these kind of events are 'newsworthy' as a spectacle which attracts media coverage. Moreover, in a document 'For an MST Communication Policy' of March 1995, the movement stresses the importance of mainstream media coverage to 'motivate militants and to broadcast to the public its achievements, especially in the areas of production and education' (Berger 1998: 108)

The MST thus has developed a more open attitude towards the mainstream media to influence the way the MST is portrayed and to establish good relations with sectors of the media. The MST has realized that restricting its communication to alternative media in order to advance its policy aims and promote its views, limits coverage and only allows it to reach an 'alternative' public sphere. It has also realized the need to have mainstream media coverage in order to reach policy-makers, to advance its policy aims, and to confirm its role as the main negotiator between different social actors to achieve land reform.

Although the movement has won significant attention, it has not been able to shape and influence the mainstream media coverage which tends to highlight its more radical form of protest – occupation – in an unsympathetic view.

Distinguishing between the coverage of the movement and of the issue (see Hammond 2004), the MST has successfully put the 'land' issue in the public and media spheres. The liberal media generally discuss agrarian reform as a matter of social justice and the MST's cause as fair. Yet, the same media are inclined to condemn their strategies and/ or disregard the movement itself. Thus, in any news piece it is possible to find simultaneously both recognition and disapproval of the movement. The editorial of the *Zero Hora* newspaper (Rio Grande do Sul, in the South of Brazil) used this frame when analysing the end of a disputed land occupation in 1993:

> There is no one with a minimal level of information who does not support agrarian reform in this country . . . On the other hand, the simple distribution of land does not represent agrarian reform. . . . It is appropriate that the leaders of the MST leave aside the passion of ideological positions.
>
> (quoted in Berger 1998: 170)

However, this seems to be a secondary concern for the movement as its focus is still on direct action to occupy farmland, which in its view is the only type of visible political pressure that will compel the government to provide land to the landless (see Stédile and Fernandes 2005).

Conclusion

The MST's central role in the struggle for land reform, and its mobilizing capacity, including the use of alternative media, have turned the movement into a signifier of social struggle against social exclusion, with the issue of agrarian reform gaining a place on the public and political agenda, and visibility in the mainstream media. Politically, the MST has achieved remarkable success as a voice of national democracy and increasing awareness among the oppressed of their citizen's rights (Gohn 1997; Rossiaud and Scherer-Warren 2000). The history of the movement, though, is not marked only by successful events, given that the MST has been criticized for its undemocratic control and a lack of transparency and accountability of its decisions and actions, which according to Navarro (2005: 15) is an obstacle to the right to participation of the landless members. For him, 'accountability, open representation and legitimacy, are simply empty rhetoric in the history of the MST'.

The movement's aims and praxis are essentially national, although engaging with global social movements in its struggle for global justice. In this scenario, the use of new ICTs by the MST is significant in helping to sustain and build global networks of solidarity among activists while simultaneously distributing information to increase understanding about the global interconnections of different local social struggles.

The repertoire of action of the MST is characterized by a focus on direct action, such as mass marches and occupations, which are successful in part due to the use of alternative media to support their organization. These actions, which are embedded with symbolic communication, express the identity of the movement. This works through forms of representation and embodied experience as 'mode of presence and engagement' (Csordas 1993: 135), which become, for instance, evident in the Mystic ritual. These types of action-communication emphasize the MST's commitment to rewriting the history of the landless people on their own terms.

In a country where the land issue is a controversial political subject, and the majority of the mainstream media are owned by the economic and political elites who, to a certain extent, define and shape the news through the use of conservative frames, it is of fundamental importance to the MST to have its own alternative media. These alternative media play a crucial role not only in the organization of its demonstrations and direct actions, but, most importantly, as 'public spheres' in which the movement's alternative philosophy and counter-hegemonic views are presented.

The communicative grammar of the movement tell us the history, subjectivities, and experiences of the landless in their 'march' for land reform and a more egalitarian Brazilian society.

Notes

1 This very brief summary of the MST's history risks oversimplifying more than 20 years of history.
2 During the period of military rule (1964–84) the Catholic Church in Brazil was an active force for radical organization and change in the rural areas. Following the official focus of the Roman Catholic Church on land tenure issues in Latin America (1961) the Brazilian episcopate published a series of educational documents to inform rural peasants that 'land is a gift of

God', and created the Pastoral Land Commission to defend landless people in the Amazon region (Wolford 2003).

3 In general, new slogans are discussed in the MST at the local level and then submitted for approval at national meetings and conferences, which are held every five years.

4 According to the Comissão Pastoral da Terra (2007), the situation of violence against farm workers in Brazil continues to give cause for concern: 'they are still suffering violence. In 2006 there was an increase of 176.92% in attempts to murder farm workers (compared to 2005). The number of imprisoned farm workers also increased from 261 in 2005 to 917 in 2006, an increase of 251.34%.'

5 http://www.mst.org.br/mst/pagina.php?cd=1.

6 The movement works with several organizations including the progressive sectors of numerous churches, in particular the Pastoral Commission for the Land of the Catholic Church, and although the majority of its members are either militant members of the Worker's Party or vote for it, the party has no voice in its internal affairs (Stedile and Fernandes 2005).

7 Tilly (1995: 56) defines 'repertoire of contention' as 'the ways that people act together in pursuit of shared interests'.

8 http://www.mst.org.br/mst/pagina.php?cd=1.

TRANSLOCALIZATION, GLOCALIZATION AND THE INTERNET: THE RADIOSWAP PROJECT

Radio is a space without walls . . . Radio is a space in time, an invisible bridge between speaker and listener that traverses vast distances in the snap of a finger, the punch of a button. It is an architectural space to be inhabited – the site of an event, an arena, a stage, a promenade, a public square, an intersection, a telephone booth, a corridor. It is a room we enter together.

(Apple 1993: 307)

Introduction

One of the major restrictions on alternative media is their confinement to the local, which traps them on one side of the local–global dichotomy. Alternative media are most often seen as small-scale and highly localized media organizations. The possibility of the sustained existence of large-scale and global alternative media is equally often put into question or even considered virtually unthinkable. This dominant mode of locality can be explained by the emphasis it receives in the interconnecting traditional media-centred approaches (see Chapter 1). The alternative media approach uses large-scale mainstream media as a reference point, almost automatically positioning alternative media on the other (small-scale) side of the binary. The community media approach draws on the dominant conceptualizations of community, which – as Leunissen (1986) argues – refer to geography and ethnicity as structuring notions of collective identities or group relations. Through this focus on territorialized communities, the community media approach also tends to privilege the local.

But when we take a closer look at the global, the local becomes unavoidably and immediately implicated. Appadurai (1993) points out that the processes of globalization have not intervened in all realms of the social, but have been concentrated in different societal spheres or *scapes*. He distinguishes five such scapes: ethnoscapes, mediascapes, ideoscapes, technoscapes and financescapes, which incorporate flows of people, cultural meanings, ideologies, technologies and capital. He argues that globalization is characterized by the disjunctures that occur in and between the scapes. In mediascapes, films, for instance, travel the world, hopping from market to market. Appadurai considers this apparent disconnection – or deterritorialization – to be one of the main characteristics of globalization. At the same time he argues that this disconnection is not total, but hides a complex interplay between the local and the global. Although the homogenizing effects of global culture exist, they are absorbed by local political and cultural economies and reappear as heterogeneous dialogues with the original versions. The homogenous and heterogeneous, and the global and the local, find themselves in permanent fields of tensions, a dynamic process that is well captured by the concept of 'glocalization' (Robertson 1995).

The specificity of alternative media complicates their direct access to the global mediascapes. This does not imply that they are completely severed from the global. Similar to the above-described logics, the argument can be made that localized alternative media do not remain unaffected by the global. Here, Howley's (2005: 267) point that 'community media rather forcefully undermined the binary opposition of the categories "local" and "global" in two discrete, but interrelated ways' is relevant. He refers to the 'historicizing and particularizing [of] the penetration of global forces into local contexts' and to the 'endless stream of variation and diversity of cultural forms and practices around the world' generated by community media. Nevertheless the dominant mode of locality seems to keep alternative media firmly locked within its 'essence' of being small-scale and a part of the local community.

This reduction structurally weakens alternative media in comparison to large-scale – and sometimes global – mainstream media. When they are so small, it is difficult for them to play their potentially enlarged societal role, which reduces their relevance. Moreover, they become vulnerable in relation to the large mainstream media organizations and the political-regulative system. Paradoxically, their strength is also to be found in their being small-scale. The close connection of alternative media with their respective local communities provides them with a diversity of content and collaborators. Their small scale makes them sensitive to the access and participation of their publics, and enables them to actually include more than token participatory practices, both at the level of content generation and management. In other words, it renders them alternatives to the mainstream.

This paradox, where the need for alternative media to (at least partially) overcome the local is combined with the equally important need to safeguard their local embeddedness, also requires a theoretical reconfiguration. For this purpose, the concept of the translocal (see Appadurai 1995) becomes relevant. In comparison to the glocal, the translocal implies an inverse approach that allows taking the local as the point of departure, and adding the global as a second component. In this way, translocalization acts as glocalization's mirror image. It allows us to retain the focus on the dynamics of the local and the global, but uses the local as a starting point.

Apart from the theoretical reconfigurations of community (which also incorporate this possibility – see Chapter 1), theoretical support for developing the translocal is found in the metaphor of the rhizome. Rhizomatic thought focuses on the hetero-geneous and ever-changing interconnections between a multiplicity of technologies, people and texts, which are explicitly articulated against the arbolic – rigid and homogeneous – structures of state and market. From this perspective, there is not necessarily any reason why the rhizome should stop at the edge of the local community. But simply enlarging the scale of operations to overcome the confinements of locality would be a self-defeating strategy in the face of the elusive and diversified identity of alternative media. To use Deleuze and Guattari's (1987) phrasing: creating an arbolic structure would simply imply the creation of a *copy* of mainstream and large-scale media, and would not generate a *map*, with its multiple entryways and adaptability.

The other characteristics of the rhizome enumerated by Deleuze and Guattari (1987) are the principles of connection, heterogeneity, multiplicity, and asignifying rupture.[1] These characteristics allow the complexities of alternative media as rhizomatic networks to be taken into account. Rhizomatic connections imply organizational structures in which alternative media organizations can remain grounded in local communities and become simultaneously engaged in translocal networks characterized by the fluid articulation of media organizations. The rhizomatic approach thus becomes instru-mental in avoiding the dichotomized positioning of alternative media in relationship to the local and the global, as it opens up ways to theorize about how the local and global touch and strengthen each other within alternative media organizations.

The role of ICTs in expanding the rhizome

Several attempts have been made by alternative media to overcome the restrictions of scale, without jeopardizing their focus on locality. One example is AMARC, the World Association of Community Radio Broadcasters, which, through its global focus, clearly transcends the local. Through its (localized) membership base, it protects its connection to the local.

Although not all attempts are linked to ICTs, they can offer an important tool to support these translocal networks. For this reason, this chapter analyses a case study where ICTs are used to exchange locally produced content among dispersed radio stations, thus broadening the scope of these alternative media.

As is the case in the reconfiguration of community, ICTs can play an important – but non-deterministic – role in the creation of these rhizomatic connections. ICTs, and more specifically networked computer communication, have been thoroughly researched through the rhizome metaphor. For instance, Spiller (2002: 96) wrote that Deleuze and Guattari's (1987) book 'is the philosophical bible of the cyber-evangelist.

This book is possibly one of the most quoted philosophical texts in connection with the technological "spacescape" that computers have created and augmented.'

More relevant to the topic of this chapter is that different types of civil society organizations have transcended geographical/national frontiers and have initiated the use of ICTs to support this construction of rhizomatic networks. Various names (and perspectives) have been used to describe this enlargement of civil society: Keck and Sikkink (1998) refer to transnational advocacy networks; Keane (2003) to global civil society; whilst Smith et al. (1997) adopt the notion of transnational social movements. Whatever name is used, ICTs are seen to play an important role within those networks of individuals and civil society organizations (Scott and Street 2001; Cammaerts 2005a).

Within the media sphere, the rise of IMCs can be seen as a fascinating example. Focusing on Indymedia, Mamadouh (2004: 488–9) describes the interconnected functioning of these IMCs and the dialectics between the local and the global as follows: 'The Indymedia websites provide platforms to mobilize activists at different scales at once, with global sites addressing a global audience and local sites addressing local ones, but both scales are entwined, constantly connected through newswires and links'.

Of course, it should be noted that ICTs are not only used to produce content. In the same article, Mamadouh (2004: 487) for instance stresses the importance of ICTs as decision-making tools for IMCs:

The Internet is a local resource for IMCs as they often run their decision-making through electronic lists, on top of regular meetings (often weekly). This resource is even more crucial to sustain the global network. The coordination activities of the global network occur through computer-mediated communication: via mailing lists and IRC chats.

These examples from the civil society realm and from the sphere of alternative (new) media raise important questions about the potentiality of alternative media to establish similar rhizomatic networks that move beyond the local, to overcome the reduction to locality and to link up with translocal and (even) transnational social struggles. In the next section of this chapter, a case study of RadioSwap, a very modest attempt to move beyond the confinement of the local and to contribute to the generation of a more translocal rhizome, is analysed (see also Carpentier et al. 2006).

Glocal alternative media?

A number of projects in Europe and the USA have focused on facilitating the exchange of audio content by alternative media organizations. For instance, the Stream on the Fly project[2] is an Austrian-based collaboration of radio stations and companies, such as Public Netbase. Following several years of trialling, they now have an operational 'open-source, station-management interface, a programme exchange platform and a portal engine for radio programme reuse' (Alton-Scheidl et al. 2005: 1). The One World Radio project, with its more than 1000 members, has become 'a global radio community sharing programmes and ideas on development'.[3]

The Programme Exchange Initiative was initiated by the British Community Media Association (CMA), and 'is particularly aimed at assisting Community Radio stations in accessing the wealth of community radio programmes that are produced each year in the UK Community Radio sector.'[4] Finally, the A-Infos radio project, based in the USA, has more than 800 radio programmes in MP3 format; its 'goal is to support and expand the movement for democratic communications worldwide. We exist to be an alternative to the corporate and government media which do not serve struggles for liberty, justice and peace, nor enable the free expression of creativity.'[5]

This case-study chapter focuses on a Belgian radio exchange project, called Radio-Swap, which is based on a project of six Belgian radio stations – Radio Campus, Urgent, Radio Panik, Radio Centraal, FMBrussel and Radio Universitaire Namuroise. RadioSwap, financed by the Belgian federal government, started on 1 January 2001. In the first phase of the project the six radio stations were supported by four academic research centres: Groupe de Réflexion sur les Processus Organisationnels (GREPO), Recherche et Diffusion de l'Information Scientifique (RDIS), Centre de Recherches Informatique et Droit (CRID) and Centrum voor Intellectuele Rechten (CIR). In the second phase of the project CRID and the Centre for Communication for Social Change (CSC)[6] and two commercial companies, Nerom NV and Info-Graphic SA, provided support.

RadioSwap's objectives

The RadioSwap project makes use of a website to organize the exchange of radio content. On this website we can also find a description of its main objective, written by the project coordinators: 'The Radioswap.net project aims to develop a technical as well as organisational system that will allow staff working for non-commercial and community radio stations – inside and outside Belgium – to exchange radio programs via the Internet' (RadioSwap 2001).

On RadioSwap's second website (Figure 9.1), which was mounted in 2002 to replace the first, the project objectives are regrouped under five headings: seeking multilingualism; directed at volunteers; giving a greater place to forms of self-management; dreaming of co-productions, partnership and news exchanges; and willing to experiment (RadioSwap 2002). The first item refers to the participatory nature of the radio stations involved; their staff work voluntarily without remuneration to produce the radio programmes.[7] The RadioSwap database is based on a participatory model, as described in the self-management item:

> The point of all of this is not to build a 'normalised network' such as some of the networks we can find in the commercial radio world. It is rather to develop a

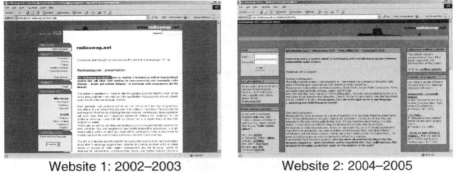

Website 1: 2002–2003   Website 2: 2004–2005

Website 3: 2006–

Figure 9.1 The RadioSwap websites.

common tool whose management would be shared and that the radio stations and their collaborators could use according to their needs in order to reinforce their singularity and specificities.

(RadioSwap 2002)

The project not only aims to 'give the radio collaborators an opportunity to spread their programs beyond their original radio' (RadioSwap 2002), but also wants to construct and enhance networks among different individuals and organizations.

Another objective of the project is to make it possible to use the system to set up co-productions between radio stations, or with outside partners. The system should allow collaborators to work together from afar on the same contents and the same programs, each one using her/his own way of working, with his/her own culture.

(RadioSwap 2002)

RadioSwap is no longer restricted to the six original founding radio stations. In April 2007 RadioSwap included 81 radio stations or affiliated organizations and 209 registered users based in Austria, Bulgaria, Canada, France, Hungary, Macedonia, the Netherlands, Portugal, Slovenia, the UK and the Czech Republic. They have uploaded 982 radio programs, which accounts for 47GB of audio.

Rhizomatic technologies?

The RadioSwap technology and procedures build on the idea of (data) self-management.[8] The password-protected interface is meant to enable radio producers to record, digitize, compress (using MP3 or Ogg Vorbis)[9] and upload the material they themselves have produced (Figure 9.2). During the upload, the users provide the necessary metadata, allowing the later use of search engines. These sound files (and their metadata) are stored on the RadioSwap server for retrieval by other radio producers. The introduction of the third website in 2006 has made available to all website visitors, not just RadioSwap members, material that is not copyright-protected.

These technologies potentially facilitate the global distribution of the uploaded material, although this is of course dependent on the goodwill of the partner radio stations to rebroadcast the material. The exchange of content allows the alternative discourses and representations to circulate far beyond the local. The Antwerp radio producers, whose radio station (Radio Centraal) is experiencing severe restrictions in broadcasting range, point to the irony of being heard in other cities, whilst facing problems 'at home', being confined within a 3 km broadcasting zone.

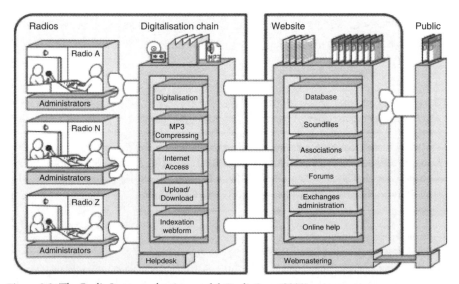

Figure 9.2 The RadioSwap production model (RadioSwap 2001).

Now you have the opportunity to have your programme broadcast in London, or Prague, or Berlin, or wherever, even in Rotterdam. If this happens, this is really funny because here we are dealing with our frequency and the too low power of the transmitter. People living three kilometres from the station are having problems getting high-quality reception, whilst people living hundreds of kilometres abroad get perfect reception.

(DR, Radio Centraal)

At the same time the RadioSwap website has considerable limitations. Most 'ordinary' users described the first two websites that were in operation from 2002 until the end of 2005 as difficult, not user-friendly, and time-consuming.[10] They also complained about others' lack of systematic and regular uploading, and about the lack of uniformity in the metadata that were provided. Despite these problems, most users do appreciate the capacity to exchange audio content and to broaden their networks, creating connections with other radio producers:

The strong points. First the material aspects, meaning the possibility to easily exchange content. The second is putting different actors in touch with each other. These contacts might only be talking to each other, or exchanging programmes. We did send representatives to international meetings, etc, and we decided to install structures for European lobbying which did not exist before.

(BD, Radio Campus)

Apart from the opportunities to exchange audio material, users valued the possibilities for collaboration and co-creation. These interactional aspects of the project are seen in most cases as important, but simultaneously described as future developments, as these quotes from two interviewees illustrate:

A means of diffusion, of multiplication and of communication. So it is an ordinary tool, and tomorrow it might become a tool for creation.

(JP, Radio Campus)

It might be the starting point for co-productions, collaborations and for the creation of joint events.

(MG, Radio Panik)

Collaboration is not only hampered by language problems – 'I think the most important problem is still language' (AvH, Radio Urgent) – but also by the lack of human, non-computer-mediated interaction. One of the Brussels producers emphasized the importance of supplementing the interface with interpersonal communication:

So, finally the site is nice, but the human contacts made before and after still remain very important. Suppose that I'm re-broadcasting a weekly programme produced by Panik. The best thing to do is to have an oral agreement with Panik about the use of jingles and such like. To make sure that the programme is online every week, on the site, the new version there on time, things like that. Because he might put it online this time, but not next week.

(KV, Radio FMBrussel)

One of the RadioSwap project coordinators confirmed this need:

We definitely need more functions that allow them to express their point of view about a broadcast that they've listened to, or to get in touch with the producer, or to get in touch with someone that has listened to it.

(PdJ, RadioSwap)

These (self-)critiques go to the heart of the problems the RadioSwap project faces. Although initiated by members of the community radio stations, RadioSwap is (at least partially) defined as being outside the radio stations. One of the producers expressed this very clearly:

It is a problem when a project comes from the outside, when it's not a project that the radio station could participate in, in the formulation of the objectives, when it is a project that one has to accept as it is.

(KB, Radio Universitaire Namuroise)

This balancing between being on the inside and the outside can be explained by the requirements of government funding and the resulting lack of continuity and uncertainty, the close involvement of people linked to academia (as illustrated in the quote below), the technology, which is still perceived as 'strange' to the core business of audio broadcasting, the lack of immediate and considerable benefits in relation to the core business, and the different needs of individual radio producers and those in charge of radio station programming. Individual radio producers usually only have one-hour slots, and are disinclined to broadcast material other than their own.

I think the website needs to be completely changed. The way it has been built makes sense from the perspective of people that work in a university, but it doesn't make sense from the perspective of the people that have to use it.

(WG, Radio Centraal)

Principally, I think that I just have one broadcast, that I produce on a regular basis. There is no need to just fill it and it was not made to be open to another broadcast[er].

(BD2, Radio Campus)

The limited involvement of the partner radio stations is considered by the project management to be problematic; they prefer to meet with committed individuals who represent equally interested partner radio organizations, but invariably have contacts with a series of people who are only mildly interested in the project. Although the project management feels that the organizations have disintegrated, it is more likely that interest in RadioSwap has waned:

We discovered little by little that we weren't facing *organizations* (Community Media or not) with whom we could construct a project starting from their expertise . . ., but only a few individuals who had agreed – sometimes unwillingly – to come once in a while to a meeting where they could only speak on their own behalf.

(DD, RadioSwap)

At the same time the RadioSwap project is still seen as a part of the alternative media world. The project's identity reinforces the core values of the participating alternative radio stations and thus serves as a tool for the construction of an alternative media identity. This process is exemplified (and symbolized) by a comment from one of the radio producers about the RadioSwap logo (see Figure 9.3):

Even the look of RadioSwap I like. It has a submarine, with a periscope. It is a clear reference to the underground. I think that we are going to stay underground, even if we are going to affirm ourselves more publicly.

(JP, Radio Campus)

The project's alternative identity is also based on the reproduction of the antagonistic positioning of the radio stations towards the so-called commercial media. These media were denied membership, as the radio producers feel very strongly about the idea that these commercial media might benefit from their work.

Just forgetting our financial situation now, last year, or whenever, I do think it is important that people don't make money from broadcasting our fragments. If something is re-broadcast, and they insert commercials before and after, well then, we're actually entitled to the money from those commercials, because we covered the production costs, however minimal.

(KV, Radio FMBrussel)

Apart from these technological, interactional, organizational and identificatory characteristics of the RadioSwap project, some users also point to some political aspects. The planned opening up of the database to the general public has raised several legal problems concerning copyright, which have been addressed by reverting to the promotion of 'copyleft' material.[11] One of the radio producers interviewed pointed to the importance of discourses that (at least attempt to) nuance the hegemony of commercial music production:

I like the initiative, because it is instrumental in the distribution of non-registered

Figure 9.3 The RadioSwap logo.

music, and of the copyleft idea. Also the distribution of reportages is very
interesting.

(DR, Radio Centraal)

In addition, the RadioSwap network is indeed seen as strengthening the alternative
radio movement:

If, thanks to Swap, we can find the right cement, the means to link 10 to 15 radio
stations, to form a strong association of alternative radio stations, we can create a
counter-force against the commercial networks. We could also have the power to
go to the French Community [one of the regional governments] and tell them:
we're 10; we're 15; we have RadioSwap; we need more frequencies. If Swap could
play this role, become a political tool, then it would become alter-radiophonic.

(JP, Radio Campus)

Evaluating RadioSwap

Four patterns of usage can be distinguished from our analysis of user practices. In a
small number of cases entire broadcasts are regularly rebroadcast by other radio stations, for example, *Rock Minute Soup*, produced by Radio Campus Brussels and
rebroadcast by Radio Universitaire Namuroise, and *Micro Ouvert*, produced by Radio
Campus Brussels and rebroadcast by Radio Campus Lille (France). Another form of
'structural' use is related to the idea of creating a RadioSwap slot in the programming
schedules of the different radio stations. Although Radio Centraal has considered this
option, it has not been implemented (yet). A third 'structural' use is related to specific
thematic needs that arise when the 'normal' programming is suspended for radiophonic or journalistic projects or festivals. In this case the RadioSwap database provides an opportunity to locate thematically relevant content. The fourth pattern of
usage is linked to individual radio producers' practices, and consists of using fragments
of downloaded material within their 'own' time slots. In all cases, radio content (regular programmes, exceptional productions, and fragments alike) crosses the borders of
the local community, as they are transposed from one community to another. Being
broadcast within the 'regular' flow of radio programmes, they become part of an
assemblage of translocal radio content.

Despite these real and planned processes of exchange, despite RadioSwap's ambi-
tion to create a community of interest that overcomes locality, and despite its contribution to the generation of rhizomatic transhegemonic media, it remains questionable
whether there is a sense of belonging, which – even in its reconceptualized versions that
enhance its fluidity – is crucial to the definition of community (Morris and Morton
1998). In other words, does RadioSwap show a degree of cross-cutting articulations
that move beyond the arbolic star-shaped network that offers nothing more than a
service to radio producers? Can we find the same participatory community-based

practices at the level of the translocal and the local, or is the translocal just an additional layer where these participatory community-based practices are abandoned?

There are a number of constraints which produce some pessimism in relation to these questions. First, the size of the network is a constraint. Although the numbers (of members, both individual and collective, and of hours of uploaded content) may at first sight be impressive, the core group of regular users is small. Moreover, as the Radia network[12] is linked to RadioSwap, a sub-community of radio artists has formed which remains relatively disconnected from the other radio producers. Secondly, the project suffers from the fallacy of a technology-centred approach to human interaction. The interface is seen as sufficient stimulation for community building, which can only considered to be illusionary. This constraint is further strengthened by the (unavoidable) top-down approach used in (applying for) the project, reducing the possibility for the radio producers to appropriate the database and adapt it to their specific needs. This approach also makes the project a target for the deterritorializing strategies of (the more radical) radio stations that usually target the state and the market. The radio producers interviewed at times appeared a disinterested and detached 'community' of self-interest; however, their remarks are only verbalizations of the structural constraints they face, and not necessarily signs of lack of interest.

The interest of the radio producers in RadioSwap is shown by their suggestions for improvements; given the lack of human interaction, it is no coincidence that the 'ordinary' user asks for additions, such as face-to-face meetings or chats, newsletters, or even a 'who's who' to give the RadioSwap members a face. Below is a comment from one radio producer, asking for more newsletters:

> A newsletter, from time to time, like the one Pierre [one of the two RadioSwap coordinators] put out a couple of times, with news on some recent events, not from RadioSwap, but from one of the other radio stations, on what they could upload. That would be good.
>
> (SC, Radio Universitaire Namuroise)

Finally, RadioSwap cannot escape from the constraints that have dogged alternative media since their origin. The lack of financial security and stability creates severe restrictions; most radio producers we interviewed were left wondering what would happen to the project once the financial support dries up.

At the same time the project should not be too harshly evaluated as it is still being developed and redeveloped.

> Everybody agrees that the interface we used for the first version was really horrible! Let's hope that the next version will be better; we are working on it, anyhow.
>
> (DD, RadioSwap)

Although the fluidity of the project creates problems for the users – 'That's the difficulty with RadioSwap, it is a project that has evolved and that was developed at the same time when it was discovered [by the users]' (MG, Panik) – it also generates room for improvement (at least for the duration of the 'formal' project, which ended in August 2006). Also, RadioSwap epitomizes the phantasm of the rhizome, and can be seen as an important materialization of the discourse of participatory media production and of rhizomatic alternative media structures.

Conclusion

Alternative media play a vital role at the level of local communities, offering their members' access to an (alternative) media system and providing them (as publics) with wide sets of alternative discourses and representations that are often missing in the mainstream media. As members of the local civil society they – and many other civil society organizations – are key societal actors, vital to the further democratization of the social and political. As localized media they often act as catalysts for a social struggles, thus occupying an important position within the local rhizomes.

At the same time they continue to face a variety of threats, which force them into a constant struggle for survival and reduce their potential strength and societal impact. Being small-scale media renders them relatively harmless, and incapable of being the 'thorns in the side of political power', to use Keane's (1991: 150) words. But their mindsets are often transnational: their programmes feature music from every continent and their connections with new social movements allow them to cover events and processes from all over the world. In this fashion they try to contribute to the alternative ideoscapes that circulate through global civil society and transnational social movements. Their sensitivity towards the problems of marginalized societal subgroups[13] allows members of those subgroups, from a diversity of nationalities and origins, to have their 'own' broadcasts and gain the ability to have their voices heard. Many of these alternative media organizations have links with national and transnational media organizations. Their broadcasts are simultaneously locally embedded, in the locally situated lives of a wide number of individuals that have reached Belgium in the slipstream of the global ethnoscapes. The organizational structures of alternative media are also often limited to the locality of their often geographically defined community. In other words, with their existence and their practices they signify how the local and global melt into the glocal.

The RadioSwap project adds another dimension to this discussion. By using the capacities of the Internet, this project aims to create a new community, besides the communities that these radio stations want to serve with their broadcasts. This community of radio producers is a new network that transcends the local, but still remains firmly rooted in it. More than simply being global, RadioSwap is – through its architecture – a translocal community of interest, based on the exchange of self-produced audio that crosses the frontiers of the local, without losing its connection to it.

Access to this community is negotiated through membership of the partner radio stations, which are open-access organizations (albeit to different degrees). Once access is granted, the radio producers can (on a voluntary basis) upload and download content, thus facilitating the circulation of alternative content and adding nodes to the rhizome. Although this form of gate-keeping creates access restrictions, it also shapes and structures the sub-rhizome RadioSwap (as part of the larger rhizome of alternative media) and thus allows for the generation of new nodes.[14]

These radio stations and radio producers remain embedded in their communities and produce the programmes that they want to produce for their communities. Through RadioSwap they are offered the opportunity to overcome localism and isolationism, and to no longer be utterly confined to the local. Although the global component is potentially present – because of the semi-global access offered by the Internet – it only provides the radio stations with limited added value. The main emphasis is on the local, as a site of embeddedness where locality is simultaneously transcended. In summary, RadioSwap is an example of glocalization, but even more of translocalization.

Most glocalization models deal with the complex dynamics of the glocal, where global flows touch local contexts. Global flows of people, money, technology, meaning and representation, and ideology all have repercussions for the local, and the ways they are incorporated demonstrates their heterogeneity and recalcitrance. But at the theoretical level, the point of departure in models of glocalization is the global, with the local added as a second layer. This perspective does not provide us with a sufficient answer to the problem of the 'erasure of place' highlighted in Dirlik (1999).

The RadioSwap project is a very modest contribution to the ever-expanding network of media organizations and other civil society organizations. It is nevertheless important because it has explicitly incorporated this unattainable – at least in the short run – horizon. RadioSwap not only illustrates the difficulties that alternative media have to face when striving for a translocal identity, it is a materialization of the need and the dream to move beyond the local rhizome, to follow the trajectory of global civil society, transnational social movements, and glocalized IMCs, and to offer a viable alternative for the global (media) market of the future.

Notes

1 To summarize these characteristics: rhizomes are fluid networks with the potential to establish a diversity of heterogeneous connections between material and discursive elements, which can be disconnected and reconnected again at all times.
2 http://sotf.berlios.de/.
3 http://radio.oneworld.net.
4 http://www.commedia.org.uk/about-cma/cmas-projects/the-showcase/programme-exchange/.
5 http://www.radio4all.net/index.php?op=about&nav=&session=.
6 As an evaluation partner of RadioSwap, the CSC conducted a series of interviews in 2004 and 2005 with the six radio station coordinators (the administrators) and 19 'ordinary' RadioSwap users. Three from this group of 'ordinary' RadioSwap users kept diaries for four

months, describing the use they made of RadioSwap. Finally, the RadioSwap coordinators received and commented upon an earlier draft of this text. This chapter is based on a qualitative analysis of all these interviews and diaries. We are grateful to the RadioSwap users and the student researchers Andries Fluit, Nathalie Gonzalez, Nathalie Colsoul, Laura Schuerwegen and Jozefien Vanhaverbeke who worked on this project.

7 During the project, the position of FMBrussel, one of the radio stations, changed when the North Belgian government decided to subsidize it. As a result, the number of voluntary staff was drastically reduced.

8 Although administrators were involved in the actual database construction, their participation was limited, despite the best efforts of the RadioSwap coordinators.

9 http://www.vorbis.com/.

10 The users especially considered the uploading procedure, with its compression and the required adding of metadata, as particularly time-consuming.

11 RadioSwap has translated the copyleft concept, which rebalances intellectual ownership and free redistribution, to the world of Belgian broadcasting.

12 The Radia network consists of nine radio stations and one programme on the Austrian public broadcaster ÖRF, all of which are involved in the production of radio art and/or experimental radio programming (see http://www.constant.irisnet.be/~sound/radia/).

13 Item 5 of the 1994 *Community Radio Charter for Europe* of AMARC states that community radio stations 'provide a right of access to minority and marginalized groups and promote and protect cultural and linguistic diversity'.

14 This argument shows the dialectics of generative/productive and restrictive power practices, as theorized by Foucault (1978).

JAMMING THE POLITICAL: REVERSE-ENGINEERING, HACKING THE DOMINANT CODES[1]

> As awareness of how the media environment we occupy affects and directs our inner life grows, some resist. The skilfully reworked billboard ... directs the public viewer to a consideration of the original corporate strategy. The studio for the cultural jammer is the world at large.
>
> (Negativland 1985/1994)

Introduction

The term 'cultural jamming' was introduced in popular discourse by the 'audio-Dada' band Negativland on a cassette recording called *JamCon'84*, released in 1985 and re-issued on CD in 1994. On the tape one of the band members referred to so-called billboard activists – altering billboards to produce subversive meanings – as the archetypical cultural jammers.

Cultural jammers 'create with mirrors' (Berry 1995) and are related to what Gramsci (1971: 417) called a 'new way of conceiving the world' and 'modifying ... popular thought and mummified popular culture'. Gramsci referred to the construction of a counter-hegemony as a strategy to challenge dominant forces and discourses in society. By placing resistance and the war of position within the realm of (mass) popular culture, Gramsci also refers to the need to translate these counter-hegemonic discourses beyond like-minded intellectuals. Lasn (2000: xvi), one of the co-founders of Adbusters, describes cultural jamming as 'a rebranding strategy – a social demarketing campaign'. According to Dery (1993) the cultural jammer is someone who 'intrude[s] on the intruders, investing ads, newscasts, and other media artefacts with subversive meanings'. In her book *No Logo*, Klein (2000: 281) refers to the cultural jam as 'interceptions – counter-messages that hack into a corporation's own method of communication to send a message starkly at odds with the one that was intended'. Klein talks of hacking and implicitly refers to hacktivism, another notion that has become commonplace in recent years to describe digital activism (Jordan and Taylor 2004).

A much cited example of a cultural jam is the well-documented *Peretti* v *Nike* case (Peretti 2001; Carty 2001). Jonah Peretti, at that time an MA student at MIT, took advantage of a stunt that Nike launched allowing customers to order custom-made shoes by adding a word or slogan that would be printed on the shoe. Peretti chose the word 'sweatshop' to be printed on his shoes, which was of course rejected by Nike. What made this a classic jam, however, was the fact that Peretti posted his correspondence with Nike on the Internet and it was promptly distributed throughout the world, causing embarrassment to Nike.

More established civil society organizations, such as Greenpeace, increasingly use cultural jamming techniques in their campaigns against corporations. A good example was their 'Stop E$$O' campaign; substituting the S's with $ signs. Esso/Exxon/Mobil decided to sue Greenpeace for infringing the copyright of its logo and for reputational damage. In reaction to the court case, which Greenpeace won, Greenpeace launched a call to the public to subvert the Esso logo in graphical jams (Greenpeace 2002). The result were cunning, often witty fake logos.[2]

Although these forms of cultural jamming are inherently political in that they react against the dominance of commodification and corporate actors within society and everyday life, the focus is on attacking and mocking the capitalist corporate brand culture. The focus in this chapter, on the other hand, is the use of cultural jamming techniques by political actors, citizens and their networks, in their political communication using alternative media within fragmented counter-public spheres, as well as aiming to hack into the mainstream public sphere. Jamming the political should therefore be seen as a way of dealing with the messiness of reality, as subverting meanings, and employing humour, mockery, satire and parody. The practice of jamming illustrates the functioning of the rhizome in two ways. First, at the level of meaning, it shows that the meanings communicated through jamming techniques deterritorialize mainstream (hegemonic) meanings, by both using and subverting these dominant meanings. Jamming simultaneously shows the instability and fluidity of meaning, and the impossibility of fixed meanings, whether they are hegemonic or counter-hegemonic. Secondly, at the level of social networks, jamming shows the complexity of these social networks, and the many fluid interconnections between civil society actors, state actors and market actors.

Some history

Jamming is not a totally new phenomenon (Hutcheon 1994; Dentith 2000); the germs of what today is called cultural or political jamming can in fact be traced back to a variety of art and subcultural movements from the beginning of the twentieth century through to the 1980s.

Cultural jamming can be applied to the optical illusions produced by surrealists, such as René Magritte, often cunningly devised to confuse the audience. Fluxus, an avant-garde art movement of the 1960s and 1970s which extended Dadaism, can also be linked to the emergence of cultural jamming.[3] It established itself as a counter-artistic movement involved with social action.

Fluxus explicitly integrated making art with cultural and socio-political criticism of society and the way it functions. The phrase 'Duchamps has qualified the object into art, I have qualified life into art' in a piece by Wolf Vostell from 1972 exemplifies this. Adoption of the name Fluxus embodies the notion of change, interdependence and dynamism, the fast-paced, non-static, ever-evolving flux that increasingly characterizes life, the world and society. Fluxus was influenced by what the composer John Cage (1966) called the need to depersonalize art, and his critique of the artist as something of a genius.

Situationism and its articulation of *détournement* is probably the most relevant reference to what today is described as cultural jamming. Guy Debord and Gil Wolman (1956) speak of the 'serious parody' in their *détournement* manual:

> It is thus necessary to envisage a *parodic-serious* stage where *the accumulation of detourned elements*, far from aiming to arouse indignation or laughter by alluding to some original work, will express our indifference toward a meaningless and forgotten original, and concern itself with rendering a certain sublimity.
>
> (Translated in Knabb 1981; emphasis added)

The very idea of the parody, with a serious undertone or overturned meanings, resonates with reversing, transgressing or subverting in the definitions quoted above. An example of Situationist art is taking old cartoons and replacing or 'situating' a different content in the speech balloons. Another much used Situationist technique is that of the (art) performance, interventions in the public space as a form of direct action, art as a political act.

Like Fluxus, the Situationist International situates art very much within the context of the everyday and of society, thereby opposing the elitist view that art is somehow detached from or transcends society and the everyday context of so-called 'ordinary' people. 'Art is revolutionary or is not.' The Situationists were very active in the 1968 spring of dissent in Paris, popularizing surrealist, but nevertheless very meaningful, slogans such as 'Soyez réalistes, demandez l'impossible!' or 'Il est interdit d'interdire'.[4] The movement was also very conscious of the increasingly important mediating role of mainstream media in distorting events, truth and experiences and at the same time commodifying them. This thesis was very much at the heart of the famous book *La Societé du Spectacle* by Guy Debord (1967/translation: Knabb 1981):

> In societies where modern conditions of production prevail, all of life presents itself as an immense accumulation of spectacles. Everything that was directly lived

has moved away into a representation. . . . In a world which really is topsy-turvy, the true is a moment of the false.

(Translated in Knabb 1981)

Other influences that have shaped cultural jamming include 'cut-up' techniques used in literature, by Brion Gysin and William Seward Burroughs amongst others (Beiles et al. 1960) and the anarchistic DIY culture within the punk movement at end of the 1970s and beginning of the 1980s (see Reid and Savage 1987). Finally, cultural jamming can also be linked to the notion of *bricolage*, defined by Hartley (2002: 22ff.), referring to French anthropologist Claude Lévi-Strauss, as 'the creation of objects with materials to hand, re-using existing artefacts and incorporating bits and pieces' (see also Deuze 2006b).

Contemporary cultural jamming and the political

While recent conceptualizations of cultural jamming, as outlined above, are directed at the corporate world and its brand culture, more overtly political jams are directed against government policies, or formal political actors, such as political parties; against undesirable behaviour in society; or even at times against minorities in society. The 'political' jam, therefore, is not inherently progressive. The 'classic' cultural jam is generally portrayed and constructed as a David and Goliath battle – the inventive 'funny' activists versus the mighty evil corporate world. *Détournement* in political communication also voices feelings of intolerance, public hatred towards a common demonized enemy, such as Osama bin Laden, and even blatant racism towards ethnic minorities.

We first analyse some examples of political jams. This first selection shows cultural jamming techniques being used by networks of citizens and civil society activists to deterrotorialize hegemonic (or arbolic, see Chapter 1) government policies and to disseminate alternative discourses, that nevertheless still contain the original meanings. As these counterhegemonic redefinitions are not stable either, we then address the appropriation of jamming techniques by more formal political actors in information or election campaigns. These cases illustrate the workings of the rhizome of meanings. Finally, we turn to the rhizome of actors, and the functioning of networks. The alternative Internet (Atton 2004), as a means of distributing political jams, is instrumental in bringing together a multitude of actors, but is not the only means of communication used to support these social networks. Showing how these networks use a diversity of communicative tools (from the street to the Internet) illustrates the workings of the rhizome. As argued in Chapter 9, the network does not stop at the edge of civil society, but clearly enters into the domains of state and market.

Jamming the political

Billboard activists, very much at the core of the cultural jamming movement, have diverted from attacks on the corporate world to the use of more overtly political messages directed against dominant political thinking. Ron English is a master of what he calls the art of subversion. His website[5] contains several examples of political jams: Picasso's famous painting *Guernica* headlined with the banner 'The New World Order', and billboards carrying the slogans 'Jihad Is Over! (If You Want It)' and 'One God, One Party – Republicans for a dissent free theocracy'. This type of activism shows that the street is still a space for political alternative discourses to be 'advertised'. In many countries radical activists use stickers to voice dissent. These types of engaged street-art[6] seek to subvert and at the same time reclaim public spaces through counter-messages.

The street is also the space where political resistance is 'performed' and articulated through demonstrations. During major demonstrations against international organizations such as the WTO, the G8, the EU, and the recent anti-war demonstrations, citizens and civil society organizations frequently use political jamming techniques to convey their subverting counter-messages. For some, the act of demonstrating becomes a performance in the sense that the Situationists perceived it. Scott and Street (2001: 42) call this 'the aestheticisation of politics'. In the different, almost carnivalesque, and sometimes even party-like demonstrations, echoes can be heard of the ironic detoured Situationist slogans used in the May 1968 protest in Paris. In the USA a protester walked around draped in a US flag, his mouth taped up, carrying a sign that said 'Patriot Act' (Cole 2003). In the UK, anti-war protesters sang 'We all live in a terrorist regime' to the tune of the 1966 Beatles song 'Yellow Submarine'. Other interlinked examples of these kinds of performative subversions are slogans such as 'Peace is Patriotic' and 'War is Terrorism' that found their way into anti-war protests across the world, which shows the transnational character of jamming, as well as its rhizomatic features.

Performance is central to activists such as the Yes Men,[7] who pioneered identity correction: 'Honest people impersonate big-time criminals in order to publicly humiliate them. Targets are leaders and big corporations who put profits ahead of everything else.' The Yes Men famously impersonated a spokesperson for the WTO selling slavery to an African business conference or pledging in the name of Dow Chemical to compensate victims of the chemical disaster in Bhopal, India, on the BBC World Service. Another activist collective adopting similar tactics is the 'Billionaires for Bush (or Gore)' campaign, directed against corporate control over politics in the USA, again hacking deep into the mainstream media. This was a deliberate tactic to catch the attention of the mainstream media and thus the public at large, as Boyd (2002: 373) – one of the activists – stated: 'if the media wanted the humour (and they did), they had to take the content too. The materials were catchy and accessible and the action model was easy to DIY. Thus the meme "spread, replicated, and mutated".' As such, the main aims of these performances are to jam the media, partially using/accepting and partially abusing/rejecting the tools of communication from the state and the market.

Just like with the more classic 'corporate' cultural jams, civil society actors also increasingly use cultural jamming techniques in their political communication and politically oriented campaigns. In the run-up to the 2003 European and regional elections in Belgium, an Antwerp-based multicultural radio station, Radio Multipop, launched a campaign to counter the propaganda by the North Belgian extreme-right party, Vlaams Blok.[8] This initiative from a semi-commercial radio station was supported by a large number of individuals and by a broad coalition of local civil society organizations, including several minority organizations, labour unions, and gay organizations. It also crossed the border between civil society and market by gaining support from some private sector actors (such as a discotheque). The 'Hate Is No Solution' campaign was set up to counter the essentialist discourses being voiced by the nationalistic extreme right party and to promote mutual understanding and respect between the different communities in Antwerp and North Belgium. While the original campaign used slogans such as 'Less Immigration, More Flanders' and 'Less Crime, More Flanders', the counter-campaign reversed this by using the same layout and colours but with a completely different message, such as 'More Heart, Less Hate' and 'More Dialogue, Less Hate'.

Forty thousand of these political jams were printed in poster form, which citizens throughout the city were encouraged to display. These posters could also be downloaded from the Internet, again demonstrating the two sides of mobilizing through the Internet, but at the same time having a visible presence in the offline world. A similar initiative was a jam of the Antwerp street signs, using the same design and length as ordinary street signs, but saying 'Without Hate Street'.

In the UK anti-war activists campaigning against the New Labour government have employed similar tactics. One group subverted the original Saatchi campaign against Labour by appropriating the slogan 'Labour Isn't Working' but adding the words 'For Peace', and replacing the line of unemployed on the original poster with a line of bombs.

The examples above demonstrate the rhizomatic behavior of the jam, breaking down and transgressing established analytical distinctions such as online/offline or alternative/mainstream. In addition, when analysing the phenomenon of jamming, it becomes apparent that this technique is not merely the prerogative of 'fringe' activists, but belongs to all actors within the political domain.

Appropriating jamming

The interconnectedness of citizens and civil society with the market and the state, characteristic of the rhizome, also runs the danger of appropriation by these other actors at times attempting to reinstate their hegemony. The dichotomy between what constitutes mainstream and alternative is also challenged.

An example of the latter is the increasing use of jamming techniques by mainstream media in their satirical broadcasts. More and more comedy shows subvert TV formats such as human interest-type programmes, infotainment, as well as traditional current affairs programmes. Examples of these are: *In de Gloria*, produced by Woestijnvis for the Dutch-speaking Belgian public broadcaster, which mocks the human interest genre; *Broken News* on the BBC, jamming TV news, as well as infotainment-type formats; or the US *The Daily Show with Jon Stewart*, who regularly uses jamming techniques.

An example of the appropriation of jamming techniques by formal political actors is their use in political marketing campaigns by political parties. In the 2001 general election campaign in the UK New Labour used fake movie posters in party election broadcasts and on huge billboards. One featured William Hague, the then Tory party leader, sporting Margaret Thatcher's hairstyle, carrying the slogan 'Get Out to Vote or They Get In'. Another poster referred to the huge number of houses being repossessed by banks due to high interest rates and read 'Return of the Repossessed', with the Tory leaders depicted as zombies, and the sub-title 'No Home Is Safe from Spiralling Tory Interest Rates'. Yet another film poster used by Labour was 'Economic Disaster II', starring Michael Portillo as Mr Boom and William Hague as Mr Bust, 'coming to a home, hospital, school and business near you' (Figure 10.1).

This use of parody in a political campaign with a serious undertone, though perceived by some observers as very populist, did strike a chord with the (young) electorate. It was intended to convince voters that the Tory party was not to be trusted, and to induce fear over a Tory victory (Smith 2001). In North Belgium, the youth organization of the socialist party (Animo) produced a 'Piss on Bush' sticker, which they placed in urinals in pubs and schools. The stickers also found their way to the toilets in the Cabinet of the socialist federal deputy prime minister. This caused a diplomatic incident

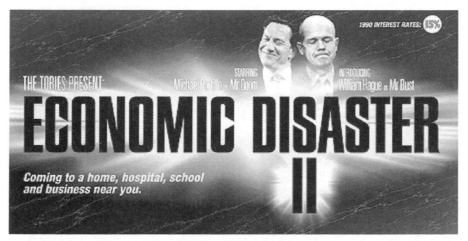

Figure 10.1 New Labour poster, 'Economic Disaster II', used in the 2001 general election (source: TBWA London. Reproduced by permission of the Labour Party).

and provoked Vito Fossella, the Republican member of Congress for New York, to comment that 'such cheap political humor at the expense of the American flag was beneath a country with such a rich heritage as Belgium' (Fosella 2005).

Finally, public information campaigns, although less prominent, have also used cultural jamming techniques to convey messages of public interest. An example of this is a controversial campaign by a Dutch semi-public organization called SIRE, focusing on the anti-social behaviour of citizens and youngsters. The title of the campaign was 'Society is You'. It used the metaphor of children's books, hacking Dick Bruna's simplified but highly successful images through similar layout and language.[9] This is similar to the *détournement* of cartoon speech balloons of the Situationists. In one of the illustrations a grandmother is depicted with the accompanying text: 'Mies sits in the tram. Here comes grandmother. "Can I sit there, I am old and a bit tired". "Piss off, you old cow", says Mies. Grandmother is crying. Mies is happy that she can remain sitting' (authors' translation). The campaign elicits emotional reactions partly through shock and by implying such behaviour is childish. Other cartoons were directed against the chanting of anti-Semitic slogans by football supporters, sexual harassment of women, or use of a mobile phone in a theatre or cinema. In addition to posters, some radio ads were produced that used children's songs.

This SIRE campaign was designed by the private advertising agency Lintas, which again demonstrates the blurring of the boundaries between civil society, formal political actors, and the private sector, to which the rhizome also refers.

Completing the circle, this campaign was hacked and mocked by activists and citizens playing around with the same children's imagery and language, but targeting different audiences, and often not so innocent or in the public interest. In a sense this could be seen as a parody of the parody or dejamming the jam, but at the same time often transgressing dangerous boundaries. One quite abhorrent example of this shows a weeping child on the left, with the following message on the right: 'Hassan is mad. He said to the girl: "you cannot see Moroccans". Girl nevertheless sees Moroccans. Hassan rapes girl with 13 friends. Well done Hassan. This is real integration' (authors' translation).

These examples show that political jams are not *per se* progressive, but can contain essentialist racist (counter-)discourses that could be considered as pertaining to anti-public spheres. Again, meaning is not stable.

The Internet as an alternative medium of distribution for jams

Recently published research on hacktivism and Internet use by activists (Meikle 2002; Jordan 2002; van de Donk et al. 2004; Jordan and Taylor 2004; Atton 2004) does not allow us to assess the extent of the distribution of cultural and political jams. However, it would be fair to say that many Internet users, worldwide, have at some time received a political jam in their mailbox. Moreover, world events, such as 9/11 and the subsequent US-led wars against the Taliban in Afghanistan and the Ba'ath regime in Iraq, have resulted in an explosion of political jams, usually distributed and dispersed through the Internet (Ellis 2002; Frank 2004). These illustrations are often delivered unsolicited via e-mail or are stored on sites dedicated to these kinds of jams and as such are very difficult to attribute to an author, which in itself is significant.

A well-known and widely distributed political jam is the Star Wars poster that has been re-engineered to become 'Gulf Wars, Episode II – Clone of the Attack'. It was produced by *MAD* magazine. Similar jams of movies or TV series featuring 9/11, Bush, Osama bin Laden or the wars in Iraq and Afghanistan include *The Matrix*, *Face/Off*, *Escape from New York*, *Natural Born Killers*, *Terminator*, and the 1980s TV series the *A-Team*. Also cartoons such as *South Park*, *The Simpsons* and *Spiderman*, and the computer games *Flight Simulator*, *SimCity* and *Tomb Raider*, have been jammed to mock recent US politics.

The technique of photo doctoring is often used to fake images: for instance, showing Saddam Hussein being presented as a DJ, or George Bush morphed with Osama bin Laden (Figure 10.2). Again less innocent examples emerge as well, such as a picture of Mecca with a plane heading towards the Kaaba with the subtitle 'An Eye for an Eye', and the like. This again shows that political jamming is not only 'performed' by progressive-democratic voices and activists, but also serves to ridicule, humiliate or victimize the common enemy or the personification of evil at that given moment in time. As Silverstone (2006: 75) states, '[e]vil is the signal expression of otherness, of the other as malevolant, in a world governed by God'. It is therefore not unsurprising that religion is a prime target in many of the essentialist jams. One example depicts Osama bin Laden with pigs – a huge insult to Muslims worldwide. Another can be seen as the *détournement* of the French sports newspaper *L'Équipe*, representing the 9/11 World Trade Center attack as goal scoring in a deadly football match between religions. It shows the cover of the sports newspaper with a picture of the burning twin towers and bearing the headline 'Allah: 1 – Jésus: 0'.

There are thousands of political jams circulating the Internet which cannot be reduced to criticism or even support for US policies in relation to Iraq or Afghanistan. They also often refer to other (local) political contexts and issues and usually combine popular culture and politics. In this context, the Internet serves very much as an alternative means of distribution and its viral characteristics allow the cultural or political jam to spread extremely quickly across borders and at minimal cost to its producers. Citizens forward these jams to their professional and/or personal networks, which spreads them even further (Frank 2004: 637; Peretti 2001).

However, it would be wrong to overemphasize the importance of the Internet. Some of the examples presented in this case study show that other media are equally, or indeed even more important, in the spreading of counter-discourses beyond the cosy circle of like-minded individuals. The counter-campaign against the extreme-right party in Antwerp had an effective and attractive website, but nevertheless also had 40,000 posters printed to ensure visibility on the city streets, and was supported by

Figure 10.2 Jamming the War on Terror source: Mullah Bush by Mister Hepburn, http://www.bushspeaks.com).

the broadcasts of Radio Multipop. The activities of the Yes Men or the 'Billionaires for Bush (and Gore)' only serve a purpose if they get exposure in the mainstream media.

Transgressing the boundaries between alternative media spheres and the mainstream public sphere, as well as between old and new media, is crucial in this regard. When referring to tactical media as a form of digital interventionism the Critical Art Ensemble (2002: 7) states that: 'By "digital" CAE means that tactical media is about copying, re-combining, and re-presenting, and not that it can only be done with digital technology'. This points to a non-deterministic perspective with regard to media, technology and society, as well as a breaking down of the dichotomies between different kinds of media, as implied by the metaphor of the rhizome.

Conclusion

Although the notions of cultural and political jamming are fairly new, they should be seen within an evolutionary perspective of the relationship between culture and politics or more specifically between art and social struggles. It also embodies the de-elitization of art and allows the citizen/activist to voice dissent, and challenge dominant discourse in society through artistic expression. In addition, patterns of discontinuity can be detected. They mostly refer to the means for distributing jams, where the alternative Internet plays a pivotal role in its ability to spread a jam very much like a virus from one community of users to another. However, the street as a stage to perform resistance and so-called old media continue to be important ways to communicate jams beyond the (often fragmented) subaltern public spheres of the Internet.

A rhizomatic approach to alternative media, as developed in Chapter 1, proves to be an adequate model to frame the notion of jamming, both in its corporate, as well as its more overtly political focus. It allows us to see the jam as nomadic, moving from anti-public spheres, to autonomous public spheres, to counter-public spheres, to the main-stream public sphere. In doing so the jam disturbs or, as Deleuze and Guattari would say, deterritorializes the status quo. Jamming also exposes the interlinkages between citizens, civil society, the state and the market, as well as the appropriation of jamming techniques by these different actors. This causes the destabilization of its counter-hegemonic nature. Finally, the practice of jamming also allows us to go beyond the dichotomous representations of old versus new media and, instead of essentializing them, to see them in conjunction and interaction with each other.

The rhizomatic approach not only metaphorically captures the way in which jamming transgresses these conceptual boundaries, it also accounts for the high variety of actors and the diversity of political strategies adopting cultural and political jamming. In our post-modern society, a world of greenwashing, spin and other newspeak – 'the true is a moment of the false' – *détournement* is no longer inherently progressive. It increasingly voices 'passionate' sentiments of hatred and violence, essentializing entire (religious) communities and populations as well. It is not neccesarily embedded in the modernist emancipatory ideals of the Enlightment,[10] and as a result it does not auto-matically aim to challenge the status quo or strive to extend rights for citizens at large. This in turn can partly be explained by its appropriation by both reactionary and mainstream actors, including market actors. Some political actors, as well as com-panies, increasingly use jamming techniques as a 'hip' political communication strat-egy, thereby reducing it to a marketing technique – unjamming the jam so to speak. Others use it to demonize and essentialize a common 'evil' enemy or ethnic/religious minority. For mainstream broadcasters jamming is often 'merely entertainment'.

It therefore remains important not be too celebratory about these phenomena and take into account Baudrillard's (1987) criticism that media, both mainstream and alter-native, create an over-saturated hyperreality that can potentially lead to the implosion of meaning, whereby the jam represents merely another 'noise' amongst existing noises.

Notes

1 This chapter is partly based on Cammaerts (2007a).
2 The result of this campaign can be seen at http://www.stopesso.org/static/logos.html.
3 A recent Adbuster campaign, 'Unbrand America', used an American flag with corporate logos instead of stars. This bears a strong resemblance to the American flag designed by Fluxus artist George Maciunas to protest against American imperialism (*U.S.A. Surpasses All The Genocide Records*, 1965).
4 These slogans translate as 'Be realistic – demand the impossible!' and 'It is forbidden to forbid'.
5 See http://www.popaganda.com/.
6 For more examples of street-art, see http://www.woostercollective.com/.
7 See http://www.theyesmen.org/.
8 Due to a conviction for disseminating persistent racist discourses, Vlaams Blok recently changed its name to Vlaams Belang, which is a change in form, but not in substance.
9 Dick Bruna is best known for his Miffy character (Nijntje in Dutch), a rabbit that seems to be universally appealing to young children.
10 In this regard, Morrow (2003) refers to the emergence of a new age of 'endarkenment'.

CONCLUSION

In referring to the classic dichotomous relationship between alternative and main-stream media, Downing (2003: 637) states that

> we must acknowledge that these more hegemonic media habits interact with alternative-media uses, both in terms of their prior communicative accumulation and simultaneously. People do not categorically switch off mainstream media in the present moment, however intense that moment, nor can they elect simply to erase their accumulated mainstream media inheritance by some magical act of will. It is normal for there to be a dynamic mental co-habitation among users between the two types of media source and their variants.

These interactions and dynamic dialectics between what is deemed to be mainstream and what is perceived to be alternative create a multiplicity and variety of alternative media that need to be fully appreciated.

In this book we have provided a comprehensive theoretical overview of the various ways to articulate relevant core concepts, presented a panoptic and multi-faceted model to understand alternative media, and highlighted a number of empirical cases that partially challenge, unsettle, or, dare we say, deterritorialize, commonplace conceptions of alternative media. We have established that the concept of alternative media is in itself a highly contested notion, and proposed four ways to approach, study and research them. Each of these approaches – community, alternative, civil society and rhizome – involves a distinct emphasis, drawing on different theoretical traditions, privileging some core notions and aspects above others. However, it is important to understand that these approaches are neither mutually exclusive nor in opposition. Each has its own merits, as well as its limitations, for studying and understanding what we call alternative media.

The key argument in this book is that in order to gain access to the complexity of these alternative media worlds, these four approaches need to be combined. There is, therefore, no one 'right' way to frame or define alternative media. Combining the different approaches enables a panoptic picture of the phenomenon that takes account of the multiplicity and diversity of alternative media initiatives, acknowledging the concepts that structure and define their identity as well as their fluidity, at a micro level of analysis.

The different approaches

The first perspective emphasizes the notion of community in describing alternative media – serving a local or dispersed community, being produced and controlled by the community – through the key idea of participation. The first case study from a community perspective focuses on the struggle for existence of community radio stations alongside the commercial and public broadcasting model. Despite fierce resistance from both commercial and/or state interests, community radio stations have slowly but surely begun to assert themselves in many countries. This does not mean that there is no longer any struggle. On the contrary; it is still necessary to struggle, not only to secure the right to transmit and to communicate, but also to sustain activities and to be able to draw on the community, whether it be local or transnational, to innovate and adapt to constantly changing circumstances. In this regard, many constraints stand out, from commercial pressures to state control or media regulation, at a technical level and in relation to content. Also, the Internet has opened up possibilities for community radio to reach beyond its immediate locality.

The second case from a community perspective involves a series of relevant studies on diasporic audiences and readers' usage of alternative media. The analysis highlighted the role of diasporic media in helping diasporic communities to overcome social and cultural exclusion. It emerges that diasporic groups have distinct uses for alternative media, depending on their particular situations, such as their reasons for migrating to a new country, differences in terms of class, age, gender, ethnicity, and so on. Diasporic audiences tend to form 'communities' bound by some degree of common political and social interests, and by ethnicity, language, and culture. Moreover, they may produce and use these media as political instruments to voice concerns about their exclusion from the main public sphere, to maintain connections with their countries of origin and to build and sustain a new local and transnational 'imagined' community. Overall, the diversity of their media practices functions to help these communities in the process of identity negotiation – individual and collective new hybrid identities – between the homeland and the host country's societies, rules, and rituals.

The second perspective focuses on the 'alternative' in alternative media, positioning it in relation to or complementing mainstream media. We addressed the challenge that the alternative blogosphere represents for mainstream journalism, particularly in times of crisis and war, when there is a dearth of reliable and unbiased information. Individual blogs are not always the ultimate in terms of neutrality and objectivity, but, exactly because of their specificity, engagement, and subjectivity, they are able to challenge hegemonic representations and discourses and articulate a more personal and, some would claim, a more genuine and passionate account of war. It is clear that the categories of 'alternative' and 'mainstream' are not rigid; they can be extremely fluid. For instance, some bloggers have been appropriated by the mainstream media and the publishing industry; others are clearly striving to strengthen the hegemonies in which they are located. In the case of military blogs, the state attempts to reassert its control in direct (censorship) as well as indirect (self-censorship) ways. Photo-blogs can serve as living memory, and the Abu Ghraib example illustrates the interaction between investigative (mainstream) journalism in this case, and the alternative online.

Alternative media are relevant channels of expression for many ethnic and religious groups, particularly those with neither access to nor representation in the mainstream public media sphere. The number of ethnic-religious media has increased enormously in the last ten years, especially in multicultural societies where they are creating mediated spaces of communication to voice their demands for social, political, cultural, and economic inclusion as well as to produce entertainment. We have argued that Q-News magazine works as a hybrid form of alternative media: it combines a political ethos – speaking for Muslims – with a commercialism, highlighting that community media and commercial, community-oriented media are not mutually exclusive. Although the journalism produced by Q-News is not fully participatory, it functions as a mediator of a local and global conversation among Muslim peers, creating new forms of political mobilization and solidarity, thus following a general trend observed in the literature of public/participatory journalism (Deuze, 2003).

Alternative media are also a part of civil society and are often embedded in activist or (new) social movements, in between the state and the market. We examined the use of the Internet by civil society actors to distribute alternative discourses and information, organize themselves and facilitate debate. The case studies illustrate the many potentials of the Internet in terms of organization, mobilization, interaction, and facilitation of debate, at both local and transnational levels. Despite this potential, there are clear indications of the considerable constraints within which these media have to operate. Regarding civil society involvement in formal policy contexts, mailing lists clearly constitute crucial tools for intra-movement networking (or mesomobilization) and the exchange of information. Furthermore, policy-oriented mailing lists are also often used to forge consensus on a common position or even to elect representatives, who are then mandated to speak in the name of civil society. However, it is precisely at the level of representation that tensions and difficulties, such as the dominance of civil society representatives from the West and the need for expert knowledge to be taken seriously at an international level of governance, are exposed. The Indymedia forum is a different case, highlighting the facilitation of much more fluid and citizen-based interaction, as well as confrontation. The contentious issue being discussed led to intense conflicts between opposing ideological views, which at times also led to flaming between participants, resulting in the disengagement of participants from the ongoing debate.

The Brazilian Landless Rural Workers' Movement's (MST) communication strategies were analysed as expressions of a particular segment of the Brazilian civil society – the landless people. The movement has an elaborate repertoire of political actions, which work through a mixture of innovative and traditional communicative forms. Its alternative media provide a democratic space to air opposing views on political and social issues and to counter the generally negative representation of the MST by the mainstream media. The movement has built a public identity through political actions, such as mass demonstrations, marches, and land occupations. These actions reinforce the identities of the members internally as *sem terra* as well as externally, while at the same time functioning as a form of communication requiring no mediation. The mystique embedded in all these political actions is the embodiment of the cultural and spiritual expression of the movement, a symbolic communication which, through the use of flags, songs, theatre, and hymns, helps to form new ideas and shape its members' behaviour. We argued that these repertoires of action form a communicative space beyond the traditional media. Although the movement has been criticized for its undemocratic control of the decision-making process, the MST has became a legitimized voice in Brazil to speak for its landless members, to speak about land reform in the public (media) sphere, and to act as a mediator between the state and the landless people in their struggle for land reform.

The fourth approach to alternative media we introduced builds on the metaphor of the rhizome, as theorized by Deleuze and Guattari (1987), which points to the fluidity of the seemingly strict boundaries that structure the other three approaches. Alternative media still carry identities that are different from their state and market counterparts, but these differences do not exclude the existence of many of the interdependencies between all three domains of the social. The RadioSwap project shows how a network of alternative radio producers transcends a number of the borders that traditionally restrict alternative media. First, the members of RadioSwap are not limited to alternative media, and include producers from other civil society organizations, and (in one case) from a public broadcaster. Secondly, and more importantly, the RadioSwap project transcends the borders of locality that often confine alternative radio stations. In its free and (potentially) worldwide distribution of radio programmes, RadioSwap enters the domain of the larger media players and their markets in a rather unique way. This uniqueness is based on the translocal nature of RadioSwap, where programmes remain firmly grounded in the local, but nevertheless (and simultaneously) move into the global.

Finally, we looked at the phenomenon of cultural and political jamming, which works by disrupting common representations, perverting them and, in the process, criticizing hegemonic views and values in society. Activists mix the use of the street, old and new media, and alternative and mainstream media to distribute their jams. Although jamming can be traced back to a number of art movements embedded in revolutionary counter-hegemonic artistic projects, cultural and political jamming is moving beyond its counter-hegemonic legacy. Increasingly, it is being co-opted by corporate and formal political actors as a hip (political) marketing tool. Furthermore, reactionary forces within society are using the technique of jamming to voice essentialist and racist discourses. This shows the nomadic nature of jamming, in moving from being counter-hegemonic to re-enforcing hegemonies, from progressive to reactionary, from alternative to mainstream and from old to new media.

A panoptic approach to alternative media

The case studies illustrate that the dichotomies (and/or trichotomies) structuring the intertwined social, cultural, and political fields, such as alternative/mainstream, civil society/state/market, are not as rigid as is often assumed. They are in fact flexible, fluid, opening up the possibility for different constellations to coexist alongside each other at times, and on other occasions closing them down again. This dialectic between openness and closure constitutes the diversity and multiplicity of public spaces that Mouffe (1999b: 757) advocates, leading to very distinct alternative 'media'; some totally independent of market or government, some dependent on the state for their resources, others drawing on advertising to finance their operations; some re-producing hegemony, others clearly counter-hegemonic; some reactionary, some reformist, some revolutionary, and others less obviously political.

From this panoptic perspective, alternative media should be seen as a multiplicity of public spaces, a colourful – but at times also contentious – myriad of media initiatives as diversified as society itself. Not everything is totally fluid, though, and concepts such as community and civil society still matter to structure and give coherence to alternative media's social reality. As such, it makes no sense to focus exclusively on the hyperfluidity of alternative media as they are also embedded in social and discursive structures, which generate a certain form of stability for their identities. Even the rhizome is structured, although its movable structures remain clearly distinct from the more arbolic structures of state and market, and their media organizations.

These arbolic structures, imposed by state and market, as well as the taken-for-granted hegemonies, have always had a considerable impact on alternative media and their ability to broadcast or distribute printed material, despite the resistance this evoked. From an (even) broader perspective, alternative media cannot function as permanent radical alterities on each of the many different societal levels. Resisting all hegemonies on all societal levels will only lead to a total detachment from the social, or to a collapse into solipsism. In this sense, alternative media are transhegemonic, and not exclusively counter-hegemonic, as they oscillate between acceptance and rejection, between resistance and compliance, between restriction and creation. At the same time, they remain rhizomatic, avoiding (or at least attempting to avoid) incorporation into the realms of state and market.

Given these restrictions, the Internet still clearly constitutes a political opportunity structure. It is not only cost-efficient in terms of use and distribution, but also opens up the public space beyond the nation-state and, thereby, to some extent bypasses, or rather escapes, state and market colonization. However, we should not ignore the increased state surveillance on the net and the tensions between decommodification (cf. open source, freeware, creative commons, peer-to-peer exchange, free podcasts) on the one hand and the hypercommodification of the Internet on the other (cf. the omnipresent banners, the cost of bandwidth, and of copy- or broadcasting rights, the crackdown on peer-to-peer networks, etc.).

The multiplicity of alternative media, the distinct positions and forms they take, can be understood from the perspective of political theorists such as Fraser (1992) and Mouffe (1993, 1994, 1999b). They stress the constitutive role of conflict and power in society and provide a role and space for the subaltern within a radical pluralistic project. However, this does not mean that the consensus model should be rejected entirely. Both consensus- and conflict-oriented models stress the need for citizens and/ or civil society to participate in these processes of dialogue, debate, and deliberation. From both perspectives, an argument can be made in favour of encouraging participation and participatory media.

Both perspectives – the agonistic or antagonistic struggle for or against hegemony and the consensus arising from constructed and sedimented hegemonies – are present in our society. Consensus, or rather compromise, can, however, only be understood as a temporary stability. Conflict can re-emerge at any time, disturbing the constructed harmony or hegemonies. This highly dialectic relationship between consensus-building, on the one hand, and the eruption of conflicts between different interests, on the other, is also needed to grasp the diversity of alternative media; some highly conflictual and radical, independent, others more consensual, at times even reinforcing dominant hegemonies. Within civil society these different positions also emerge. As Laclau and Mouffe (1985: 170) point out, the strength of social movements in present-day democratic societies is partly dependent on the ability of very diverse organizations and activists, with different strategies, to construct a 'new historic bloc in which a plurality of economic, social and cultural aspects are articulated', to identify common aims and to articulate a common identity whilst at the same time also respecting difference, 'combining strategic and partial incorporation with continued resistance and independent critique', as exemplified in Servaes and Carpentier's (2005: 10) notion of the Janus-head of civil society organizations (and activism).

Strategies to strengthen alternative media

All this requires an enabling environment for alternative media, not merely from a purely regulatory perspective, but also at the social, political, and cultural levels, in allowing resistance and the voicing of dissent in the social and political realms. In this sense, our book is a political project: it reinforces the importance of acknowledging the diversity of alternative media in the study (and elaboration) of media and communication policies, as well as their role in politics, in everyday life, and in strengthening democracy. Also, it reaffirms the need to recognize the vibrant history and sustained presence of alternative voices in developing theory relating to democracy, citizenship, media, and communication. As part of our politics, then, we identify (in a nonprescriptive way), two sets of strategies to provide an enabling environment and thereby strengthen the presence of alternative media in society,[1] and ultimately of participation and democracy.

These two sets of strategies are different, but not mutually exclusive. The first set is aimed at strengthening the niches that alternative media occupy, often caught in the uneasy position between market and state. The second focuses more on the societal context in which alternative media operate: by enlarging the network (or rhizome), alternative media can be part of a broader movement and their democratic function within civil society can be exposed to a higher degree.

In order to improve the position of 'their' alternative media, several countries have established media funds, specifically oriented towards direct financing of projects, privileging alternative media.[2] Very different kinds of participatory media projects could receive support, thereby strengthening the alternative media spaces in print, over the airwaves, on television, and on the Internet. These (community) media funds could also function at a more transnational level, allowing alternative media from a specific continent or different continents to apply for direct project subsidies or support transnational networks. Such funds could be cross-subsidized by a small percentage of the advertising revenues of the public and/or commercial media.

A second point related to strengthening of the niches in which alternative media operate, is the need for high-quality legislation and regulation and their enforcement in different countries and continents, embedded within local political, social, and cultural contexts. This legislation should not be limited to the protection of human rights (in its widest sense), but needs to recognize the specificities and differences of alternative media on the technical, organizational, and content-related levels, at the same time allowing for the establishment of strategic alliances with public mainstream media. In this regard, the agenda of communication rights is highly relevant, not just for the nonaligned countries that originally defended them, but for all countries (see Cammaerts and Carpentier, 2007).

At the same time, policies should be oriented towards the important role of alternative media in deepening the levels of democratization and in promoting a vibrant civic culture (Dahlgren 2000), thereby aiming to enlarge the network or rhizome. This democratic function relates to their role as a nodal point in the network of civil society. The first step towards improving the strength of the rhizome is improving the network between the different alternative media themselves, an aim that could be realized through the structural (financial) support for the representative national and international organizations of the alternative media. This would allow these representative organizations (and others) to increase the number of their 'regional offices', to organize the exchange of content, and the ability to exchange alternative media staff. In these ways, contacts and links between alternative media collaborators/producers within a particular country as well as from different countries and/or continents might be established (as the RadioSwap project, discussed in Chapter 9, shows), thus stimulating organizational learning and networking. Furthermore, the number of connections between alternative media and non-media civil organizations should be increased. Project funding specifically aimed at stimulating voluntary collaboration between media and non-media organizations should be prioritized, while as the same time acknowledging the potential conflicts of interest (and of organizational cultures) among these different organizational types. Exchange of content and other contacts between the staff – working on compatible issues – of these different organizations should be encouraged. This would increase the opportunities for partnerships between media and non-media organizations and the explicit media-centredness that (in part) continues to characterize most media organizations (to the detriment of their society-centredness).

Finally, the importance of connections between public (and other) mainstream media and alternative media should be stressed. The rhizomatic approach allows the rigid separations created by the antagonistic position towards mainstream media and towards the market and the state, to be breached. Moreover, it enables collaboration with public mainstream media, which would be beneficial for both parties if carried out with the utmost respect for the individual identities of the actors involved. The establishment of partnerships between public broadcasters and alternative media firstly would strengthen alternative media, which are sometimes in very vulnerable positions, and allow them to broaden their public sphericules. Such partnerships would also enable public broadcasters to extend beyond their existing limits and innovate, in response to the challenges from digital media. The achievements and limitations of alternative media in facilitating and realizing access, participation, self-representation, self-management, community cohesion, civil empowerment, societal and discursive diversity, pluralism, and democracy should be considered a knowledge reservoir that can and should be accessed by public broadcasters and should be mobilized in the face of a radical pluralistic democracy.

These different strategies, if implemented with the greatest respect for diversity and specificity, would allow alternative media to remain in a position where they can (continue to) serve their communities, act as an alternative to mainstream media (discourses), promote/advocate democratization in the media and (through the media) in society, and function as a crossroads in civil society.

Notes

1 What follows is partly based on Carpentier et al. (2003b).

2 Good examples are the French *Fonds de Soutien à l'Expression Radiophonique* and the South Belgian *Fonds d'Aide à la Création Radiophonique*, that redistribute a taxation on advertising revenues for audiovisual media. Both can be translated as 'support funds for radiophonic expression or creation' (cf. Chapter 3).

GLOSSARY

Agonism: A conflictual relationship that constructs 'the other' as an adversary and not an enemy, whereby debate and confrontation become a possibility.

AM: Amplitude modulation, a way to broadcast radio. Unlike frequency modulation (FM), AM produces radio waves that can travel a long way due to their amplitude. The disadvantage of AM is poor sound quality.

AMARC: Association Mondiale des Radiodiffuseurs Communautaires (http://www.amarc.org/), the international association of community radio broadcasters. It has almost 3000 members from 106 countries, and covers all five continents. It is organized regionally and has a fairly light overarching International secretariat based in Quebec, Canada. AMARC represents the interests of the community radio sector at the regional as well as global level of governance.

Antagonism: A conflictual relationship that constructs 'the other' as an enemy to be destroyed. Antagonism renders debate impossible.

Arbolic: Gilles Deleuze and Félix Guattari juxtapose the arbolic to the rhizomatic. While the rhizome is a heterogeneous, non-hierarchical and ever-changing network, the arbolic describes homogenous, hierarchical and sedentary ways of thinking. In this book the arbolic also refers to the organizational frameworks that characterize the mainstream media.

Articulation: Articulation is the practice of establishing a relationship between different elements such that their identity is modified through the articulatory practice itself (see Laclau and Mouffe 1985: 105).

Balance: Balance is one of the components that support journalistic objectivity, which often consists of reporting the opposing positions in a specific debate. More elaborate versions of balance take the multiplicity of positions into account and/or focus on the diversity of arguments rather than the actors' positions (termed 'argumentative balance').

Citizenship: Citizenship refers primarily to the rights and obligations of citizens within given geographical boundaries. Citizenship can be considered inclusive while at the same time excluding 'the other', the non-citizen. In these times of increased globalization, citizenship is no longer bounded by geographical location or communities of birth, but can be expanded towards (sub)cultural and political identities that stretch beyond the nation-state. Examples of these unbounded notions of citizenship are cultural citizenship, cosmopolitan or post-national citizenship and ecological citizenship.

Civic culture: Civic culture was introduced into democratic theory to account for learning about politics beyond the formal political culture. It relates to participation in various kinds of associations of a political but also cultural nature. From this broad perspective on the political, a vibrant civic culture is deemed an essential feature of a healthy democracy. As such, decentralized models of democracy emphasize the importance of civic culture.

Co-creation: Co-creation refers to the creative-collaborative process in which different social actors with different societal (often professional) positions take part on the basis of a (relatively) equal power balance.

Commercial radio: Commercial radio is based on mainstream formats, and aims to appeal to the widest possible or narrowest niche audience. Its income is derived from advertising. Commercial radio often operates in networks in order to minimize production costs.

Communication rights: Communication rights are the current articulation of the right to communicate as introduced in the UNESCO MacBride report of 1980 (see International Commission for the Study of Communication Problems 2004). Communication rights are considered to be a human right and relate to the access of citizens to information, to communication tools and participation in the media. Adoption of a communication rights discourse enables a link with citizenship rights discourses. At the same time, communication rights emphasize the importance of media diversity, participatory media, equal access to ICTs, etc.

Community: The concept of community includes those forms of communality in the spheres of work, neighbourhood, politics, and other areas with a presence in the social life of individuals. These communities are structured around a sense of collective goals and shared meaning, thus providing a means for social interaction and face-to-face relations in physical spaces. However, modern forms of community organized around social relations might be endangered by consumerism, media, ICTs, and heterogeneous living in global metropolitan centres which have reshaped traditional notions of communities to include 'virtual' or 'artificial' communities. The central criticism of the ideal of community – virtual or not – is that it homogenizes members of a certain community, for example an 'ethnic' community, thereby denying difference and conflict.

Contingency: Contingency is opposed to necessity, and refers to the potential fluidity and changeability of the identities of processes or entities.

Copyleft: The concept of copyleft was developed by the Free Software Movement, and is 'a general method for making a program or other work free, and requiring all modified and extended versions of the program to be free as well' (see http://www.fsf.org/licensing/essays/copyleft.html). Copyleft is a method of ensuring that intellectual work (and all deduced versions of it) can circulate freely, without the constraints of copyright. It was developed in order to prevent public domain software becoming copyrighted material at a later stage, owned by people other than the original programmers.

Counter-hegemony: Gramsci's (1971) work on hegemony points to the opportunity for the 'common-sense' ideas – ideologies – of capitalist society to be challenged by subordinate groups. In the cultural sphere, for example, conventional and dissident meanings – ideologies – can coexist in popular culture, media, styles of dress, dance, and so on.

Cyberization: Cyberization refers to a process by which an activity or everyday practice becomes mediated by the Internet or other ICTs.

Cyberspace: William Gibson (1984: 67) coined the word cyberspace in his famous novel *Neuromancer*. He described it as 'a consensual hallucination' of an 'unthinkable complexity. Lines of light ranged in the nonspace of the mind, clusters and constellations of data.' Since then cyberspace has become a common metaphor for the online realm. As a result it constructs a dichotomy between what happens in the online as opposed to the offline world.

Democracy: Democracy is a form of government and governance based on the premise that the people or citizens rule. The precise articulation of how this should then be organized and formalized is essentially contested. It could be argued that democracy, like participation, is an empty signifier, making it impossible to stabilize or fixate its precise meaning and articulation. Within this war of position, decentralized articulations can be opposed to centralized elitist models, and conflict-oriented approaches to consensual ones.

Detachment: Detachment is one of the strategies used to construct journalistic neutrality, which is in turn one of the components that support journalistic objectivity. Detachment implies the absence of journalistic involvement in reporting. Extreme forms of detachment have been criticized as being 'bystander journalism'.

Deterritorialization: Deterritorialization is the capacity to subvert existing (hierarchical) structures from within. In *A Thousand Plateaus* (1987), Gilles Deleuze and Félix Guattari link deterritorialization to the rhizome.

Détournement: Détournement is a French word that was introduced by Situationism, a post Second World War art movement in France and Belgium. It is used to describe the 'serious parody' and the inversion of meanings (see Debord and Wolman 1956). Currently, the notion of *détournement* is used to describe forms of hacktivism such as cultural jamming.

Diaspora: Etymologically, the term 'diaspora' comes from the Greek *diaspeirein*, meaning 'to disperse' or 'scatter'. It refers to the dispersion of peoples belonging to one nation and/or with a common culture, who have settled outside their countries of origin, suffer alienation in their new place of belonging, maintain a strong ethnic community in the host country, and have close bonds with their homeland. Diaspora is more than a reference to the flow of people around the globe; it involves a politics of oppression and counter-assertion including a sense of resistance to full assimilation by the host nation.

Diasporic communities: Diasporic communities describe communities in terms of being strategic alliances rather than groups whose origins are the same. Stratified by class, education, occupation, religious affiliation, cultural interests, urban or rural background, and so forth, diasporic communities are constituted as much by difference and division as by commonality and solidarity.

Digitization: Digitization is the process of transforming cultural content into a digital and computerized format, based on a discrete set of points.

Essentialism: Essentialism is the intellectual position that claims that a process or entity has a stable set of characteristics, which are essential to its existence.

Flaming: Flaming refers to offensive postings on forums, newsgroups or even mailing lists. Flames typically do not intend to further discussion or debate, but to disrupt it by being abusive and refusing to accept counter-arguments. The disruption occurs when the flame escalates into a flame war, often leading to the end of the forum or disengagement by those participating in it.

FM: Frequency modulation, a way to broadcast radio. Unlike amplitude modulation (AM), FM produces radio waves that cannot travel further then the horizon, some 50 km. FM radio is of higher sound quality than AM.

Fringe: Fringe refers to the alternative, non-mainstream, and non-conformist edge of popular as well as avant-garde culture.

Gate-keeping: Gate-keeping is the practice of selection exercised by specific media actors (individuals or organizations, often within a professional context), with the objective of reducing the amount and protecting the quality of the information passing through the 'gate', based on criteria established by the media system itself.

Globalization: Globalization refers to the increased connectivity and integration of a wide variety of actors and spheres on a global scale, resulting in the compression of space and time.

Glocalization: Glocalization refers to the interconnection of the processes of globalization and localization. Popularized by Roland Robertson, the concept emphasizes how global processes are influenced (and sometimes subverted) by local applications, interpretations and adaptations.

Hegemony: This concept owes much to the writings of Antonio Gramsci. Hegemony, from the Greek word for 'rule' or 'leadership', expresses the ways ideology works in modern capitalist societies. A state of hegemony is accomplished when a specific social group establishes a consensus, which makes the power of the dominant group seem 'natural', accompanied by its ideas, institutions, and hierarchies. However, hegemony is a dynamic and constant process of renegotiation and redefinition of the ruling class's legitimacy and leadership, which can also be challenged, for example in moments of crises – popular demonstrations – when the subordinate groups can withdraw their support as the ideologies of the subordinate groups are not accommodated within the process of negotiation. Hegemony through consensus – as opposed to coercion – is constructed, maintained, and exercised through institutions such as the media, the family, the education system, and religion. These institutions might play a fundamental role in providing ideological frameworks for understanding the hegemonic order of society and the world as 'natural'.

Homo sacer: Literally, the sacred man in Latin, but meaning being ostracised by society, stripped of any rights – even the right to live. The Italian philosopher Giorgio Agamben (1988) used the metaphor of this ambiguous status in Roman society to point to the current predicament of stateless people, refugees, and asylum seekers.

Hybrid identity: This relates to the mixed identities of persons or ethnic groups, particularly those resulting from the historical encounters of Western culture (and forms of rule/power) with other peoples and cultures in colonial times, and more recently by immigration. The experience of 'hybrid identities' was viewed as being the consequence of the continued hegemony of white colonization, and implied exclusion and suffering. In more recent analyses, the ideas of hybridity and mixedness not only defy essentialist accounts of 'racial' identity, origins, and belonging, but also recognize the internal differences within mixed identities as well as the connections between those identities.

Hyperreality: Hyperreality is a notion that was introduced by semioticians such as Jean Baudrillard and Umberto Eco to signal a post-modern condition in which it is difficult to distinguish what is real from what is a simulation – often an enhanced reality.

Identity: Rather than a static and one-dimensional phenomenon, contemporary identities are fluid or intentionally defined, and in either case likely to be subject to ongoing negotiation in a number of elements, whether religion, ethnicity, language, gender, or nationality. In its dynamism, then, identity is defined not as essences or roots but as 'ongoing projects of becoming' or routes (Hall 1996). In addition, identities are constrained by multiple structures of power; for example, different religions can shape the nature of political regimes and regulate the behaviour and beliefs of individuals and groups. Identities also entail individual agency and must be grasped within a historical context (see Karner 2007).

Ideological model of war: The ideological model of war is based on a bipolar and antagonistic construction of the identities involved in a conflict, where the self is defined as inherently good and the enemy is articulated as inherently evil.

Ideology: Ideology is a contested and slippery concept. In common-sense terms, it relates to the realm of ideas and beliefs. Theoretically, Karl Marx applied it to refer to the ideas of the ruling class, which would always be the dominant ideas in a society. Ideology then is a set of ideas intended to serve the vested interests of the ruling class. The concept was refined by the Italian political thinker Antonio Gramsci and the French philosopher Louis Althusser, drawing on Marx's work. Gramsci relocated the discussion of ideology, at least partially, from the economic to the cultural sphere, in which the 'mediation' between 'real life' and ideologies takes place. For Gramsci, ideology is found in the 'common-sense' views operating at the ordinary daily life level and particularly through language, which reproduce both ruling-class ideas and progressive thinking. For Althusser ideology is a set of values, which provides a form of practical knowledge to help individuals to make sense of the world.

Information and communication technologies: Information and communication technologies (ICTs) are networked technologies that enable the convergence of information provision (the press, audiovisual media content, etc.), telecommunication and informatics. Often the term ICTs is used as a synonym for the Internet. However, mobile telephones, MP3 players, and satellite technology are also increasingly being categorized as ICTs.

Infotainment: Infotainment joins two signifiers that until recently were kept very separate, namely information and entertainment. The use of this term signals the increased interpenetration of both media genres: more entertainment in news broadcasts, but also more information in entertainment programmes.

Internet governance: The Internet is a global medium, but its root file, comprising most common domain names and basic routeings, is controlled by a US-based semi-private organization, the Internet Corporation for Assigned Names and Numbers (ICANN). Internet governance deals with how this global information and communication network is managed and which actors should or do exert oversight. Internet governance was among the most contentious issues debated during the WSIS. Oversight remains with ICANN, but a permanent Internet Governance Forum was established. This forum, comprising state, market and civil society actors, can debate any issue relating to internet governance, but has an advisory role only.

Jamming: Jamming was used to indicate disruption and interference to military radio communication signals. It was first practised by the German Army in the First World War and perfected by the Krestyaninova Section of the Soviet Ministry of Communications during the cold war. The term is used in connection with the Citizen Band (CB) culture to refer to the hijacking of radio broadcasts or interruptions to ongoing conversations. Cultural jamming entered popular discourse through the 'audio-Dada' band Negativland's cassette recording entitled *JamCon'84*, which was released in 1985 and reissued on CD in 1994. It refers to *détournement* as a counter-technique to the dominant consumer brand-oriented culture.

MacBride report: The so-called MacBride report was the final report of the UNESCO

International Commission for the Study of Communication Problems, published in 1980 and reissued in 2004. It is a highly critical report which warns of the dangers of media concentration and denounces the asymmetrical flows of information between North and South. The report called for a more balanced New World Information and Communication Order (NWICO) and introduced the right to communicate. The NWICO and the right to communicate were highly debated at the time and led to the USA and the UK withdrawing from UNESCO. UNESCO officially abandoned the NWICO in 1989.

Mailing lists: Mailing lists are e-mail-based tools that allow any subscriber to the list to post a message to all other subscribers. Some mailing lists have a moderator who serves as a gate-keeper to what gets forwarded and what does not; others are unmoderated. Mailing lists have become powerful tools for mobilization, networking practices, deliberation, and the distribution of very specialized and/or alternative information and discourses.

Media-centred media models: Models that theorize, describe and/or explain media structures, practices, and ideologies in ways that treat the media system as isolated from society and other societal systems.

Mesomobilization: The concept of mesomobilization refers to networking between civil society organizations and was introduced by Gerhards and Rucht (1992).

Metadata: Metadata are structured data describing other data in order to facilitate the retrieval or utilization of the latter.

Mil-blogs: Mil-blogs are the weblogs of soldiers, whether on tours of duty or not. They have to some extent replaced the writing of letters to the 'home front', and are accessible to many more people than family and close friends.

Objectivity: Objectivity is a multilayered value that supports the journalistic claim to truth. Following Westerståhl (1983), we can distinguish two core dimensions, factuality and impartiality, each of which has two components. The components of factuality are relevance and truthfulness; the components of impartiality are balance and neutrality.

Opsec: Operational security usually refers to the non-disclosure or classifying of factual information that could jeopardize specific military operations.

Parody: In Greek poetry, parody referred to the satirical, mocking imitation of a style or narrative of a well-known epic poem. The parody became a frequently used technique in literature, film, theatre, visual arts, and music.

Performance: Performance can mean many things; here it mainly refers to performance art, whereby the performance and the artists in the process of performing become the artwork itself. It gained prominence in the 1960s and 1970s, but can be traced back to Dadaism.

Pim Fortuyn: When Pim Fortuyn emerged on the Dutch political scene, he was by all standards a peculiar and polarizing figure. Dutch society and politics have always been marked by a high degree of political correctness and an integrative, consensual culture. Fortuyn broke with that tradition and combined an extreme *dandyesk* libertarianism with virulent anti-Islam discourses, thereby disrupting the implicit Dutch political codes. His rhetorical talents and polarizing anti-establishment discourses thrust him centre-stage in the May 2002 Dutch political campaign, during which he was fatally shot when leaving a TV studio in Hilversum by a radical environmentalist activist.

Policy: A policy is an articulation of general principles on which a government or public body bases its actions. The concrete implementation of a policy reveals itself in the precise regulatory arrangements that are decided upon.

Power: Causal models of power focus on decision-making processes and the ability of actors to achieve their objectives despite the resistance of others. Later versions of these models also incorporate the ability to implement non-decisions (at a manifest level) and no decisions (at a latent level). Strategic models of power emphasize the strategic behaviour of social actors combined with the inability of these actors to decide on the 'ultimate' outcome of their strategies, as counter-strategies will always impact on this negotiative power process.

Public broadcasting service: A public broadcasting service aims to provide citizens with accurate and balanced information, to educate citizens, and to entertain them. In most European countries public radio and TV held a monopoly on broadcasting until the 1990s when commercial radio and TV were allowed. In some countries the public service broadcaster is financed by commercial advertising, in others citizens pay a licence fee, and in yet others there is a mixed system of public and private sources of funds.

Public sphericules: This is a spatial metaphor for the fragmentation of the traditional public sphere and describes the increase of 'plural' public spheres in modern societies enhanced by ICTs. This phenomenon points to the decline of individual and community political participation in the public sphere as well as criticizing the traditional ideal of the 'public sphere' as a united and perfect political sphere. Public sphericules can be constituted within one nation-state, but they can also be transnational. They are small, and independent 'communities of information and participation', and formed by groups with common affinities and interests, which help these communities to restore a place for do-it-yourself politics – participation and recognition (see Gitlin 1998).

Regulation: Regulation is the practical implementation of policies through legislation and rules. It refers to the institutions and instruments with the power to enforce those rules. In relation to media and communication regulation, it enables, restricts, and is resisted simultaneously. Its implementation is policed by – ideally – independent regulatory bodies with the public interest at heart.

Relationism: Relationism is the intellectual position that claims that the identity of a process or entity is dependent on a wide range of other processes or entities, and that the set of characteristics is changeable over space and time.

Resistance: Resistance is the practice of non-acceptance, oriented against a dominant other. Resistance is relational and an indistinguishable component of power.

Rhizome: Rhizome is an organic metaphor developed by Gilles Deleuze and Félix Guattari to describe a heterogeneous, non-hierarchical and ever-changing network. The characteristics of the rhizome listed by Deleuze and Guattari (1987) are: connection, heterogeneity, multiplicity, asignifying rupture, cartography and decalcomania. The implication is that any point of a rhizome can be connected to any other point, but that the points are not necessarily connected, that in a rhizome there is no unity to serve as a pivot, that a rhizome might be ruptured, but will regenerate, that it is an adaptable map with multiple entryways. In this book the term 'rhizomatic' is used to capture the mobility and contingency of the organizational frameworks that characterize alternative media.

Self-management: Self-management relates to structural participation by citizens or communities in media organizations. This is opposed to content-related participation, where media professionals retain ultimate control over selection or editing. Self-management implies that a community or citizens have full control of their own self-representation and the editing and distribution of their self-produced content.

Society-centred media models: These are models that theorize, describe, and/or explain media structures, practices, and ideologies in ways that embed the media system in society as a whole and include the relationships of the media system with other societal systems.

Sweatshop: Originally used to describe small or medium-sized companies producing fabrics, clothing, footballs, etc. whose workers received very low wages and worked in deplorable conditions. Child labour is often associated with sweatshops, but this need not necessarily be the case.

Tactical media: Tactical media are a form of *détournement* that goes momentarily inside the mainstream media frame to turn against it with a vengeance. De Certeau (1984: xix) defines a tactic as 'insinuat[ing] itself into the other's place, fragmentarily, without taking it over in its entirety, without being able to keep it at a distance'. The tactical use of media is seen here as a provocative act of resistance towards corporate, state or interstate actors.

Third voice: The third voice refers to groups, organizations, and communities independent of market and state. They ideally voice the interests of citizens from a non-institutional and not-for-profit and civil society perspective.

Translocalization: Similar to glocalization, translocalization describes how local processes are influenced by other processes that exceed the local. However, in contrast to glocalization, translocalization takes the local (and not the global) as its starting point, to show how localized processes transcend the local while at the same time remaining embedded in it.

Transnational media: Until the early 1980s, media systems in Western countries worked mostly inside their national borders with control over the number of foreign programmes shown. Two factors have worked to change this scenario: firstly, the new media regulatory mechanisms (media policies) driven by economic market interests aimed at expanding audiovisual spaces and markets beyond the boundaries of national communities; secondly, the rise of new distribution technologies, such as satellite television, which made transnational broadcasting systems a reality and, consequently, created new transnational and global audiovisual markets. The Internet has an important role as a transnational platform for the production and dissemination of information and entertainment. These new audiovisual spaces now co-exist across the old national media landscapes.

Transnationalism: Transnationalism refers to social practices that transcend the national (and the nation-state), but at the same time remain – in contrast to internationalism – embedded in the national and the realities of nation-states.

Weblog: A weblog or blog is an online diary that allows its author to share his or her views on a variety of issues with a potentially global audience. Not all blogs are political in the strict sense, but many can be classified as such if a broad definition of the political is used. Also elite persons have adopted the weblog as a way to communicate independently.

Wikipedia: A wiki is an open-source online platform that allows for the storing of information on any subject. It makes extensive use of hyperlinks. Another feature is that its content is provided and updated by an online community of users. In principle any user can amend or supplement the postings of others, potentially producing richer and more balanced information on the subject. The most famous wiki is Wikipedia, an online encyclopedia produced by its users. Wikipedia, however, suffers from a difficult tension between the openness of the system and editorial control.

WSIS: The World Summit on the Information Society was an ITU-organized world summit held in two stages, phase 1 in 2003 in Geneva and phase 2 in 2005 in Tunis. The WSIS was charged with responding to growing concerns about a range of issues related to the information society (UN Resolution 56/183, December 2001). The WSIS was innovative in terms of participation as it was the first world summit to which civil society was granted access to the preparatory process. Although not very successful in terms of its impact on the formal outcomes of the Summit, civil society did manifest itself as an important actor in the process, developing counter-discourses (WSIS Civil Society Plenary, 2003) and enacting strategies of resistance both inside and outside the summit (see Cammaerts and Carpentier 2005).

ACRONYMS

AM	Amplitude modulation
CAE	Critical Art Ensemble
CD	Compact disc
CID	Criminal Investigation Command
CMA	Community Media Association
CRA	Community Radio Association
CRID	Centre de Recherches Informatique et Droit [Research Center for Informatics and Law]
CRIS	Communication Rights In the Information Society
CSC	Communication for Social Change
DIY	do it yourself
DVD	Digital versatile disc
EU	European Union
FACR	Fonds d'Aide à la Création Radiophonique [Fund to Aid Radiophonic Creations]
FCC	Federal Communication Commission
FM	Frequency modulation
ICTs	Information and Communication Technologies
IG	Internet governance
IMCs	Independent media centres
MST	Movimento dos Trabalhadores Rurais Sem Terra
NWICO	New World Information and Communication Order
OECD	Organization for Economic Cooperation and Development
UN	United Nations
UNESCO	United Nations Educational, Scientific and Cultural Organization
WGIG	Working Group on Internet Governance
WSIS	World Summit on the Information Society

FURTHER READING

Chapter 1: Four approaches to alternative media

Community and participation

- Wasko, J. and Mosco, V. (eds) (1992) *Democratic Communications in the Information Age*. Norwood, NJ: Ablex.
- Couldry, N. (2002) *Media Rituals: A Critical Approach*. London: Routledge.
- Howley, K. (2005) *Community Media. People, Places, and Communication Technologies*. Cambridge: Cambridge University Press.
- Fraser, C. and Estrada, S. R. (2001) *Community Radio Handbook*. Paris: UNESCO. http://www.unesco.org/webworld/publications/community_radio_handbook.pdf.

Alternative media

- Atton, C. (2002) *Alternative Media*. London: Sage.
- Rodriguez, C. (2001) *Fissures in the Mediascape: An International Study of Citizens' Media*. Creskill, NJ: Hampton Press.
- Downing, J., with T.V. Ford, G. Gil and L. Stein (2001) *Radical Media. Rebellious Communication and Social Movements*. London: Sage.
- Kidd, D. (1999) The value of alternative media, *Peace Review* 11(1): 113–19.

Civil society

- Cohen, J.L. and Arato, A. (1992) *Civil Society and Political Theory*. Cambridge, MA: MIT Press.

- Alexander, J.C. (ed.) (1998) *Real Civil Societies. Dilemmas of Institutionalization*. London: Sage.
- Rodriguez, C. (2001) *Fissures in the Mediascape. An International Study of Citizens' Media*, Cresskill, NJ: Hampton Press.
- Hintz, A. (2007) Civil society media at the WSIS: a new actor in global communication governance?, in B. Cammaerts and N. Carpentier (eds), *Reclaiming the Media: Communication Rights and Expanding Democratic Media Roles*. Bristol: Intellect, pp. 243–64.

Rhizome

- Deleuze, G. and Guattari, F. (1987) Introduction: Rhizome, in *A Thousand Plateaus. Capitalism and Schizophrenia*, Minneapolis: University of Minnesota Press, pp. 3–25.
- Sakolsky, R. (1998) Introduction: Rhizomatic radio and the great stampede, in R. Sakolsky and S. Dunifer (eds) *Seizing the Airwaves: A Free Radio Handbook*. Oakland, CA: AK Press. http://www.infoshop.org/texts/seizing/intro.html.

Chapter 3: Community approaches in Western radio policies

- Fairchild, C. (2001) *Community Radio and Public Culture. Being an examination of media access and equity in the nations of North America*. Cresskill, NJ: Hampton Press.
- Girard, B. (ed.) (1992) *A Passion for Radio: Radio Waves and Community*. Montreal: Black Rose Books. http://www.comunica.org/passion/.
- Jankowski, N., Prehn, O. and Stappers, J. (eds) (1992) *The People's Voice. Local Radio and Television in Europe*. London, Paris, and Rome: John Libbey and Company Ltd.
- Lewis, P. (ed.)(1993) *Alternative Media: Linking Global and Local*. Paris: UNESCO.

Chapter 4: Diasporas and alternative media practices

- Banja, S. (2006) *Reading Bollywood: The Young Audience and Hindi Films*. Basingstone: Palgrave Press.
- Bird, S.E. (2003) *The Audience in Everyday Life: Living in a Media World*. London: Routledge.
- Fisher, C. (2006) *Black & Black: Urban Youth Films and the Multicultural Audience*. Madison, WI: Scarecrow Press.
- Karner, C. (2007) *Ethnicity and Everyday Life*. London: Routledge.

Chapter 5: Blogs in the second Iraqi War: alternative media challenging the mainstream?

- Mirzoeff, N. (2005) *Watching Babylon. The War in Iraq and Global Visual Culture*. New York: Routledge.
- Sontag, S. (2003) *Regarding the Pain of Others*. New York: Farrar, Straus and Giroux.

- Taylor, P.M. (1995) *Munitions of the Mind: A History of Propaganda from the Ancient World to the Present Era*. Manchester: Manchester University Press.
- Zelizer, B. and Allan, S. (2002) (eds) *Journalism after September 11*. New York: Routledge.

Chapter 6: Ethnic-religious groups and alternative journalism

- Georgiou, M. (2006) *Diaspora, Identity and the Media: Diasporic Transnationalism and Mediated Spatialities*. Cresskill, NJ: Hampton Press.
- Jerkins, H. (2006) *Convergence Culture*. New York: NYU Press.
- Riggins, S. (1992) *Ethnic Minority Media: An International Perspective*. London: Sage.
- Rodriguez, A. (1999) *Making Latino News: Race, Language, Class*. Thousand Oaks, CA: Sage.

Chapter 7: Online participation and the public sphere: civil society mailing lists and forums

- Dahlgren, P. (2005) The Internet, public spheres, and political communication: dispersion and deliberation, *Political Communication*, 22: 147–62.
- Dahlberg, L. (2001) The Internet and democratic discourse: exploring the prospects of online deliberative forums extending the public sphere, *Information, Communication & Society*, 4(4): 613–33.
- Wilhelm, A. (2000) *Democracy in the Digital Age: Challenges to Political Life in Cyberspace*. London: Routledge.
- Hill, K.A. and Hughes, J.E. (1998) *Cyberpolitics: Citizen Activism in the Age of the Internet*. Lanham, MD: Rowman and Littlefield.

Chapter 8: The Brazilian Landless Rural Workers' Movement : identity, action, and communication

- Phillips, P. (2003) *The Project Censored Guide to Alternative Media and Activism*. New York: Seven Stories Press.
- Prashad, V. and Ballve, T. (eds) (2006) *Dispatches from Latin America: On the Frontlines against Neo-liberalism*. Cambridge, MA: South End Press.
- Radford, B. (2003) *Media Myth Makers: How Journalists, Activists, and Advertisers Mislead Us*. New York: Prometheus Books.
- Tilly, C. and Tarrow, S. (2007) *Contentious Politics*. Boulder, CO: Paradigm.

Chapter 9: Translocalization, glocalization and the Internet: the RadioSwap project

- Appadurai, A. (1995) The production of locality, in R. Fardon (ed.) *Counterworks: Managing the Diversity of Knowledge*. New York: Routledge, pp. 204–25.

- Atton, C. (2004) *An Alternative Internet*. Edinburgh: Edinburgh University Press.
- Couldry, N., and Curran, J. (2003) *Contesting Media Power: Alternative Media in a Networked World*. Lanham, MD: Rowman and Littlefield.
- Jankowski, N., and Prehn, O. (2001) *Community Media in the Information Age: Perspectives and Prospects*. Cresskill, NJ: Hampton Press.

Chapter 10: Jamming the political: reverse-engineering, hacking the dominant codes

- Scott, A. and Street, J. (2001) From media politics to e-protest? The use of popular culture and new media in parties and social movements, in F. Webster (ed.) *Culture and Politics in the Information Age, A New Politics?* London: Routledge, pp. 32–51.
- Knabb, K. (1981) *Situationist International Anthology*, Berkeley CA: Bureau of Public Secrets. http://www.bopsecrets.org/SI/index.htm.
- Lasn, K. (2000) *Culture Jam: How to Reverse America's Suicidal Consumer Binge – and Why We Must*. New York: Quill.
- Frank, R. (2004) When the going gets tough, the tough go photoshopping: September 11 and the newslore of vengeance and victimisation, *New Media & Society*, 6(5): 633–58.

REFERENCES

Agamben, G. (1988) *Homo Sacer: Sovereign Power and Bare Life* (translated by D. Heller-Roazen). Stanford, CA: Stanford University Press.

Aksoy, A. and Robins, K. (2000) Thinking across spaces; transnational television from Turkey, *European Journal of Cultural Studies*, 3(3): 343–65.

Aksoy, A. and Robins, K. (2003) Banal transnationalism: The difference that television makes, in K.H. Karim (ed.) *The Media of Diaspora*. London: Routledge, pp. 89–104.

Alam, S. (2005) Recognizing Israel or selling out?, *Q-News*, 364: 24.

Allan, S. (1999) *News Culture*. Buckingham: Open University Press.

Allan, S. (2002) Reweaving the Internet: Online news of September 11, in B. Zelizer and S. Allan (eds) *Journalism after September 11*. New York: Routledge, pp. 119–40.

Almeida, P.D. and Lichbach, M.I. (2003) To the Internet, from the Internet: Comparative media coverage of transnational protests, *Mobilization*, 8(3): 249–72.

Alton-Scheidl, R., Micsik, A., Pataki, M., Reutz, W., Schmidt, J. and Thurner, T. (2005) StreamOnTheFly 2005: A peer-to-peer network for radio stations and podcasters. Paper presented at the 1st International Conference on Automated Production of Cross Media Content for Multi-channel Distribution (AXMEDIS), Florence, 30 November–2 December.

AMARC Europe (1994) *One Europe – Many Voices. Democracy and Access to Communication.* Conference report, AMARC-Europe Pan-European Conference of Community Radio Broadcasters, Ljubljana, Slovenia, 15–18 September. Sheffield: AMARC.

Ameli, S.R., Marandi, S.M., Ahmed, S., Kara, S. and Merali, A. (2005) *The British Media and Muslim Representation: The Ideology of Demonisation*. London: Islamic Human Rights Commission. http://www.ihrc.org.uk/file/1903718317.pdf (accessed 25 January 2007).

Amnesty International (2003) Iraq: The US must ensure humane treatment and access to justice for Iraqi detainees. Press release, 30 June. http://www.amnestyusa.org/countries/iraq/document.do?id=80256AB9000584F680256D52005AC567 (accessed 25 January 2007).

Anderson, B. (1983) *Imagined Communities: Reflections on the Origin and Spread of Nationalism*. London: Verso.

Ang, I. (1991) *Desperately Seeking the Audience*. London/New York: Routledge.

Ansari, A. (2005) Postscript: Panning Panorama, *Q-News*, 364: 15.

Appadurai, A. (1990) Disjuncture and difference in the global economy, *Public Culture*, 2(2): 1–24.

Appadurai, A. (1993) Disjuncture and difference in the global cultural economy, in B. Robbins (ed.) *The Phantom Public Sphere*. Minneapolis: University of Minnesota Press, pp. 269–95.

Appadurai, A. (1995) The production of locality, in R. Fardon (ed.) *Counterworks: Managing the Diversity of Knowledge*. London: Routledge, pp. 204–25.

Apple, J. (1993) The art of radio, in N. Strauss (ed.) *Radiotext(e)*. New York: Semiotext(e), pp. 307–9.

Arato, A. (1981) Civil society against the state: Poland 1980–81, *Telos*, 47: 23–47.

Atton, C. (2002) *Alternative Media*. London: Sage.

Atton, C. (2003) Ethical issues in alternative journalism, *Ethical Space*, 1(1): 26–31.

Atton, C. (2004) *An Alternative Internet*. Edinburgh: Edinburgh University Press.

Atton, C. (2005) Sourcing routines and representation in alternative journalism: a case study approach, *Journalism Studies*, 6(6): 347–59.

Bailey, O.G. (2007) Latin Americans, identities, and media in Britain, in O.G. Bailey, M. Georgiou and R. Harindranath (eds) *Transnational Lives and the Media: Re-imagining Diaspora*. London: Palgrave.

Bailey, O.G. and Harindranath, R. (2005) Racialized 'other': the representation of asylum seekers in the news media, in S. Allan (ed.) *Journalism: Critical Issues*. Maidenhead: Open University Press, pp. 274–86.

Bailey, O.G. and Harindranath, R. (2006) Ethnic minorities, cultural difference, and the cultural politics of communication, *International Journal of Media and Cultural Politics*, 2(2): 299–316.

Balibar, B. (1991) The nation form, in E. Balibar and I. Wallerstein (eds) *Race, Nation, Class*. London: Verso, pp. 1–24.

Banja, S. (2006) *Reading Bollywood: The Young Audience and Hindi Films*. Basingstone: Palgrave Press.

Barber, B. (1984) *Strong Democracy: Participatory Politics for a New Age*, 4th edn. Berkeley and Los Angeles: University of California Press.

Barber, B. (2003) Which technology and which democracy?, in H. Jenkins and Thorburn, D. (eds) *Democracy and New Media*. Cambridge, MA: MIT Press, pp. 33–48.

Barnett, C. (2003) *Culture and Democracy: Media, Space and Representation*. Edinburgh: Edinburgh University Press.

Barry, B. (2001) *Culture and Equality: An Egalitarian Critique of Multiculturalism*. Cambridge: Polity Press.

Baudrillard, J. (1987) *The Ecstacy of Communication*. New York: Semiotext(e).

Beiles, S., Burroughs, W.S., Corso, G. and Gysin, B. (1960) *Minutes to Go*. Paris: Two Cities Editions.

Benford, R.D. and Snow, D.A. (2000) Framing processes and social movements: an overview and assessment, *Annual Review of Sociology*, 26: 611–39.

Benjamin, M. (2006) Salon exclusive: The Abu Ghraib files. Salon.com, 16 February. http://www.salon.com/news/feature/2006/02/16/abu_ghraib/index.html (accessed 25 January 2007).

Benson, R. (2003) Commercialism and critique: California's alternative weeklies, in N. Couldry and J. Curran (eds) *Contesting Media Power: Alternative Media in a Networked World*. Lanham, MD: Rowman and Littlefield, pp. 111–28.

Berger, C. (1998) *Campos em confronto: a terra e o texto*. Porto Alegre: Universidade Federal do Rio Grande do Sul Press.

Berrigan, F.J. (1977) *Access: Some Western Models of Community Media*. Paris: UNESCO.

Berrigan, F.J. (1979) *Community Communications: The Role of Community Media in Development*, Reports and Papers on Mass Communication no. 90. Paris: UNESCO.

Berry, C. (1995) The letter U and the numeral 2, *Wired*, 3.01 (January).

Beveridge, Lord (1951) *Report of the Broadcasting Committee – 1949*, Cmnd 8116. London: HMSO.

Billig, M. (1995) *Banal Nationalism*. London: Sage.

Bird, S.E. (2003) *The Audience in Everyday Life: Living in a Media World*. London: Routledge.

Blackwell, C.W. (2003) Athenian democracy: an overview, in C.W. Blackwell (ed.) *Dēmos: Classical Athenian Democracy* The Stoa: A Consortium for Scolary Publication in the Humanities. http://www.stoa.org/projects/demos/home (accessed 25 January 2007).

Bourdieu, P. (1985) The social space and the genesis of groups, *Theory and Society*, 14(6): 723–44.

Boyd, A. (2002) Truth is a virus: Meme warfare and the Billionaires for Bush (or Gore), in S. Duncombe (ed.) *Cultural Resistance*, London: Verso, pp. 369–78.

Brecht, B. (1983) Radio as a means of communication: a talk of the function of radio, in A. Mattelart and S. Siegelaub (eds) *Communication and Class Struggle – Volume 2: Liberation, Socialism*. New York and Paris: International General and International Mass Media Research Center, pp. 169–71.

Buzzell, C. (2005) *My War: Killing Time in Iraq*. New York: GP Putnam's Sons.

Cage, J. (1966) *Silence: Lectures and Writings*. Cambridge, MA: MIT Press.

Caldwell, J. T. (2003) Alternative media in suburban plantation culture, *Media, Culture and Society*, 25: 647–67.

Calhoun, C. (1992) Introduction: Habermas and the public sphere, in C. Calhoun (ed.) *Habermas and the Public Sphere*, pp. 1–48. Cambridge, MA: MIT Press.

Cammaerts, B. (2005a) ICT-usage among transnational social movements in the networked society – to organise, to mobilise and to debate, in R. Silverstone (ed.) *Media, Technology and Everyday Life in Europe: From Information to Communication*. Aldershot: Ashgate, pp. 53–72.

Cammaerts, B. (2005b) Through the looking glass: Civil society participation in the WSIS and the dynamics between online/offline interaction, *Communications & Strategies*, Special Issue, WSIS Tunis: 151–74.

Cammaerts, B. (2007a) Jamming the political: beyond counter-hegemonic practices, *Continuum*, 21(1): 71–90.

Cammaerts, B. (2007b) Media and communication strategies of glocalised activists: beyond media-centric thinking, in B. Cammaerts and N. Carpentier (eds) *Reclaiming the Media: Communication Rights and Expanding Democratic Media Roles*. Bristol: Intellect, pp. 265–88.

Cammaerts, B. and Carpentier, N. (2005) The unbearable lightness of full participation in a global context: WSIS and civil society participation, in J. Servaes and N. Carpentier (eds) *Towards a Sustainable Information Society: Beyond WSIS*. Bristol: Intellect, pp. 17–49.

Cammaerts, B. and Carpentier, N. (eds) (2007) *Reclaiming the Media. Communication Rights and Democratic Media Roles*. Bristol: Intellect.

Cammaerts, B. and Van Audenhove, L. (2005) Online political debate, unbounded citizenship and the problematic nature of a transnational public sphere, *Political Communication*, 22(2): 179–96.

Cammaerts, B., Van Audenhove, L., Nulens, G. and Pauwels, C. (eds) (2003) *Beyond the Digital Divide: Reducing Exclusion and Fostering Inclusion*, Brussels: VUB Press.

Carpentier, N. (1994) ORCA: De paradox van de kleinschaligheid, *Samenleving en Politiek*, 1(8): 40–6.

Carpentier, N. (2003) BBC's Video Nation as a participatory media practice. Signifying everyday life, cultural diversity and participation in an on-line community, *International Journal of Cultural Studies*, 6(4): 425–47.

Carpentier, N. (2004) The identity of the television audience: Towards the articulation of the television audience as a discursive field, in N. Carpentier, C. Pauwels and O. Van Oost (eds), *Het On(be)grijpbare Publiek / The Ungraspable Audience*. Brussels: VUB Press, pp. 95–122.

Carpentier, N. (2007a) Expanding community media beyond the confinements of locality. Translocalism and the growth of the communicative rhizome, media and change, in E. Vartanova (ed.) *The Media and Changes*. In press.

Carpentier, N. (2007b) Fighting discourses. Discourse theory, war and representations of the 2003 Iraqi War, in Sarah Maltby and Richard Keeble (eds) *Communicating War: Memory, Media and Military*. Cambridge: Cambridge Scholars Press. Bury St Edmunds: Abramis. In press.

Carpentier, N. (2007c) Participation and interactivity: changing perspectives. The construction of an integrated model on access, interaction and participation, in V. Nightingale and T. Dwyer (eds) *New Media Worlds*. Sydney, Oxford University Press. In press.

Carpentier, N. and Cammaerts, B. (2006) Hegemony, democracy, agonism and journalism: An interview with Chantal Mouffe, *Journalism Studies* 7(6): 964–75.

Carpentier, N., Lie, R. and Servaes, J. (2003a) Making community media work, in J. Servaes (ed.) *Approaches to Development. Studies on Communication for Development*. Paris: UNESCO.

Carpentier, N., Lie, R. and Servaes, J. (2003b) Is there a role and place for 'community media' in the new remit?, in G.F. Lowe and T. Hujanen (eds) *Broadcasting and Convergence: New Articulations of the Public Remit*. Gothenburg: Nordicom, pp. 239–54.

Carpentier, N., Lie, R. and Servaes, J. (2003c) Community media – muting the democratic media discourse?, *Continuum*, 17(1): 51–68.

Carpentier, N., with Colsoul, N., Gonzalez, N., Fluit, A., Schuerwegen, L. and Vanhaverbeke, J. (2006) *Een gebruikersevaluatie van het RadioSwap-Project uit de periode 2004–2005*. Brussel: CSC-KUB.

Carruthers, S. (2000) *The Media at War. Communication and Conflict in the Twentieth Century*. London: Macmillan.

Carty, V. (2001) The Internet and grassroots politics: Nike, the athletic apparel industry and the anti-sweatshop campaign, *Tamara*, 1(2): 34–47.

Casey, E. (1997) *The Fate of Place*. Berkeley: University of California Press.

Castells, M. (1996) *The Information Age – Economy, Society, and Culture. Vol. I: Rise of the Network Society*. Cambridge, MA and Oxford: Blackwell.

Cecil, M. (2000) Editor's introduction, *Journal of Communication Inquiry*, 24(4): 355–56.

Chelebi, M. (2005) Travelcard to Heaven, *Q-News*, 364: 9.

Chesters, G. and Welsh, I. (2006) *Complexity and Social Movements: Multitudes at the Edge of Chaos*. London: Routledge.

Cheval, J.-J. (1997) *Les radios en France. Histoire, état et enjeux*. Rennes : Editions Apogée.

Christiansen, C.C. (2004) New media consumption among immigrants in Europe: The relevance of diaspora, *Ethnicities*, 4(2): 185–207.

Christopoulou, N. and De Leeuw, S. (2005) Children making media: Constructions of home and belonging, in J. Knörr (ed.) *Childhood and Migration. From Experience to Agency*. Bielefeld: Transcript Verlag, pp. 113–35.

ChuckO (2002) The sad decline of Indymedia, *Infoshop News*, 8 December. http://www.infoshop.org/inews/article.php?story=02/12/08/2553147 (accessed 25 January 2007).

Clark, D.B. (1973) The concept of community: a reexamination, *Sociological Review*, 21: 397–417.

Coggins, S.-A. M. (2004) On blogs, blogging and bloggers from the Iraqi blogger-turned-author. http://weblogs.about.com/od/bestofblogsdirectory/a/salampax2.htm (accessed 25 January 2007, later removed).

Cohen, A.P. (1985) *The Symbolic Construction of Community*. London: Routledge.

Cohen, J.L. and Arato, A. (1992) *Civil Society and Political Theory*. Cambridge, MA: MIT Press.

Cole, L. (2003) On the aestetic agenda of the antiwar movement, *Post Road Magazine*, no. 7. http://www.postroadmag.com/7/criticism/OnAestheticAgenda.phtml (accessed 25 January 2007).

Comedia (1984) The alternative press: the development of underdevelopment. *Media, Culture and Society*, 6(2): 95–102.

Comissão Pastoral da Terra (2007) Dados da CPT revelam que impunidade mantém violência no campo. http://www.cptnac.com.br/?system=news&action=read&id=1835&eid=248 (accessed 11 June 2007).

Community Learning and Development Partnership (2004) Notes from Community Radio Meeting, 12 May, Newbattle Community Learning Association, Midlothian. http://www.midlothianradio.org.uk/12maynotes.htm (accessed 25 January 2007).

Cooper, C. (2004) Army blogger's tales attract censors' eyes, *Wall Street Journal*, 9 September: B1.

Corner, J. (1996) Reappraising reception: Aims, concepts and methods, in J. Curran and M. Gurevitch (eds) *Mass Media and Society*. London: Arnold, pp. 280–304.

Couldry, N. (2002) *Media Rituals: A Critical Approach*. London: Routledge.

Couldry, N. (2003) Beyond the hall of mirrors? Some theoretical reflections on the global contestation of media power, in N. Couldry and J. Curran (eds) *Contesting Media Power: Alternative Media in a Networked World*. Lanham, MD: Rowman and Littlefield, pp. 39–54.

Couldry, N. and Curran, J. (eds) (2003) *Contesting Media Power: Alternative Media in a Networked World*. Lanham, MD: Rowman and Littlefield.

Cox, R.W. (1999) Civil society at the turn of the millennium: prospects for an alternative world order, *Review of International Studies*, 25(1): 3–28.

Critical Art Ensemble (2002) *Digital Resistance*. New York: Autonomedia.

Csordas, T. (1993) Somatic modes of attention, *Cultural Anthropology*, 8(2): 135–56.

Cunningham, S. (2001) Popular media as public 'sphericules' for diasporic communities, *International Journal of Cultural Studies*, 4(2): 131–47.

Cunningham, S. and Sinclair, J. (eds) (2000) *Floating Lives: The Media and Asian Diasporas*. St Lucia: University of Queensland Press.

Curran, J. and Park, M.-J. (2000) *De-Westernizing Media Studies*. London: Routledge.

Dahlberg, L. (2001) The Internet and democratic discourse: Exploring the prospects of online deliberative forums extending the public sphere, *Information, Communication & Society* 4(4): 613–33.

Dahlgren, P. (2000) The Internet and the democratisation of civic culture, *Political Communication*, 17(4): 335–40.

Dahlgren, P. (2005) The Internet, public spheres, and political communication: dispersion and deliberation, *Political Communication*, 22: 147–62.

Dale, S. (1996) *McLuhan's Children: The Greenpeace Message and the Media*. Toronto: Between the Lines.

Dalle, M. (2006) Les radios libres, utopie 'deleuzoguattarienne', *French Cultural Studies*, 17(1): 55–72.

Dayan, D. (1999) Media and diasporas, in J. Gripsrud (ed.) *Television and Common Knowledge*. London: Routledge, pp. 18–33.

De Block, L., Buckingham, D., Holzwarth, P. and Niesyto, H. (eds) (2004) Visions across cultures: Migrant children using visual images to communicate. Report for EC-funded project CHICAM (Children In Communication about Migration).

de Certeau, M. (1984) *The Practice of Everyday Life*. Berkeley: University of California Press. http://www.ubu.com/papers/de_certeau.html (accessed 25 January 2007).

De Leeuw, S. and Rydin, I. (2007) Diasporic mediated spaces, in O.G. Bailey, M. Georgiou and R. Harindranath (eds) *Transnational Lives and the Media: Re-imagining Diaspora*. London: Palgrave.

DeBatto, D. (2004) Whitewashing torture? Salon.com, 8 December. http://dir.salon.com/story/news/feature/2004/12/08/coverup/index.html (accessed 25 January 2007).

Debord, G. (1967) *La Societé du spectacle*. Paris: Buchet/Chastel. Translated as *The Spectacle Society*. http://www.nothingness.org/SI/debord.html (accessed 25 January 2007).

Debord, G. and Wolman, G.L. (1956) Mode d'emploi du détournement, *Les Lèvres Nues*, no. 8. http://membres.lycos.fr/gviolet/Detournement.html (accessed 25 January 2007).

Deleuze, G. and Guattari, F. (1987) *A Thousand Plateaus. Capitalism and Schizophrenia*. Minneapolis: University of Minnesota Press.

della Porta, D. and Diani, M. (1999) *Social Movements: An Introduction*. Malden, MA: Blackwell.

della Porta, D., Andretta, M., Mosca, L. and Reiter, H. (2006) *Globalization from Below; Transnational Activists and Protest Networks*. Minneapolis: University of Minnesota Press.

DeLuca, K.M. and Peeples, J. (2002) From public sphere to public screen: democracy, activism, and the 'violence' of Seattle, *Critical Studies in Media Communication*, 19(2): 125–51.

Dentith, S. (2000) *Parody*. London: Routledge.

Dery, M. (1993) *Culture Jamming: Hacking, Slashing and Sniping in the Empire of Signs*. Open Magazine pamphlet series. Westfield, NJ: Open Media.

Deuze, M. (2003) The web and its journalisms: Considering the consequences of different types of news media online, *New Media & Society*, 5(2): 203–30.

Deuze, M. (2005) Towards professional participatory storytelling in journalism and advertising, *First Monday*, 10(7). http://www.firstmonday.org/issues/issue10_7/deuze/index.html

Deuze, M. (2006a) Ethnic media, community media and participatory culture, *Journalism*, 7(3): 262–80.

Deuze, M. (2006b) Participation, remediation, bricolage: Considering principal components of a digital culture, *The Information Society*, 22: 63–75.

Dirlik, A. (1999) Place-based imagination: Globalism and the politics of place, *Review: A Journal of the Fernand Braudel Center*, 22(2): 151–87.

Downey, J. and Fenton, N. (2003) New media, counter publicity and the public sphere, *New Media and Society*, 15(2): 185–202.

Downing, J. (2003) Audiences and readers of alternative media: the absent lure of the virtually unknown, *Media, Culture & Society* 25(5): 625–45.

Downing, J. and Husband, C. (2005) *Representing Race: Racisms, Ethnicities and Media*. London: Sage.

Downing, J., with Ford, T.V., Gil, G. and Stein, L. (2001) *Radical Media: Rebellious Communication and Social Movements*. London: Sage.

Drijvers, J. (1992) Belgium: So many ways to run a railroad, in N. Jankowski, O. Prehn and J. Stappers (eds) *The People's Voice: Local Radio and Television in Europe*. London, Paris, and Rome: John Libbey and Company, pp. 104–22.

Dunn, R.G. (1998) *Identity Crises: A Social Critique of Postmodernity*. Minneapolis: University of Minnesota Press.

Eagleton, T. (1991) *Ideology: An Introduction*. London: Verso.

Ellis, B. (2002) Making Big Apple Crumble: The role of humor in constructing a global response to disaster, *New Directions in Folkore*, 6. http://www.temple.edu/isllc/newfolk/bigapple/bigapple1.html (accessed 25 January 2007).

Escobar, A. (2000) Place, power, and networks in globalisation and postdevelopment, in K.G. Wilkins (ed.) *Redeveloping Communication for Social Change. Theory, Practice and Power*. Lanham, MD: Rowman and Littlefield.

Fairchild, C. (2001) *Community Radio and Public Culture. Being an examination of media access and equity in the nations of North America*. Cresskill, NJ: Hampton Press.

Fish, S. (1980) *Is There a Text in This Class? The Authority of Interpretative Communities*. Cambridge, MA: Harvard University Press.

Fisher, C. (2006) *Black & Black: Urban Youth Films and the Multicultural Audience*. Madison, WI: Scarecrow Press.

Fleras, A. and Kunz, J. C. (2001) *Media and Minorities*. Toronto: TEP.

Fonds d'Aide á la Création Radiophonique (2005) Bilan du Fonds d'aide à la création radiophonique. Brussels: Ministère de la Communauté Française.

Fosella, V.J. (2005) Rep. Fossella criticizes top Belgium official for childish anti-American prank. Press Release, 25 February. http://www.house.gov/fossella/Press/press2005/pr050225_belgium. html (accessed 25 January 2007).

Foucault, M. (1975) *Discipline and Punish: The Birth of the Prison*. New York: Random House.

Foucault, M. (1978) *The History of Sexuality, Vol. I: An Introduction*, translated by Robert Hurley. New York: Pantheon.

Foucault, M. (1980) *Power/Knowledge*. Brighton: Harvester Wheatsheaf.

Frank, R. (2004) When the going gets tough, the tough go photoshopping: September 11 and the newslore of vengeance and victimisation. *New Media & Society*, 6(5): 633–58.

Fraser, C. and Estrada, S. R. (2001) *Community Radio Handbook*. Paris: UNESCO. http://www.unesco.org/webworld/publications/community_radio_handbook.pdf (accessed 25 January 2007).

Fraser, N. (1990) Rethinking the public sphere, *Social Text*, 25/26: 56–80.

Fraser, N. (1992) Rethinking the public sphere: A contribution to the critique of actually existing democracy, in C. Calhoun (ed.) *Habermas and the Public Sphere*. Cambridge, MA: MIT Press, pp. 109–42.

Freire, P. (1970) *Pedagogy of the Oppressed*. New York: Continuum.

Galtung, J., Jacobsen, C.G. and Brand-Jacobsen, K.F. (2001) *Searching for Peace*. London: Pluto Press.

Gamson, W.A. and Wolfsfeld, G. (1993) Movements and media as interacting systems, *Annals of the American Academy of Political and Social Movements*, 526: 114–27.

Georgiou, M (2006) *Diaspora, Identity and the Media: Diasporic, Transnationalism and Mediated Spatialities*. Cresskill, NJ: Hampton Press.

Georgiou, M. (2005) Diasporic media across Europe: Multicultural societies and the universalism-particularism continuum. *Journal of Ethnic and Migration Studies*, 31(3): 481–98.

Gerhards, J. and Rucht, D. (1992) Mesomobilization. Organizing and framing in two protest campaigns in West Germany, *American Journal of Sociology*, 98: 555–96.

Gibson, W. (1984) *Neuromancer*. London: Grafton.

Gillespie, M. (1989) Technology and tradition: Audio-visual culture among South Asian families in West London, *Cultural Studies*, 3 (2): 226–39.

Gillespie, M. (1994) *Television, Ethnicity and Social Change*. London: Routledge.

Gillespie, M. (ed.) (2005) *Media Audiences*. Maidenhead: Open University Press.

Gilroy, P. (1987) *There Ain't No Black in the Union Jack*. London: Hutchinson.

Girard, B. (ed.) (1992) *A Passion for Radio: Radio Waves and Community*, Montréal: Black Rose Books. http://www.comunica.org/passion/ (accessed 25 January 2007).

Gitlin, T. (1998) Public spheres or public sphericules, in T. Liebes and J. Curran (eds) *Media, Ritual and Identity*. London: Routledge, pp. 168–74.

Gohn, M. d. G. (1997) *Os Sem Terra, ONGs e Cidadania*. São Paulo: Cortez.

Gore, A. (1994) The global information infrastructure: forging a new Athenian age of democracy, *Intermedia*, 22(2): 4–7.

Gramsci, A. (1971) *Selections from the Prison Notebooks of Antonio Gramsci*. London: Lawrence and Wishart.

Greenpeace (2002) StopE\$\$O parody logo competition, 24 July. http://activism.greenpeace.org/cybercentre/gpi/Climate/1027510006/1027510006.html (accessed 25 January 2007).

Guattari, F. (1978) Les radios libres populaires, *La Nouvelle Critique*, 115: 77–9.

Gumucio, D.A. (2001) *Making Waves*. New York: Rockefeller Foundation.

Habermas, J. (1992) Further reflections on the public sphere, in C. Calhoun (ed.) *Habermas and the Public Sphere*, Cambridge, MA: MIT Press, pp. 421–61.

Hall, S. (1992a) The question of cultural identity, in S. Hall, D. Held and T. McGrew (eds) *Modernity and its Futures*. Cambridge: Polity Press, pp 210–322.

Hall, S. (1992b) The West and the rest, in S. Hall and B. Gieben (eds) *Formations of Modernity*. Cambridge: Polity Press/Open University Press, pp. 275–332.

Hall, S. (1996) Signification, representation, ideology: Althusser and the post-structuralist debates, in J. Curran, D. Morley and V. Walkerdine (eds) *Cultural Studies and Communications*. London: Arnold, pp. 10–33.

Hall, S. (ed.) (1997) *Representation: Cultural Representations and Signifying Practices*. London: Sage.

Hallin, D.C. and Mancini, P. (2004) *Comparing Media Systems: Three Models of Media and Politics*. Cambridge: Cambridge University Press.

Hammond, J. L. (1999) Law and disorder: The Brazilian Landless Farm Workers' Movement, *Bulletin of Latin American Research*, 18(4): 469–89.

Hammond, J. L. (2004) The MST and the media: Competing images of the Brazilian Landless Farmworkers' Movement, *Latin American Politics & Society*, 46(4): 61–90.

Harcup, T. (2005) 'I'm doing this to change the world': Journalism in alternative and mainstream media, *Journalism Studies*, 6(3): 361–74.

Hardt, M. and Negri, A. (2004) *Multitude: War and Democracy in the Age of Empire*. New York: Penguin Press.

Harnecker, M. (2003) *Landless People: Building a Social Movement*. São Paulo: Expressão Popular Press.

Hartley, J. (2002) *Communication, Cultural and Media Studies: The Key Concepts*, 3rd edn. London: Routledge.

Hartley, J. and McKee, A. (2000) *The Indigenous Public Sphere*. Oxford: Oxford University Press.

Held, D. (1987) *Models of Democracy*. Cambridge: Polity Press.

Hemmati, M. (2002) *Multi-Stakeholder Processes for Governance and Sustainability*. London: Earthscan.

Hersh, S. M. (2004) Torture at Abu Ghraib: American soldiers brutalized Iraqis. How far up does the responsibility go?, *The New Yorker*, 10 May. http://www.newyorker.com/fact/content/?040510fa_fact (accessed 25 January 2007).

Hill, K.A. and Hughes, J.E. (1998) *Cyberpolitics: Citizen Activism in the Age of the Internet*. Lanham, MD: Rowman and Littlefield.

Hillery, G.A. (1955) Definitions of community: areas of agreement, *Rural Sociology*, 20: 111–24.

Hilliard, R. L. and Keith, M. C. (2005) *The Quieted Voice: The Rise and Demise of Localism in American Radio*. Carbondale: Southern Illinois University Press.

Hintz, A. (2007) Civil society media at the WSIS: a new actor in global communication governance?, in B. Cammaerts and N. Carpentier (eds) *Reclaiming the Media: Communication Rights and Expanding Democratic Media Roles*. Bristol: Intellect, pp. 243–64.

Hockenberry, J. (2005) The blogs of war, *Wired*, 13.08. http://www.wired.com/wired/archive/13.08/milblogs_pr.html (accessed 25 January 2007).

Hoffman, E. (1997) The new nomads, in A. Anciman (ed.) *Letters of Transit. Reflections on Exile, Identity, Language and Loss*, New York: New Press in collaboration with New York Public Library, pp. 41–63.

Hollander, E. (2000) Online communities as community media. A theoretical and analytical framework for the study of digital community networks, *Communications: The European Journal of Communication Research*, 25(4): 371–86.

Howarth, D. (2000) *Discourse*. Buckingham: Open University Press.

Howley, K. (2005) *Community Media. People, Places, and Communication Technologies*. Cambridge: Cambridge University Press.

Husband, C. (1994) *A Richer Vision. The Development of Ethnic Minority Media in Western Democracies*. Paris: UNESCO.

Hutcheon, L. (1994) *Irony's Edge – The Theory and Politics of Irony*. London: Routledge.

International Commission for the Study of Communication Problems (2004) *Many Voices, One World – Towards a New, More Just, and More Efficient World Information and Communication Order*. Lanham, MD: Rowman & Littlefield. First published by UNESCO in 1980.

International Committee of the Red Cross (2004) Report of the International Committee of the Red Cross (ICRC) on the treatment by the coalition forces of prisoners of war and other protected persons by the Geneva Conventions in Iraq during arrest, internment and interrogation, February. http://www.globalsecurity.org/military/library/report/2004/icrc_report_iraq_feb2004.pdf (accessed 25 January 2007).

Jacobson, T. L. (1998) Discourse ethics and the right to communicate, *Gazette*, 60(5): 395–413.

Jankowski, N. (1994) International perspectives on community radio, in *AMARC-Europe, One Europe – Many Voices. Democracy and Access to Communication*. Conference report, AMARC-Europe Pan-European Conference of Community Radio Broadcasters, Ljubljana, Slovenia, 15–18 September. Sheffield: AMARC, pp. 2–3.

Jankowski, N. (2003) Community media research: a quest for theoretically-grounded models, *Javnost – The Public*, 10(1): 5–14.

Jankowski, N., Prehn, O. and Stappers, J. (eds) (1992) *The People's Voice. Local Radio and Television in Europe*. London, Paris and Rome: John Libbey and Company.

Janoski, T. (1998) *Citizenship and Civil Society: A Framework of Rights and Obligations in Liberal, Traditional and Social Democratic Regimes*. Cambridge: Cambridge University Press.

Janowitz, M. (1967) *The Community Press in an Urban Setting. The Social Elements of Urbanism*. Chicago: University of Chicago Press.

Jerkins, H. (2006) *Convergence Culture*. New York: NYU Press.

Johnson, H.B. (1987) Portuguese settlement, 1500–1580, in L. Bethell (ed.) *Colonial Brazil*. Cambridge: Cambridge University Press, pp. 1–39.

Jones, S.G. (1995) Understanding community in the information age, in S.G. Jones (ed.) *CyberSociety: Computer-Mediated Communication and Community*. London: Sage, pp. 10–35.

Jordan, T. (2002) *Activism! Direct Action, Hactivism and the Future of Society*. London: Reaktion Books.

Jordan, T. and Taylor, P. A. (2004) *Hacktivism and Cyberwars: Rebels with a cause?* London: Routledge.

Karner, C. (2007) *Ethnicity and Everyday Life*. London: Routledge.

Keane, J. (1991) *The Media and Democracy*. Cambridge: Polity.

Keane, J. (1998) *Democracy and Civil Society*. London: University of Westminster Press.

Keane, J. (2003) *Global Civil Society?* Cambridge: Cambridge University Press.

Keck, M.E. and Sikkink, K. (1998) *Activists beyond Borders: Advocacy Networks in International Politics*. Ithaca, NY: Cornell University Press.

Kellner, D. (1992) *The Persian Gulf TV War*. Boulder, CO: Westview Press.

Kellner, D. (2004a) On digital photomania and media spectacle, *Blog Left: Critical Interventions Warblog*, 9 May. http://www.gseis.ucla.edu/courses/ed253a/2004/05/dk-on-digital-photomania-and-media.php (accessed 25 January 2007).

Kellner, D. (2004b) Globalization, technopolitics and revolution. http://www.gseis.ucla.edu/faculty/kellner/essays/globalizationtechnopoliticsrevolution.pdf (accessed 6 June 2007).

Kenney, P. (2003) *A Carnival of Revolution: Central Europe 1989*. Princeton, NJ: Princeton University Press.

Kidd, D. (1999) The value of alternative media, *Peace Review*, 11(1): 113–19.

Kitchin, R. (1998). *Cyberspace: The World in the Wires*. Chichester: Wiley.

Klein, N. (2000) *No Logo: No Space, No Choice, No Jobs, Taking Aim at the Brand Bullies*. London: Flamingo.

Knabb, K. (1981) *Situationist International Anthology*. Berkeley, CA: Bureau of Public Secrets. http://www.bopsecrets.org/SI/index.htm (accessed 25 January 2007).

Kymlicka, W. (2001) *Politics in the Vernacular*. Oxford: Oxford University Press.

Laclau, E. (1996) *Emancipations*. London: Verso.

Laclau, E. and Mouffe, C. (1985) *Hegemony and Socialist Strategy: Towards a Radical Democratic Politics*. London: Verso.

Langman, L. (2005) From virtual public spheres to global justice: A critical theory of internetworked social movements, *Sociological Theory*, 23(1): 42–74.

Lasn, K. (2000) *Culture Jam: How to Reverse America's Suicidal Consumer Binge – and Why We Must*. New York: Quill.

Leunissen, J. (1986) 'Community' en 'Community Development' bij de Australische Aborigines, in M. Van Bakel, A. Borsboom and H. Dagmar (eds) *Traditie in Verandering: Nederlandse Bijdragen aan Antropologisch Onderzoek in Oceanië*. Leiden: DSWO Press, pp. 57–82.

Lewis, P. (ed.) (1993) *Alternative Media: Linking Global and Local*, Reports and Papers on Mass Communication No.107. Paris: UNESCO.

Lindlof, T. R. (1988) Media audiences as interpretative communities, *Communication Yearbook*, 11: 81–107.

Livingstone, S. and Lunt, P. (1994) *Talk on Television, Audience Participation and Public Debate*. London: Routledge.

Macdonald, L. (1994) Globalising civil society: interpreting international NGOs in Central America, *Millenium: Journal of International Studies*, 23(2): 267–85.

MacKinnon, R. (2004) The World-Wide Conversation: Online participatory media and international news. The Joan Shorenstein Center on the Press, Politics and Public Policy, Working Paper Series, no.2004–02.

MacPherson, C.B. (1966) *The Real World of Democracy*. Oxford: Oxford University Press.

MacPherson, C.B. (1973) *Democratic Theory: Essays In Retrieval*. Oxford: Clarendon Press.

MacPherson, C.B. (1977) *The Life and Times of Liberal Democracy*. Oxford: Oxford University Press.

Magaldi, C. (2002) Foreign music as national symbol: Carlos Gomes's Opera Il Guarany (1870) as an Icon of Brazilianness. Paper presented at Annual meeting of the American Musicological Society and Society for Music Theory, Columbus, OH, 10–11 March.

Malik, A.R. (2007) Take me to your leader: Post-secular society and the Islam industry, *Eurozine* (23 April). *http://www.eurozine.com/articles/2007–04–23-armalik-en.html* (accessed 6 June 2007).

Mamadouh, V. (2004) Internet, scale and the global grassroots: geographies of the Indymedia network of independent media centres, *Tijdschrift voor Economische en Sociale Geografie*, 95(5): 482–97.

Marshall, B. (1991) Communication and politics: feminist print media in English Canada, *Women's Studies International Forum* 18(4): 430–74.

Martin-Barbero, J. (1993) *Communication, Culture and Hegemony. From the Media to Mediations*. London: Sage.

Marx, K. (1975) On the Jewish Question, in K. Marx and F. Engels, *Collected Works*, Vol. 3. London: Lawrence and Wishart, pp. 146–74.

Mattelart, A. (1983) Introduction: for a class and group analysis of popular communication practices, in A. Mattelart and S. Siegelaub (eds) *Communication and Class Struggle – Volume 2: Liberation, Socialism*. New York/Paris: International General/International Mass Media Research Center, pp. 17–67.

McAdam, D., Tarrow, S. and Tilly, C. (2001) *Dynamics of Contention*. Cambridge: Cambridge University Press.

McCarthy, R. (2003) Salam's story, *The Guardian*, 30 May. http://www.guardian.co.uk/Iraq/Story/0,2763,966819,00.html (accessed 25 January 2007).

McChesney, R. (1999) *Rich Media, Poor Democracy: Communication Politics in Dubious Times*. Urbana-Champaign: University of Illinois Press.

McClure, K. (1992) On the subject of rights: pluralism, plurality and political identity, in C. Mouffe (ed.) *Dimensions of Radical Democracy: Pluralism, Citizenship, Community*. London: Verso, pp. 108–25.

McDonald, K. (2006) *Global Movements: Action and Culture*. Oxford: Blackwell.

McNair, B. (1998) *The Sociology of Journalism*. London: Arnold.

McNair, B., Hibberd, M. and Schlesinger, P. (2003) *Mediated Access Broadcasting and Democratic Participation in the Age of Mediated Communication*. Luton: University of Luton Press.

Meikle, G. (2002) *Future Active: Media Activism and the Internet*. New York: Routledge.

Melluci, A. (1996) *Challenging Codes: Collective Action in the Information Age*. Cambridge: Cambridge University Press.

Melzer, E.J. (2005) Gay Iraqi laments life after invasion – Americans form gay support group in Baghdad. WashingtonBlade.com, 19 August. http://www.washingtonblade.com/2005/8–19/news/national/iraq.cfm (accessed 25 January 2007).

Merton, R.K. (1968) *Social Theory and Social Structure*. New York: The Free Press.

Meyer, D. S and Minkoff, D. C. (2004) Conceptualizing political opportunity, *Social Forces* 82(4): 1457–92.

Ministère de la Communauté Française (1987) Décret sur l'audiovisuel, Namur, 17 July.

Mirzoeff, N. (2005) *Watching Babylon. The War in Iraq and Global Visual Culture*. New York: Routledge.

Morley, D. (1990) Changing paradigms in audience studies, in E. Seiter, H. Borchers, G. Kreutzner and E.M. Warth (eds) *Remote Control: Television, Audiences and Cultural Power*. London: Routledge.

Morley, D. (1992) *Television, Audiences and Cultural Studies*. London: Routledge.

Morris, A. and Morton, G. (1998) *Locality, Community and Nation*. London: Hodder and Stoughton.

Morrow, L. (2003) *Evil: An Investigation*. New York: Basic Books.

Mouffe, C. (1981) Hegemony and ideology in Gramsci, in T. Bennett, G. Martin, C. Mercer and J. Woollacott (eds.) *Culture, Ideology and Social Process: A Reader*, Milton Keynes: Open University Press, pp. 219–34.

Mouffe, C. (1993) *The Return of the Political*. London: Verso.

Mouffe, C. (1994) For a politics of nomadic identity, in G. Robertson, M. Mash, L. Tickner, J. Bird, B. Curtis and T. Putnam (eds) *Travellers' Tales: Narratives of Home and Displacement*. Abingdon and New York: Routledge, pp. 105–13.

Mouffe, C. (1997) *The Return to the Political*, London: Verso.

Mouffe, C. (1999a) Carl Schmitt and the paradox of liberal democracy, in C. Mouffe (ed.) *The Challenge of Carl Schmitt*. London: Verso, pp. 38–53.

Mouffe, C. (1999b) Deliberative democracy or agonistic pluralism?, *Social Research*, 66(3): 746–58.

Naficy, H. (1993) *The Making of Exile Cultures: Iranian Television in Los Angeles*. Minneapolis: University of Minnesota Press.

Naficy, H. (2003) Narrowcasting in diaspora, in K.H. Karim (ed.) *The Media of Diaspora*. London: Routledge, pp. 51–62.

Nahdi, F. (2003) Editorial, *Q-News*, 351: 3.

Navarro, Z. (2005) Transforming rights into social practices? The landless movement and land reform in Brazil, *IDS Bulletin*, 36(1): 129–37.

Negativland (1985/1994) *Over the Edge, Vol. 1: JamCon'84*. CAS (SST 223)/CD (re-issue, Seeland 004).

Negri, A. (1999) *Insurgencies: Constituent Power and the Modern State*. Minneapolis: University of Minnesota Press.

Norris, P. (2001) *Digital Divide? Civic Engagement, Information Poverty and the Internet in Democratic Societies*. Cambridge: Cambridge University Press. http://www.pippanorris.com/ (accessed 25 January 2007).

Nostbakken, D. and Morrow, C. (eds) (1993) *Cultural Expression in the Global Village*. Penang: Southbound.

Ó Siochrú, S. and Girard, B., with A. Mahan (2002) *Global Media Governance: A Beginners Guide*. Lanham, MD: Rowman and Littlefield.

Ofcom (2005) The Community Radio Fund: Policy statement, 7 January. http://www. ofcom.org.uk/consult/condocs/crf/crf_statement/ (accessed 25 January 2007).

Olorunnisola, A.A. (2002) Community radio: participatory communication in Postapartheid South Africa, *Journal of Radio Studies* 9(1): 126–45.

O'Sullivan-Ryan, J. and Kaplun, M. (1979) *Communication Methods to Promote Grass-roots Participation*. Paris: UNESCO.

Pacifica Foundation (1946) Articles of Incorporation, 19 August. http://www.pacifica.org/ governance/460819_PacificaOriginalBylaws.html (accessed 25 January 2007).

Parekh, B. (2000) *Rethinking Multiculturalism: Cultural Diversity and Political Theory*. New York: Palgrave.

Partridge, S. (1982) *NOT the BBC/IBA: The Case for Community Radio*. London: Comedia.

Pateman, C. (1970) *Participation and Democratic Theory*. Cambridge: Cambridge University Press.

Pateman, C. (1985) *The Problem of Political Obligation. A Critique of Liberal Theory*, Cambridge: Polity Press.

Peretti, J. (2001) My Nike adventure, *The Nation*, 9 April. http://www.thenation.com/ doc.mhtml?i=20010409&s=peretti (accessed 25 January 2007).

Pérez-Díaz, V. (1998) The public sphere and a European civil society, in J.C. Alexander (ed.) *Real Civil Societies. Dilemmas of Institutionalization*. London: Sage, pp. 211–38.

Phillips, P. (2003) *The Project Censored Guide to Alternative Media and Activism*. New York: Seven Stories Press.

Popple, K. (1995) *Analysing Community Work*. Buckingham: Open University Press.

Portes, A., Guarnizo, L.E. and Landolt, P. (1999) The study of transnationalism: Pitfalls and promise of an emergent research field. *Ethnic and Racial Studies*, 22(2): 217–37.

Powell, R. (1965) *Possibilities for Local Radio*. Birmingham: Centre for Contemporary Cultural Studies, Birmingham University.

Prashad, V. and Ballve, T. (eds.) (2006) *Dispatches from Latin America: On the Frontlines against Neo-liberalism*. Cambridge, MA: South End Press.

Prehn, O. (1992) From small scale utopism to large scale pragmatism, in N. Jankowski, O. Prehn and J. Stappers (eds) *The People's Voice. Local Radio and Television in Europe*, London, Paris and Rome: John Libbey and Company, pp. 247–68.

Putnam, R. D. (1993) *Making Democracy Work*. Princeton, NJ: Princeton University Press.

Putnam, R.D. (2000) *Bowling Alone: The Collapse and Revival of American Community*. New York: Simon and Schuster.

Quraishi, M. (2005) *Muslims and Crime: A Comparative Study*. London: Ashgate.

Radford, B. (2003) *Media Myth Makers: How Journalists, Activists, and Advertisers Mislead Us*. New York: Prometheus Books.

Radio Gazelle (1992) Radio Gazelle: Multi-cultural radio in Marseille, in B. Girard (ed.) *A Passion for Radio: Radio Waves and Community*, Montréal: Black Rose Books, pp. 132–5. http://www.comunica.org/passion/ (accessed 25 January 2007).

RadioSwap (2001) Radioswap.net: presentation. http://www.radioswap.net/index.php (accessed 25 January 2007).

RadioSwap (2002) Introduction. http://www.radioswap.net/about.html (accessed 25 January 2007).

Radway, J. (1991) *Reading the Romance: Women, Patriarchy and Popular Literature*. Chapel Hill: University of North Carolina Press.

Reid, J. and Savage, J. (1987) *Up They Rise. The Incomplete Works of Jamie Reid*. London: Faber and Faber.

Reyes Matta, F. (1986) Alternative communication: solidarity and development in the face of transnational expansion, in R. Atwoord and E. McAnany (eds) *Communication and Latin American Society. Trends in Critical Research 1960–1985*, Madison: University of Wisconsin Press, pp. 190–214.

Rheingold, H. (2001) Mobile virtual communities, 9 July. http://www.receiver.vodafone.com/06/articles/index02.html (accessed 25 January 2007).

Riggins, S. (1992) *Ethnic Minority Media: An International Perspective*. London: Sage.

Rigoni, I. (2005) Challenging notions and practices: The Muslim media in Britain and France, *Journal of Ethnic and Migration Studies*, 31(3): 563–80.

Rimbert, P. (2005) *Libération de Sartre à Rothschild*. Paris: Raisons d'Agir.

Robertson, R. (1995) Glocalisation: time-space and heterogeneity-homogeneity, in M. Featherstone, S. Lash and R. Robertson (eds) *Global Modernities*. London: Sage, pp. 25–44.

Robins, K. and Aksoy, A. (2005) New complexities of transnational media cultures, in O. Hemer and T. Tufte (eds) *Media and Glocal Change: Rethinking Communication for Development*. Buenos Aires and Gothenburg: Clacso and NORDICOM, pp. 41–58.

Rodriguez, A. (1999) *Making Latino News: Race, Language, Class*. Thousand Oaks, CA: Sage.

Rodriguez, C. (1996) Shedding useless notions of alternative media, *Peace Review*, 8(1): 63–8.

Rodriguez, C. (2001) *Fissures in the Mediascape: An International Study of Citizens' Media*. Cresskill, NJ: Hampton Press.

Rossiaud, J. and Scherer-Warren, I. (2000) *A Democratização Inacabável: As Memorias do Futuro*. Petropolis, Rio de Janeiro: Vozes.

Sakolsky, R. (1998) Introduction: Rhizomatic radio and the great stampede, in R. Sakolsky and S. Dunifer (eds) *Seizing the Airwaves: A Free Radio Handbook*. Oakland, CA: AK Press. http://www.infoshop.org/texts/seizing/intro.html (accessed 25 January 2007).

Sakolsky, R. (2001) The LPFM fiasco: Micropower radio and the FCC's low power Trojan horse, *Lip Magazine*, 17 January. http://www.lipmagazine.org/articles/featsakolsky_77.htm (accessed 25 January 2007).

Sakolsky, R. and Dunifer S. (eds) (1998) *Seizing the Airwaves: A Free Radio Handbook*, Oakland, CA: AK Press. http://www.infoshop.org/texts/seizing/toc.html (accessed 25 January 2007).

Salam Pax (2003) *The Baghdad Blog*. London: Guardian Books/Atlantic Books.

Salam Pax (2005) *Iraq – The Baghdad Blogger*. Guardian Films.

Schmitt, C. (1980) *Legalität und Legitimität*, 3rd edn. Berlin: Duncker and Humblot.

Schumpeter, J.A. (1942) *Capitalism, Socialism, and Democracy*. New York/London: Harper & Brothers.

Scott, A. and Street, J. (2001) From media politics to e-protest? The use of popular culture and new media in parties and social movements, in F. Webster (ed.) *Culture and Politics in the Information Age: A New Politics?* London: Routledge, pp. 32–51.

Seligmann, R. (1998) *PROCERA: Programa Especial de Credito Para Reforma Agrária*. Brasília, DF: Instituto Nacional de Colonização e Reforma Agrária.

Servaes, J. (1999) *Communication for Development. One World, Multiple Cultures*. Cresskill, NJ: Hampton Press.

Servaes, J. and Carpentier, N. (2005) Introduction: Steps to achieve a sustainable information society, in J. Servaes and N. Carpentier (eds) *Deconstructing WSIS: Towards a Sustainable Agenda for the Future Information Society*. Bristol: Intellect, pp. 5–16.

Siemering, W. (2000) Radio, democracy and development: Evolving models of community radio, *Journal of Radio Studies*, 7(2): 373–8.

Silverstone, R. (1999) *Why Study the Media?* London: Sage.

Silverstone, R. (2006) *Media and Morality: On the Rise of the Mediapolis*. Cambridge: Polity Press.

Sinclair, J. and Cunningham, S. (2000) Go with the flow: Diasporas and the media, *Television and New Media*, 1(1): 11–31.

Sinclair, J., Yue, A., Hawkins, G., Pookong, K. and Fox, J. (2000) Chinese cosmopolitanism and media use, in S. Cunningham and J. Sinclair (eds) *Floating Lives: The Media and Asian Diasporas*. St Lucia: University of Queensland Press, pp. 35–8.

Singer, R. (1978) Ethnic newspapers in the United States. Paper Presented at the annual meeting of the Association for Education in Journalism, Seattle, WA, 13–16 August.

Sjöberg, M. (ed.) (1994) *Community Radio in Western Europe*. Sheffield: AMARC-Europe.

Smelser, N. (1962) *Theory of Collective Behaviour*. London: Routledge & Kegan Paul.

Smith, G. (2001) The 2001 General Election: Factors influencing the brand image of political parties and their leaders, *Journal of Marketing Management* 17(9–10): 989–1006.

Smith, J., Chatfield, C. and Pagnucco, R. (eds) (1997) *Transnational Social Movements and Global Politics*, Syracuse, NY: Syracuse University Press.

Sontag, S. (1973) *On Photography*. New York: Farrar, Straus and Giroux.

Sontag, S. (2003) *Regarding the Pain of Others*. New York: Farrar, Straus and Giroux.

Sontag, S. (2004) Regarding the torture of others, *New York Times Magazine*, 23 May. http://www.truthout.org/cgi-bin/artman/exec/view.cgi/9/4592 (accessed 25 January 2007).

Spiller, N. (ed.) (2002) *Cyber_reader. Critical Writings for the Digital Era*, London: Phaidon.

Spivak, G. (1988) Can the subaltern speak?, in L. Grossberg and C. Nelson (eds.) *Marxism and the Interpretation of Culture*. Urbana-Champaign: University of Illinois Press, pp. 271–313.

Sreberny, A. (2005) 'Not only, but also': Mixedness and media, *Journal of Ethnic and Migration Studies*, 31(3): 443–59.

Stédile, J. P. and Fernandes, B. M. (2005) *Brava Gente: a trajetoria do MST e a luta pela terra no Brasil*, São Paulo: Fundação Perseu Abramo.

Sterling, C. H. and Kittross, J.M. (2002) *Stay Tuned: A History of American Broadcasting*, 3rd edn. Mahwah, NJ: Lawrence Erlbaum Associates.

Szerzynski, B. (2002) Ecological rites: ritual action in environmental protest, *Theory, Culture and Society*, 19(3): 51–69.

Tarrow, S. (1999) *Power in Movement: Social Movements and Contentious Politics*. Cambridge: Cambridge University Press.

Taylor, C. (1992) *Multiculturalism and the 'Politics of Recognition'*. Princeton, NJ: Princeton University Press.

Taylor, C. and Whittier, N. (1992) Collective identity in social movement communities: Lesbian feminist mobilization, in A. Morris and C. Muller (eds) *Frontiers in Social Movement Theory*, New Haven, CT: Yale University Press, pp. 104–29.

Taylor, P. M. (1995) *Munitions of the Mind: A History of Propaganda from the Ancient World to the Present Era*. Manchester: Manchester University Press.

Thomas, P. (1994) Participatory development communication: philosophical premises, in S.A. White, with K.S. Nair and S. Ascroft (eds) *Participatory Communication: Working for Change and Development*. Beverly Hills, CA: Sage, pp. 49–59.

Thompson, J. B. (1995) *The Media and Modernity. A Social Theory of the Media*. Cambridge: Polity Press.

Tilly, C. (1982) Britain creates the social movement, in J. Cronin and J. Schneer (eds) *Social Conflict and the Political Order in Modern Britain*. London: Croom Helm, pp. 21–51.

Tilly, C. (1984) Social movements and national politics, in C. Bright and S. Harding (eds) *Statemaking and Social Movements: Essays in History and Theory*, Ann Arbor: University of Michigan Press.

Tilly, C. (1995) *Popular Contention in Great Britain – 1758–1834*. Cambridge, MA: Harvard University Press.

Tilly, C. and Tarrow, S. (2007) *Contentious Politics*. Boulder, CO: Paradigm.

Tönnies, F. (1963) *Community and Society*. London: Harper & Row.

Touraine, A. (1981) *The Voice and the Eye: An Analysis of Social Movements*. Cambridge: Cambridge University Press.

Tuchman, G. (1972) Objectivity as a strategic ritual: an examination of newsmen's notions of objectivity, *American Journal of Sociology*, 77: 660–79.

Tumber, H. and Palmer, J. (2004) *Media at War: The Iraq Crisis*. London: Sage.

Turner, G. (1992) *British Cultural Studies: An Introduction*. London: Routledge.

Van Cuilenburg, J. and McQuail, D. (2000) Media policy paradigm shifts: in search of a new communications policy paradigm, in B. Cammaerts and J.-C. Burgelman (eds) *Beyond Competition: Broadening the Scope of Telecommunication Policy*, Brussels: VUB Press, pp. 111–30.

van de Donk, W., Loader, B.D., Nixon, P.G. and Rucht, D. (eds.) (2004) *Cyberprotest: New Media, Citizens and Social Movements*. London: Routledge.

Verba, S. and Nie, N. (1987) *Participation in America: Political Democracy & Social Equality*. Chicago: University of Chicago Press.

Vlaams Commissariaat voor de Media (2005) Beslissing nr.2005/044 inzake: bezwaarschrift van VZW Radio Centraal (Radio Centraal) uit Antwerpen (dossier-nr. 2005/0291), 20 May.

Walker, J. (2001) *Rebels on the Air – An Alternative History of Radio in America*. New York: New York University Press.

Wall, M. (2005) 'Blogs of war': Weblogs as news, *Journalism*, 6(2): 153–72.

Walzer, M. (1998) The idea of civil society. A path to social reconstruction, in E.J. Doinne Jr. (ed.) *Community Works: The Revival of Civil Society in America*. Washington, DC: Brookings Institution Press, pp. 124–43.

Wasko, J. and Mosco, V. (eds.) (1992) *Democratic Communications in the Information Age*. Norwood, NJ: Ablex.

Webwereld (2004) Racisme op condoleanceregisters Van Gogh, 2 November. http://www.webwereld.nl/articles/13898 (accessed 25 January 2007).

Wenger, E. (1998) *Communities of Practice. Learning, Meaning and Identity*. Cambridge: Cambridge University Press.

Wenger, E., McDermott, R., Snyder, W.M. (2002) *Cultivating Communities of Practice*, Boston: Harvard Business School Press.

Westerståhl, J. (1983) Objective news reporting, *Communication Research* 10: 403–24.

White, C.S. (1997) Citizen participation and the Internet: Prospects for civic deliberation in the information age, *Social Studies*, 88(1): 23–8.

White, T.H. (2003) *United States Early Radio History*. http://earlyradiohistory.us/index.html (accessed 25 January 2007).

Wilhelm, A. (2000) *Democracy in the Digital Age: Challenges to Political Life in Cyberspace*. London: Routledge.

Williams, K. (1992) Something more important than truth: ethical issues in war reporting. In A. Belsey and R. Chadwick (eds) *Ethical Issues in Journalism and the Media*. London: Routledge, pp.154–70.

Williams, R. (1976) *Keywords. A Vocabulary of Culture and Society*. London: Fontana.

Wolford, W. (2003) Producing community: The MST and land reform settlements in Brazil. *Journal of Agrarian Change*, 3(4): 500–20.

Working Group on Internet Governance (2005) Report of the Working Group on Internet Governance, June, Château de Bossey. http://www.wgig.org/docs/WGIGREPORT.pdf (accessed 25 January 2007).

World Summit for the Information Society (WSIS) (2003) *Plan of Action*. Geneva: ITU. http://www.itu.int/wsis/ (accessed 25 January 2007).

Wray, S. (1998) *Rhizomes, Nomads, and Resistant Internet Use*. http://www.thing.net/~rdom/ecd/RhizNom.html (accessed 25 January 2007).

WSIS Civil Society Plenary (2003) Civil Society declaration: Shaping information societies for human needs, 8 December, Geneva. http://www.itu.int/wsis/docs/geneva/civil-society-declaration.pdf (accessed 25 January 2007).

Zelizer, B. and Allan, S. (2002) (eds) *Journalism after September 11*. New York: Routledge.

Zhang, K. and Xiaoming, H. (1999) The Internet and the ethnic press: a study of electronic Chinese publications. *Information Society*, 15(1): 21–30.

INDEX

Page numbers in *italics* refer to tables, g refers to glossary.